DOLLARS & SENSE

MAKING THE MOST OF WHAT YOU HAVE

WILSON J. HUMBER

NAVPRESS

BRINGING TRUTH TO LIFE

NavPress Publishing Group

P.O. Box 35001, Colorado Springs, Colorado 80935

The Navigators is an international Christian organization. Jesus Christ gave His followers the Great Commission to go and make disciples (Matthew 28:19). The aim of The Navigators is to help fulfill that commission by multiplying laborers for Christ in every nation.

NavPress is the publishing ministry of The Navigators. NavPress publications are tools to help Christians grow. Although publications alone cannot make disciples or change lives, they can help believers learn biblical discipleship, and apply what they learn to their lives and ministries.

© 1993 by The Navigators
All rights reserved. No part of this publication may be reproduced in any
    form without written permission from NavPress, P.O. Box 35001,
    Colorado Springs, CO 80935.
Library of Congress Catalog Card Number:
    93-4097
ISBN 08910-97414

Second printing, 1993

Editor: Lynn Stanley

Some of the anecdotal illustrations in this book are true to life and are included with the permission of the persons involved. All other illustrations are composites of real situations, and any resemblance to people living or dead is coincidental.

This publication is designed to provide accurate and authoritative information in regard to the subject matter covered. It is sold with the understanding that the author and the publisher are not engaged in rendering legal, accounting, or other professional service. If legal advice or other expert assistance is required, the services of a competent professional person should be sought. *From a Declaration of Principles jointly adopted by a Committee of the American Bar Association and a Committee of Publishers.*

Unless otherwise identified, all Scripture quotations in this publication are taken from the *HOLY BIBLE: NEW INTERNATIONAL VERSION*® (NIV®). Copyright © 1973, 1978, 1984 by International Bible Society. Used by permission of Zondervan Publishing House. All rights reserved. Other versions used include: the *New American Standard Bible* (NASB), © The Lockman Foundation 1960, 1962, 1963, 1968, 1971, 1972, 1973, 1975, 1977; and *The Living Bible* (TLB), © 1971 owned by assignment by the Illinois Regional Bank N.A. (as trustee), used by permission of Tyndale House Publishers, Inc., Wheaton, IL 60189.

Humber, Wilson J.
    Dollars and sense : making the most of what you have / Wilson
J. Humber.
        p.   cm.
    ISBN 0-89109-741-4
    1. Finance, Personal.   I.   Title.
HG179.H85   1993
332.024—dc20   93-4097
                                                                        CIP

Printed in the United States of America

FOR A FREE CATALOG OF
NAVPRESS BOOKS & BIBLE STUDIES,
CALL 1-800-366-7788 (USA)
or 1-416-499-4615 (CANADA)

CONTENTS

*To the three most important assets of my life,
the diamonds I treasure whether life is glittering or gloomy,
I dedicate this book:*

*Jeanie, your love, wisdom, and faithfulness
make it all worthwhile.*

*JT, it's an honor to be your dad and to share your name.
I trust these principles will shine from your life
as you move into the future.*

*John, nothing brings more happiness to this dad
than seeing you walking day by day with the Lord
and growing into His likeness.*

*I know you know it, but I want to say,
"I love you all."*

ACKNOWLEDGMENTS

The process of authoring a book involves a great deal of time, effort, and pleasure to get thoughts into print.

Candy Harris, your willingness to spend many hours translating my scratch on to the word processor deserves a gold medal. Your encouragement, positive attitude, and hard work are greatly appreciated.

Lynn Stanley, you would win a gold medal if there were an Olympics for writers. Thanks for your coaching, faith, persistence, and help with the deadlines.

Tim Kimmel, had it not been for your kind words and help, this book would have remained forever on my shelf. Your counsel, lifestyle, and love are a testimony that cannot be disputed.

Last, but not least, to the irrepressible James J. Lake, the eternal optimist, I owe a huge debt. You encouraged me to get involved, to grow into a position of leadership. When the roof fell in, you taught me to see the sky, not the devastated house. The Lakeism "If you don't like the outlook, try the uplook" will ring in my heart forever.

May God richly bless and prosper you all.

ONE

FINDING THE BALANCE

■

*"No one can serve two masters.
Either he will hate the one and love the other,
or he will be devoted to the one and despise the other.
You cannot serve both God and Money."*
MATTHEW 6:24

Money and finance affect every aspect of our lives. The way we handle money affects us spiritually, emotionally, and, unless we're aware of the principles God designed for its use, even physically.

Contrary to popular opinion, the Bible *is* relevant for today's economy and our complex financial system. In His Word, God promises to provide all that we need. And He *does* provide it. The problems begin when we fail to manage that provision carefully.

All the principles outlined in this book have their foundation in the Bible. If you apply them to your life, you will begin to put a permanent end to your financial problems.

THE POWERFUL EFFECTS OF ATTITUDES AND ACTIONS

In this, the richest country on earth, the majority of people at age sixty-five have no assets. If you randomly selected one hundred men, all age twenty-one, and followed them until age sixty-five, thirty-six of them would have died, and fifty-four of them would have less than $1,000 in assets. Five of the men would still be dependent upon continued work, relatives, friends, and/or charity for their financial survival. Of the remaining five, four would be financially independent and one would be "rich," owning assets over $250,000.

The reason most people have no assets when they reach retirement age is twofold: *attitudes* and *actions*. Of the almost two thousand Bible verses dealing with money and possessions, two-thirds relate to attitudes and one-third deal with actions. Our actions related to money and possessions affect our wages, savings, and spending. In the pages ahead, we'll look at the principles for work and earnings, savings and debt, housing, transportation, insurance, investing, and giving. However, although our actions determine the success or failure of our financial life, our *attitudes* toward money are most important to God.

One-third of the parables of Jesus teach us lessons about money and possessions. The major emphasis is on attitude. The secondary emphasis is on actions, because once we have a proper biblical attitude, our actions will naturally be correct. By contrast, if we're controlled by worldly attitudes, our actions will usually be the reverse of what God expects and desires from us.

What is *your* attitude toward money in general? Do your attitudes conform to biblical standards? This chapter will help you explore those questions.

Since our individual circumstances vary, learning to balance our attitudes is a unique challenge for each of us. Whether we're rich, poor, or somewhere in the middle, we all have one thing in common: our needs, wants, and desires will be more completely fulfilled if we follow biblical guidelines and principles.

In contrast to *laws*, which are exact and require clear obedience ("Speed Limit 55," for example), guidelines and principles are *boundaries*, designed to promote our health and safety (as in "Dangerous Curve Ahead"). The biblical principles in this book are clear and easy to understand. They cover 95 percent of everything you need to know about money and its use. By the time you have finished reading, you will have learned how to work toward achieving financial independence by age sixty-five.

THE THREE A'S OF BIBLICAL TRUTH
Following biblical guidelines and principles is fundamentally necessary for achieving financial independence. *How* to follow them is described in the "Three A's":

> Acquire
> Assimilate
> Apply

These terms refer to *biblical principles* concerning our attitudes toward, and management of, money. As you read and study the passages of Scripture relating to money and possessions, you *acquire* knowledge. When you incorporate the knowledge you've acquired through repetition of biblical truths, you begin to *assimilate* truth. As you act on this assimilated truth, you *apply* it to your life. The Bible encourages us to make this application:

Do not merely listen to the word, and so deceive yourselves. Do what it says. (James 1:22)

Do not conform any longer to the pattern of this world, but be transformed by the renewing of your mind. Then you will be able to test and approve what God's will is—his good, pleasing and perfect will. (Romans 12:2)

As a financial counselor, I can tell you that it's extremely exciting to see financial *and* spiritual transformation occur when those who acquire knowledge have the wisdom to apply it to their lives. My prayer is that *you* will acquire, assimilate, and apply biblical truth to your life. The goal is not knowledge *acquired*, but knowledge *applied*—resulting in life change.

SIX REASONS WHY PEOPLE HAVE MONEY PROBLEMS

All money problems arise from one or more of these six potential problems:

1. Sin nature
2. Brainwashing (in the world's materialistic attitudes)
3. Ignorance of the truth
4. Ignorance of our financial condition
5. Disobedience of the truth
6. Lack of planning and foresight

The Problem of Our Sin Nature

The Bible has much to say about our struggle against our sin nature and the power of life in the Spirit. Paul describes this struggle in his letter to the Romans:

We know that the law is spiritual; but I am unspiritual, sold as a slave to sin. I do not understand what I do. For what I want to do I do not do, but what I hate I do. . . . I have the desire to do what is good, but I cannot carry it out. . . . Now if I do what I do not want to do, it is no longer I who do it, but it is sin living in me that does it. (Romans 7:14-20)

Brainwashing

Biblical truth is opposite the world's message. Expect the Bible to contradict what you have been taught as truth:

"For my thoughts are not your thoughts
neither are your ways my ways," declares the LORD.
"As the heavens are higher than the earth,
so are my ways higher than your ways
and my thoughts than your thoughts." (Isaiah 55:8-9)

Ignorance of the Truth

Ignorance of the truth is lack of correct information, not lack of intelligence. As the prophet Hosea said, speaking to Israel, "My people are destroyed from lack of knowledge" (Hosea 4:6). During the reign of Josiah, Hilkiah, the high priest, discovered the Bible in the temple. Josiah had Scripture read to the people and made a covenant to obey the truth. This led to a period of revival and reform for Judah. Time after time the Bible tells us to learn and apply God's truth. It's the only way to freedom.

Ignorance of Our Financial Condition

Ask any individual how accurate his knowledge is of his financial condition. Could he tell you how much he spends each month? Does he know his net worth (total assets owned less total liabilities)? How much does he owe on credit cards, car payments, or home? What does he pay in interest each month?

Most people (95 percent) have no idea what their financial condition is. They think they spend less than they do, they underestimate their debt, and they have no idea how much interest they pay every month. Do you see the potential for problems?

Disobedience of the Truth

If you are aware of scriptural principles and guidelines, do you obey them? Read the twenty-eighth chapter of Deuteronomy. You will find that obedience is blessed and disobedience is punished. And in the New Testament James writes, "Anyone . . . who knows the good he ought to do and doesn't do it, sins (James 4:17). Jesus said, "If anyone loves me, he will obey my teaching" (John 14:23).

Lack of Planning and Foresight

The sixth reason people experience financial problems is that they fail to plan and do not look realistically into the future. This is *the major problem* for most Christians. Much of what follows in this book will help you learn to plan for your financial future.

As you read this book, it's imperative for you to remember that *the world's truth will almost always oppose biblical truth*. Because all the principles given here are biblically based, you can expect much of what you learn here about balanced financial planning to oppose what you've always been taught and what you've always believed is right.

THREE TRUTHS FOR SOUND FINANCIAL PRACTICE

You may already know which of the six potential problems are the root causes of your financial woes. Finding solutions for them requires establishing the right priorities.

Setting priorities is a spiritual matter involving decisions and commitments according to Scripture that are right for you individually. These decisions can be made only through prayer. When you express to God your desire to put your financial life in order according to His will, He will give you the wisdom you need to make the right decisions. Once your priorities are straight, His Spirit will empower you to follow through with the commitments you make in your effort to change. Once biblical priorities become part of the way you live, think, and feel, you will be able to make right decisions about money matters.

PRINCIPLE 1—GOD OWNS ALL YOU HAVE

A major truth we must remember is that *God owns everything*, and we are merely His stewards. Many Scriptures confirm this fact:

> The earth is the LORD's and everything in it,
> the world, and all who live in it. (Psalm 24:1)

> "The silver is mine and the gold is mine," declares the LORD Almighty. (Haggai 2:8)

> Remember the LORD your God, for it is he who gives you the
> ability to produce wealth. (Deuteronomy 8:18)

In Matthew 25:14-30, Jesus tells the parable of the talents. A careful reading of this passage reveals the following lessons about God's ownership and our stewardship:

First, we must recognize that we are "servants," and therefore only managers of assets that belong to God, entrusted to us by Him.

Second, our job as servant will not last forever. Our time period will be terminated, either by our physical death or by the Lord's return.

Third, our Master expects wise management from us. The two servants who doubled their master's money each received the same praise, even though their results were different. The "wicked and lazy" servant simply buried his master's money instead of managing it.

Fourth, we are accountable to our Master. The faithful servants were encouraged and rewarded; the poor servant was chastised and punished.

Fifth, we are given only what we can handle—no more, no less. Some of us receive five talents, some two, and still others only one. We are responsible for managing only what we have.

The world teaches us to think *my* house, *my* car, *my* bank account. But in reality, all of them are *God's*, and merely *entrusted to us* to manage. We must therefore learn to manage them using *His* rules, for *His* glory.

Handling someone else's money is a great responsibility, requiring the skill of a spiritually mature person. The concept of stewardship recognizes that everything we get comes to us from God, entrusted to us for *temporary* use. By remembering our role as manager (i.e., steward) of another's assets, we will become better managers of what we have. This is what biblical money management is all about.

PRINCIPLE 2—GOD CONTROLS ALL YOU HAVE

A second foundational truth regarding finances is that *God is in total control*. He is sovereign over all.

> Yours, O LORD, is the greatness and the power
>   and the glory and the majesty and the splendor,
> for everything in heaven and earth is yours.
> Yours, O LORD, is the Kingdom;
>   you are exalted as head over all.

Wealth and honor come from you;
    you are the ruler of all things.
In your hands are strength and power
    to exalt and give strength to all. (1 Chronicles 29:11-12)

His dominion is an eternal dominion;
    his kingdom endures from generation to generation.
All the peoples of the earth
    are regarded as nothing. He does as he pleases
    with the powers of heaven
    and the peoples of the earth.
No one can hold back his hand
    or say to him: "What have you done?" (Daniel 4:34-35)

Sound money decisions begin with accepting these truths regarding God's ownership and sovereignty.

PRINCIPLE 3—GOD PROVIDES ALL YOU NEED

Third, we must know that *God always meets our needs.* In the Gospel of Luke, Christ tells us not to worry about our needs. He points out that as God provides for the birds and even the lilies of the field, He will also meet the needs of His children, one day at a time. This is in striking contrast to the world's anxiety about daily needs:

> "For the pagan world runs after all such things, and your Father knows that you need them. But seek his Kingdom, and these things will be given to you as well." (Luke 12:30-31)

This passage is God's promise to meet your needs—not your wants. A need is anything required for you to fulfill God's plan for your life. As you consider your finances and how you're going to make changes, remember that *needs* are much different from *wants.*

Why These Truths Matter in the Real World

These three truths—God owns all, controls all, and provides all—have important implications for everyday life.

First, since the goods are God's, *He can take all of them at any time, for any reason.* A steward has no rights, only responsibilities. If the Lord chose to take everything from you right now, what would your response be? Would you be able to say what Job did? "The Lord gave and the Lord has taken away. Blessed be the name of the Lord" (Job 1:21, NASB). If you have *already* lost everything you had, was yours a biblical response? If you've only lost *most* of it, are you focusing on what you have, giving thanks with contentment? Or are you focusing on what you *had* in a spirit of discontent?

Second, *every financial, investment, or spending decision is a spiritual decision.* Most people never consider the fact that there are spiritual implications to the way they spend money. Every time you write a check, use a credit card, or make any expenditure, you're making a spiritual decision. Think, pray, and seek God's guidance before you spend any of His money, because you're accountable to Him for what you do with it.

YOUR RESPONSIBILITY AS GOD'S STEWARD
Based on these three foundational truths of God's ownership, control, and provision, your responsibility as a steward of God's assets is *commitment* and *trust*. Your commitment must be *to manage everything God has entrusted to you by His rules, for His glory.* Then you must *trust God for the outcome.*

Your responsibility is not limited to the realm of finance, however. Stewardship extends to every asset you possess: time, talent, treasure, relationships, and even the gospel itself.

For example, let's look at the asset of time. There are 168 hours in a week. If you sleep 8 hours a night, that's 56 hours from your week. Work, including commuting and the time it takes you to get ready, consumes another 50 hours or more. Another 14 is consumed by eating three meals a day. If you subtract the time you have left after these duties, you have 48 hours per week of discretionary time. It's your job to manage this time well, because you're accountable to God for what you do with the time He gives you.

Whether it's time, money, or something else, the same reality holds true: *Use it, or lose it.* Without a plan, time and money will slip through your fingers, and you'll have nothing to show for your efforts. But if you treat time and money as resources, given to you to manage for God's glory, the results will be dramatically different.

Failure to plan is planning to fail. In order to stay spiritually balanced and still have time for family and friends, physical well-being, and personal and financial commitments, you must prioritize your life.

Success doesn't happen automatically; it always requires time, effort, and planning. If you're not moving forward, you're either standing still or going backward.

I encourage you to take the time right now to prioritize your life. In order of importance, list the following categories: "Spiritual," "Family," "Physical," "Financial," "Relationships," and "Personal." Next to each category, write down one thing you know you should do to develop in that area. If you *begin today* to act on your ideas, the result will be a more balanced life.

YOUR CHOICES AS GOD'S STEWARD

"Do not store up for yourselves treasures on earth, where moth and rust destroy, and where thieves break in and steal. But store up for yourselves treasures in heaven, where moth and rust do not destroy, and where thieves do not break in and steal. For where your treasure is, there your heart will be also. The eye is the lamp of the body. If your eyes are good, your whole body will be full of light. But if your eyes are bad, your whole body will be full of darkness. If then the light within you is darkness, how great is that darkness! No one can serve two masters. Either he will hate the one and love the other, or he will be devoted to the one and despise the other. You cannot serve both God and Money." (Matthew 6:19-24)

These verses deal with our attitudes toward *luxuries*. The verses immediately following this passage (6:25-34), in which Christ promises that God will provide for us, address our attitudes toward *necessities*. This is the distinction between needs and wants.

Matthew 6:19-24 presents three fundamental choices that we must make in order to carry out our role as God's steward. Think of them as these three questions, which you must answer in order to be a responsible steward:

1. *Where will you store up treasure, in heaven or on earth?* Your answer will determine not only the direction of your life, but your final reward as well.
2. *Is your life focused on heaven, or on earth—the hereafter, or the here and now?* Your choice here will determine how you allocate the precious resources of your time, talent, and treasure.

3. *Who is your master, God or money?* Do you devote your
   free time, your thoughts, your dollars, and your talents
   to serving God? Or does your quest for material success
   devour your discretionary hours?

If you correct your spiritual perspective through answering these questions, you will gain financial contentment.

During seven years of college and graduate school, I was programed in the value of establishing specific goals and objectives.
Management by objectives was the only way to be successful. A
"successful" business generated fame, fortune, prestige, and power.
Happiness belonged to the self-actualized person who ran a successful
business—the person who had everything the world could offer.

Furthermore, I was told that "successful" people had within them
a sort of "divine discontent." No matter how much they accomplished,
they were challenged to do more and acquire more—and always more
quickly. Sayings such as "When you're green you're growing, but when
you're ripe you're rotting," and "If you're not getting bigger and better
you're not any good," were repeated to me over and over, until I finally
accepted them as truth. That's the world's way.

But the world's way stands in stark contrast to God's way, as Paul
explained to Timothy when he described the contentment at the heart
of the Christian life:

Godliness with contentment is great gain. For we brought nothing into the world, and we can take nothing out of it. But if we
have food and clothing, we will be content with that. People
who want to get rich fall into temptation and a trap and into
many foolish and harmful desires that plunge men into ruin and
destruction. For the love of money is a root of all kinds of evil.
Some people, eager for money, have wandered from the faith
and pierced themselves with many griefs. (1 Timothy 6:6-10)

This passage provides an exact definition of the goal of the Christian: *godliness with contentment*. The thrust of our Christian life should
be the development of godliness so we can learn to be content. Although
it's right and valuable to set goals, discerning and setting *Christlike*
goals is the essence of the Christian life.

Paul also reminds us in this passage that those things that appear
permanent and important to us today are not relevant to our final desti-

nation, which is eternal life in Christ. We should be content if we simply have food and clothing.

It's vitally important for us to keep money in perspective. To some, having money is, in itself, symbolically impressive—a matter of status and power. No doubt, there are just as many poor people who crave money as there are rich people who want more. In fact, the Bible says that many people disguise their financial status: "Some people pretend to be rich, but have nothing. Others pretend to be poor, but own a fortune" (Proverbs 13:7, NASB).

Many people in this country don't think of themselves as rich because they selectively compare themselves to others. Yet 4.5 billion people on this planet—three quarters of the world's population—lack adequate food and shelter. Therefore, although as individuals we may not be considered "rich" by the standards of our materialistic culture, as Christians we can't exempt ourselves from the Scriptures in which Jesus emphasizes the difficulty of "rich" people entering the Kingdom of Heaven. Are you content with food and covering, or do you think you "need" more? Do you realize how rich you are in the eyes of the world?

As God's stewards, our fundamental choice is to concentrate on what we *have* rather than on what we *lack*. This concentration develops contentment and an attitude of thankfulness, which truly honors God. But contentment must be learned, as Paul indicates:

> I am not saying this because I am in need, for I have learned to
> be content whatever the circumstances. I know what it is to be
> in need, and I know what it is to have plenty. I have learned the
> secret of being content in any and every situation, whether well
> fed or hungry, whether living in plenty or in want. I can do every-
> thing through him who gives me strength. (Philippians 4:11-13)

PRINCIPLE 4—LEARN TO BE CONTENT

The power to concentrate on what we have, not on what we lack, is a gift from God, given to those who *ask* Him for it.

Are you seeking godliness in your life, or material success? Are you learning contentment by giving thanks for what you have right now, or are you harboring feelings of discontent by dwelling on what you lack?

Over three thousand years ago, Joshua said, "Choose for yourselves today whom you will serve [money or God], . . . But as for me and my household, we will serve the LORD" (Joshua 24:15). What or whom will *you* serve? Contentment is a choice. Look at what you have and give thanks.

PRINCIPLE 5—BEWARE OF MATERIALISM

In the following section, you'll read about seven symptoms of the disease of materialism. Use these questions to check your current attitudes and actions regarding money. The insights you gain will help you learn where you're out of balance with biblical principles. Those insights, in turn, will help you identify which of the many practical suggestions in this book are especially timely for your circumstances right now.

SYMPTOMS OF MATERIALISM: A SELF-CHECK

To most people, money represents material possessions, or pleasure. That focus leads to the spiritual disease called "materialism." To see if you're infected, examine yourself for these common symptoms:

Symptom 1: Are You Caught Up in the Money Acquisition Game?
Some people think of life as a game and money as just a way of keeping score. Is your primary goal to reach the top of the career mountain? Are you as devoted to God and His Word as you are to getting to the top?

Ninety-five percent of the population will lose the "money game" altogether because life isn't a game; it's a training ground. In a balanced biblical perspective, money is a tool in our hands, given to us to be used for the glory of God. "Whoever loves money never has money enough," warned Solomon; "whoever loves wealth is never satisfied with his income" (Ecclesiastes 5:10). That's why it's so important that we manage money according to God's principles.

Symptom 2: Are You Feeling Greedy?
In our materialistic world, greed is quite acceptable. We're told there's nothing wrong with wanting more. In fact, we're encouraged to desire a better lifestyle and to aspire to a higher standard of living. Advertisers train us to buy "newer" and "better" products in order to enhance our status with others. There's nothing wrong, the world says, with wanting a larger home in a nicer neighborhood, a bigger yard, better landscaping, a pool, and maybe even a tennis court. According to this thinking, it's *normal* to want more.

But here's what Jesus says: "Watch out! Be on your guard against all kinds of greed; a man's life does not consist in the abundance of his possessions" (Luke 12:15).

We can easily get so caught up in the world and its values that we begin to fix our attention on money and possessions instead of fixing our eyes on Jesus, who instructed us to seek God's Kingdom and His right-eousness *first*. It's a lie to think that more "things" will bring us joy.

If you catch yourself saying or thinking, "I'll be satisfied when I have more money . . . another car . . . more clothes . . . a bigger house . . ." then repeat this wisdom from the Bible: *Those who love money will never have enough!* If you believe the lie that security lies in wealth, then learn the *truth*: "*God* is our refuge and strength, an ever-present help in trouble" (Psalm 46:1).

Symptom 3: Do You Envy Others for What They Have?

Keeping up with the next guy has become the American way of life. Do you long to have what your neighbor has? Do you find yourself feeling a little depressed because your friends can afford to send their children to private schools, while you struggle just to make ends meet? Are you sick of playing on the municipal course while your neighbor Richie Rich golfs at an exclusive country club?

If these things bother you, you're suffering from envy. You need a shot of the tenth commandment: "You shall not covet your neighbor's house. You shall not covet your neighbor's wife, or his manservant or maidservant, his ox or donkey, or anything that belongs to your neigh-bor" (Exodus 20:17). A sure way to infect yourself and those around you with materialistic discontent is to compare what you have with what your neighbor has. If quarrels and bickering are common in your home, perhaps you need a dose of James, too

> What causes fights and quarrels among you? Don't they come from your desires that battle within you? You want something but don't get it. You kill and covet, but you cannot have what you want. You quarrel and fight. You do not have, because you do not ask God. When you ask, you do not receive, because you ask with *wrong motives*, that you may spend what you get on your pleasures. (James 4:1-3, emphasis added)

Symptom 4: Are You Aching to Get Rich Quick?

State lotteries tempt millions of people with the prospect of getting rich quick. Multilevel marketing and "pyramid" schemes are yet another way in which people can indulge their desire to make money while expending as little energy as possible. Every day, countless business opportunities are sold to eager buyers with the promise that the buyer can practically sit home and wait for the "bills" to walk in his front door! Many of these schemes begin right inside our local churches.

Because greed has become socially acceptable, we sometimes forget to call it what it is: *sin*. And even though sins like greed and envy may seem relatively harmless, they are still serious in the eyes of God: "For of this you can be sure: No immoral, impure or *greedy* person—such a man is an idolater—has any inheritance in the kingdom of Christ and of God" (Ephesians 5:5, emphasis added).

According to God's Word, the way to make money is to work at all things diligently, as unto the Lord.

Symptom 5: Have You Been Acting a Little Selfish Lately?

It's easy to become infected by the selfishness promoted in our society. Countless "self-help" books really teach us to self-destruct, because they encourage "me-first" attitudes that turn our gaze *in*ward, when we should be looking *up*ward.

The biblical response to "me first" is found in Mark 9:35: "If anyone wants to be first, he shall be last of all and servant of all." The world encourages us to claw our way to the top; the Bible encourages us to humble ourselves before God, who will "lift" us up in His good time (1 Peter 5:6). The system trains us to hold on to what we have at all costs; the Word of God says, "Give and it will be given to you; good measure, pressed down, shaken together, they will pour into your lap. For with the measure you use, it will be measured to you" (Luke 6:38, NASB).

Symptom 6: Is Your Equilibrium Off?

Are you having trouble balancing your financial life? Many people dedicate their lives to seeking wealth, attaining possessions, and winning jobs and titles that they think will make them "successful" in various business and financial arenas. At the other extreme, some people make excuses for their lack of effort while they remain financially dependent on others.

From God's perspective, both extremes are wrong. There are dangers in wealth, and there are dangers in poverty. Rich and poor alike have at least one thing in common: Both suffer from the disease (and dis-ease) of materialism, and both share some or all of the symptoms.

Symptom 7: Are You Looking for Someone to Blame?
We have a natural urge to justify ourselves to others, and we often do it by making excuses for what we consider to be our failures: If I had a better education . . . if I had come from a more supportive environment . . . if I had the opportunities that others have had . . . if I hadn't married so young . . . if I had been born with natural advantages . . . the list goes on and on.

If we're not blaming ourselves, we're blaming someone else. Sometimes we blame those in authority for the condition of our finances—the boss, corporate politics, the government, coworkers, parents, a spouse. Maybe we're upset with the system in general because we don't have "enough."

In reality, we must all take responsibility for ourselves and accept God's sovereignty in all situations: "For there is no authority except from God and those which exist are established by God" (Romans 13:1).

Therefore, rationalizing that people are the cause of our financial problems completely ignores the truth of our responsibility and refuses to recognize that God is sovereign over all the people, circumstances, and conditions of our lives.

Excuses are a reflexive response to most of life's problems. They may be natural, but they are not admirable. What's most important to recognize is that excuses arise from the world's conditioning, and we must recognize them immediately for what they are: lies from the devil. Because Satan rules this earth, our struggle is with him. Self-examination of feelings, beliefs, and priorities is the first step in recovery from financial ailments. After years of brainwashing by the world, it takes some real effort to re-program biblical truth into our minds so we can begin to replace the lies of the world system with God's truth.

The symptoms of materialism are like those of many other diseases: we may be walking around with them without realizing it. This is why self-examination is important. If you're suffering from any symptoms of materialism, the prescription for cure is found in the Bible: all you need to do is take it literally, every day.

FROM BONDAGE TO JOY
To cure your ailing finances, begin by knowing God's thoughts on money and possessions so you can respond according to His will. Forget every lie you've learned about how to define success and deal with money. Start changing your thoughts, attitudes, and feelings to eliminate negative input (what the world has taught you about "things")

and replace it with positive input (God's Word). Then continue to dwell on the positive input by studying and repeating God's Word to yourself until it becomes a way of life.

In a recent poll, *USA Today* found that only 11 percent of Americans read the Bible daily. More than half read the Bible less than once a month or not at all. In a separate poll, the Barna Research Group found that only 18 percent of evangelical Christians read the Scriptures daily, and almost one in four people who profess to be Christians *never* read them!

Commit to reading the Bible every day. If you don't have time to read, listen to God's Word on cassette tapes while driving to and from work. In an average year, I hear the entire Bible four times that way. Study the Bible consistently; there are dozens of study aids available, if you need them. Take a Bible study at your church or a course at a local Bible college or seminary. Consider one of the fine correspondence courses currently available. Memorize Scripture and meditate on God's Word daily.

The remaining chapters of this book will focus on making you aware of, and teaching you how to apply, biblical financial principles in the following areas of your life: earning, saving, debt, spending, investing, and giving. Though each area will be treated as a separate topic, they are all fundamentally affected by one thing: *your attitude*. Learning biblical principles for earning, giving, saving, and spending money is not the most difficult part of becoming a faithful steward. The most difficult challenge is developing godly *attitudes* toward acquiring and using money.

Most of the New Testament letters, from Romans through 3 John, can be divided into one of two areas: *doctrine* or *application*. We have a tendency to skip the doctrine, which trains us how to think biblically, and move into the application, which tells us how to live. But *you can't live what you don't first know and believe*. If you study Jesus' teachings in the gospels, you'll find that He was more interested in *attitudes* than actions.

If the attitude of *your* heart is to do things God's way, you'll welcome the information you're about to receive. You'll be excited about applying these principles to your life, and you'll work at making them a habit. Then you're in for quite a ride as you watch how the application of God's principles can change your life from one of financial bondage to one of freedom and joy as He transforms you more closely into the image of Christ. I encourage you to start *now* on the adventure of building a new financial life on the guidelines in God's Word.

WORK AND EARNINGS

■

Lazy hands make a man poor,
but diligent hands bring wealth.
PROVERBS 10:4

Several years ago when I examined my job, all I could see was that I was helping the rich get richer. The majority of people who came to see me had a great deal of money. As I worked with them, I watched them become even wealthier.

But as I had grown in my knowledge of finance over the years, I had also grown in my knowledge of God's Word. As a Christian, I began asking myself, "What am I doing for the Kingdom and glory of God as an investment counselor?" I even considered retirement and thought about attending seminary so I could do something "more useful" for the Lord.

However, as I thought, prayed, and reflected on my life, God made it clear to me that a pastor is no more important or valuable to Him than an investment counselor; *it's what the investment counselor does with his time that's important to God.* I could bloom where I was planted and allow the Lord to work through me.

Once I looked around to see how God could use me, I saw several opportunities. For example: I had many clients who had no relationship with or belief in God. There were teaching opportunities at my church. Several Christian organizations were seeking biblical financial counsel and professional expertise. My two-hour commute to and from work gave me an opportunity to learn more about the Bible from cassette tapes.

But the truth was driven home to stay when I had an opportunity to share the gospel with an eighty-four-year-old client, who prayed to receive Christ. Ten days later, he was taken home to meet his Master. Even today, I thank God for the privilege of being used by Him because I was obedient and available. If I live to be eighty-four myself, I'll never forget the look on that gentleman's face (or his wife's!) after he prayed to receive Christ.

THE MYTH OF SACRED/SECULAR CAREERS
For the Christian, there should be no distinction between the "secular" jobs of the world and the "sacred" jobs of the ministry. All jobs are sacred to God. He has called us to perform those tasks in order that He might be glorified through us. If you're available and willing, you can begin to bear fruit right now, exactly where you're planted.

This chapter will examine key principles about work and earnings in the Bible and then look at specific applications of these principles for issues related to managing income.

THE BIBLICAL NATURE OF WORK—DILIGENCE
The Bible has a great deal to say about our work ethic. The attitude we have toward our work is of primary importance to God, and the book of Proverbs repeatedly uses the word *diligence* in connection with it. Diligence implies faithfulness and working hard at our assigned tasks. It is often contrasted with the word *slothful*, which means "lazy." A diligent person expends steady, earnest, and energetic effort. A slothful person is apathetic, indifferent, inconsistent, and habitually lazy.

The Bible pictures a diligent person as wise: "He who gathers crops in summer is a wise son, but he who sleeps during harvest is a disgraceful son" (Proverbs 10:5).

A diligent worker will prosper: "He who works his land will have abundant food, but he who chases fantasies lacks judgment" (Proverbs 12:11).

Diligent effort is rewarded: "Diligent hands will rule, but laziness ends in slave labor" (Proverbs 12:24).

The diligent worker plans ahead: "A prudent man sees danger and takes refuge, but the simple keep going and suffer for it" (Proverbs 22:3).

Diligence will be honored: "He who tends a fig tree will eat its fruit, and he who looks after his master will be honored" (Proverbs 27:18).

Principle 6—Have the Proper Attitude Toward Work

According to biblical principles, our motivation for work is based on our relationship with God. This is what shapes our attitudes toward our work. In Ecclesiastes, work is described as a blessing:

> Then I realized that it is good and proper for a man to eat and drink, and to find satisfaction in his toilsome labor under the sun during the few days of life God has given him—for this is his lot. Moreover, when God gives any man wealth and possessions, and enables him to enjoy them, to accept his lot and be happy in his work—this is a gift of God. (Ecclesiastes 5:18-19)

Therefore, no matter what kind of work we do, we are to do it diligently, accepting it as a blessing from God.

A man stopped at a construction site. He approached a bricklayer and asked him what he was making.

"Union wages," the bricklayer replied. "Sixteen-fifty-five an hour."

Halfway down the block, a second bricklayer was working. The man approached him and asked what he was making.

"A wall," the man responded.

The man then approached a third bricklayer and asked him the same question. The third mason replied, "I'm making a great cathedral to glorify God."

All three worked at the same job, but their different responses reflected the different attitudes of their hearts toward their work. Which of these responses most closely parallels your own attitude toward your job?

Principle 7—Acknowledge Your Dependence on God in Your Work

When Joseph was sold into slavery and taken to Egypt, he was purchased as a slave by an Egyptian named Potiphar, who recognized a difference in Joseph's attitude:

> The LORD was with Joseph and he prospered, and he lived in the house of his Egyptian master. When his master saw that the LORD was with him and that the LORD gave him success in everything he did, Joseph found favor in his eyes and became

his attendant. Potiphar put him in charge of his household
and he entrusted to his care everything he owned. (Genesis
39:2-4)

When we acknowledge our dependence upon God, our attitude
will be obvious to all, and God will be glorified. By contrast, the "self-
made" man works under the delusion that he can control his own fate.
In truth, there is no such thing as a "self-made" man. The Bible tells us
to remember that God is the one who gives us the ability to produce
wealth (Deuteronomy 8:18).

Five Scriptural Lessons on Work and Earnings
The Bible teaches five central lessons about work and earnings.

1. God owns everything, and we are to be faithful stewards of
all that He entrusts us with. In chapter 1 we explored the foundational truths of God's ownership, provision, and control of all
material goods.

2. We are to work as if we are working for God, because we are His
servants. No matter what we "work" at—our profession, our ministry
activities, our efforts in self-improvement—we should keep in mind that
we are working in obedience to God's command.

When I'm tempted to slack off, I'm reminded that I work for God,
and though I may be able to neglect some responsibility without anyone
ever knowing, *God* will know.

3. Christ is our boss. He has "called" us to the job we have right
now. He places us exactly where we need to be in order for Him to
fulfill His plan in our lives and the lives of those we touch.

God is no respecter of job status; we're all equal in His eyes. A
godly waitress or manual laborer is no less important to God than a
celebrity or the president of a large corporation. Instead of *position*, God
values *availability*. Our challenge is to accept our work as a calling from
God for as long as it lasts, glorifying God through a Christlike example
in our work. Our work is our testimony: "Let your light shine before
men in such a way that they may see your good works, and glorify your
Father who is in heaven" (Matthew 5:16).

4. We are to treat others fairly, justly, and with dignity because we
are all created by God, in His image.

5. There are two rewards for a job well done. One comes in the
here and now (our paycheck) and the second comes in the hereafter
(eternal life in Christ). Rewards (and working to get them) are biblical.

It's all right to work for them, as long as we recognize the danger of making rewards our priority.

PRINCIPLE 8—BE THANKFUL FOR WHAT YOU HAVE

Offering thanks for what you have and refusing to focus on what you lack is the secret to contentment in your work and life. If you continually give thanks for the job you have and concentrate on becoming excellent at your tasks, the Lord will reward you for your obedience.

Perhaps you have already chosen to focus on the things of God and store up treasures in Heaven. If so, I commend you. But I also warn you that it's a rare, wise, and discerning person who can avoid the temptations of a materialistic lifestyle. "Be of sober spirit, be on the alert. Your adversary, the devil, prowls about like a roaring lion, seeking someone to devour" (1 Peter 5:8, NASB). Even Christians with the purest of motives can never let their guard down.

PRINCIPLE 9—TAKE TIME FOR REST, RECREATION, AND RELAXATION

Forty years ago, efficiency experts verified the validity of balancing work with periods of rest. Instead of giving employees increased time away from work (vacations), experts found that efficiency and output increased when working periods were interspersed with periods of rest and time away from work stations.

The Bible has plenty to say about the relationship of work and rest. In the Ten Commandments, God established the Sabbath as a day of rest from six days of labor. This commandment reflected His work as Creator in toiling for six days and resting on the seventh. Jesus knew and acted upon the wisdom of taking time to rest and refresh Himself during His earthly ministry. After the disciples returned from a preaching tour, Jesus noticed that "so many people were coming and going that they did not even have a chance to eat." So He said to them, "Come with me by yourselves to a quiet place and get some rest" (Mark 6:31).

Efficiency experts have simply confirmed the wisdom of biblical counsel to balance our lives with time for work and time for rest. When you're tempted to work that seventh day, or to work during holidays and vacations, realize that you aren't really going to increase your productivity. Ultimately, you'll *decrease* it through overload. When your life is balanced with work and rest, you'll find that "the blessing of the LORD brings wealth, and he adds no trouble to it" (Proverbs 10:22).

GODLY AMBITION CAN LEAD TO BETTER PAY

Contentment and maintaining the proper balance of work and rest do not rule out ambition, however. There's nothing wrong with godly ambition. The Bible encourages us to seek excellence. It teaches us that the trademarks of a Christian worker are quality, service, and value. Godly ambition brings glory to God because service to others honors Him. But self-serving ambition, which strives after riches, fame, fortune, and power, is *not* biblical and will ultimately lead to ruin and destruction.

Part of godly ambition is seeking to improve in your professional field. This can lead to higher pay.

Some groups of professionals, such as doctors, dentists, and lawyers, earn wages far above the average. Generally, this is because their professions require a far-above-average investment of time and money for education. Such professions (and certainly many others) require tremendous effort and persistence. Even after completing their degrees, these professionals are required to spend from five to twenty hours per week just to keep current in their fields because of the explosion of information and technology.

By following this example and committing five hours per week to becoming tops in your field, it's possible to increase your earnings substantially. Investing time and money in your career will make you a more valuable and marketable professional.

For example, a hospital orderly could advance to a better-paying job in the medical field by taking classes in his spare time. College is not just for young people fresh out of high school. Increasing numbers of adults are enrolling in college courses and specialized professional training classes. Having taught in college, I know from experience that adults are generally better students because they're mature, hard-working, and goal-oriented. Most of them continue to work full time while taking two or three courses each semester.

Do you realize that by taking three courses each semester and two during the summer, you can get a college degree in only six years? Once you have a bachelor's degree, you can earn a master's degree in less than half that time. Your payoff for further education will be increasing your earning power as your extra effort becomes a key to open many doors of opportunity that may now be locked against you. If you're working five days at a current job, you might consider setting aside a sixth day each week committed to self-development in this area.

When I began as an investment advisor in 1970, I met with three of the most successful people I could find in my field because I wanted to know how to become successful myself. All three gave me the same advice: Because the area of finance is diverse—including insurance, investments, taxation, and law—to become a really competent general practitioner I'd have to study about twenty hours per week for five years. At the time I was unmarried and had no family responsibilities, but it was still difficult to study twenty hours on top of working full time.

Four years later, I married. By the time my son JT was born, all I could manage was fifteen hours per week. But five years from the time I started, I was in the top 2 percent of my field. My field of investment, tax, and estate planning is continually changing, so keeping current still requires studying for ten to fifteen hours each week.

I've invested a lot of time, effort, and money over the last twenty years in staying up to date in my field, but my payoff is a successful private practice that pays me ten times as much as I was earning twenty years ago.

If you don't currently have a plan in place to improve yourself, I encourage you to decide when, what, and how you plan to begin.

FAMILIES: ONE INCOME OR TWO?
One of the most important decisions newly married couples face is whether they will be a one-income or two-income family. This decision will have profound effects on the marriage and on any children who come later. It should be made only after the couple has set the priorities of their life together. If young marrieds decide that both partners will work, they must be prepared to make adjustments if and when children enter the marriage.

DINKS is a term coined to describe childless couples who are both working (Dual Income No Kids). Their dual income may allow them to qualify for their dream home, furnish it on credit, and fill their closets with a financed wardrobe. Perhaps they each drive a nice car. Everything is wonderful until the wife learns she's about to have a child. Suddenly, their $45,000 income will drop to $25,000, and they won't be able to fulfill their financial obligations. They're left with two unpleasant choices: finding day care for the baby so the wife can be employed outside the home, or changing their lifestyle dramatically so they can live within their reduced income. Many of these young couples end up in painful counseling sessions because they didn't take the time to plan for a decrease in income once children arrived.

The Bible says, "If anyone does not provide for his relatives, and especially for his immediate family, he has denied the faith and is worse than an unbeliever" (1 Timothy 5:8). The problem comes in attempting to define the phrase *provide for*. Does provision mean basic needs of food, clothing, and shelter? Or does it mean two nice cars in the driveway and designer clothing in the closet? Your answer will have a tremendous effect on your family, your work, your free time, and your spiritual and physical life. Because 80 to 90 percent of a child's personality is formed by the age of six, couples must decide whether a second car or a larger home is worth the psychological price their child will have to pay for their absence during his or her formative years.

Couples who can afford to do so can avoid much distress by choosing early on to live on the husband's income and bank the wife's, rather than living on both incomes and spending everything. In some instances, both spouses must work, even after children join the family. But please think about the two-income question—especially during the first six years of your child's life. Investing time and effort in a child's training and development glorifies God. If you can't decide, pray continually, and *listen* until the Lord makes His will clear to you.

How Much Does a Second Income Really Pay?

If you're a two-income family by habit, and you're trying to decide whether or not you can survive financially on one income, it might help you to calculate the net pay of the employed wife. Let's see what the net pay (that is, what you have left over after the costs associated with her job) is on a salary of $15,000 per year.

First, let's subtract some immediate deductions from the gross yearly salary in order to establish a net spendable amount.

Gross salary	$15,000.00
Giving	– $1,500.00
FICA (Federal Insurance Contributions Act)	– $1,126.50
Federal, state, and local taxes	– $4,500.00
Net salary	$7,873.50

Now we have take-home pay of $7,873.50 per year, or $656.13 per month. Let's see what's left of this salary after we figure out how much has to go to expenses associated with this job.

Net yearly salary	$7,873.50
Transportation	– $1,500.00
Child care	– $1,000.00
Clothing	– $1,000.00
Meals out	– $1,000.00
Net pay after expenses	$3,373.50

The spouse's net pay of $3,373.50 yields a monthly sum of $281.13—or $1.69 per hour! And, realistically, you won't really net $1.69 per hour because by the weekend, you'll both be too tired to clean and you'll end up hiring someone to help with cleaning. You'll rationalize that it costs only $50 and it gives you more quality time with the kids. But if you do that only twice a month, you'll see another $1200 per year trickle through your finger tips. And if you take an expensive family vacation to try to make up for all the time you don't normally get to spend together, you could easily put a thousand dollars on your credit card, which will charge you 18 to 21 percent interest. Add to that an extra $750 or so you wouldn't normally spend for birthdays and Christmas, and you're lucky if you're ahead by a few dollars each month at the end of the year. Once couples recognize these realities, many of them reevaluate the desirability of a two-income household.

Benefits of Moms at Home

Our society has devalued young mothers who want to stay at home and raise their own children. But in truth, there's no job on earth more significant in God's eyes than nurturing the children He's blessed you with, and training them up in the way they should go.

Families with Mom at home can save money by spending time studying grocery ads and clipping coupons. Hundreds of dollars per year can be saved by shopping garage sales, or perhaps even making some clothing items, instead of buying everything new. Hundreds more can be saved by making meals at home instead of going out to eat several times a week.

There are many possibilities for earning money while managing a home full-time. For example, I know a single mother who teaches music lessons in her home four hours a day and six hours on Saturday. She is able to earn $14,000 to $15,000 in yearly income. Some women are able to earn as much or more by making clothing and doing alterations. Some women baby-sit; others use their creative talents to manufacture and market various goods and services.

I don't mean to imply that every woman who manages a home and cares for children ought to take on income-producing work as well. But those who are considering working outside the home, or who are already doing so, might find it helpful in evaluating their situation to run a comparison of their net pay to the costs and sacrifices incurred by that job.

Special Challenges for Single Moms and Widows

The most traumatic cases I see in counseling are single moms with small children. Without job skills, it's almost impossible for them to maintain a household and provide adequately for basic needs. If work is a necessity, jobs are scarce. If the single mother's lucky enough to find a job, she can seldom earn enough to have anything left after paying for housing and child care.

The financial impact of divorce is almost always traumatic. In many cases, the woman has no marketable job skills if she's been out of the work place for a number of years while bearing most of the responsibility for caring for the children. She may receive a property settlement and/or child support for a period of time, but she's definitely handicapped financially, especially if her ex-spouse can't or won't live up to his financial commitments.

Divorce is a tragic event, but it happens. For that reason, it's wise for every woman to acquire marketable job skills early in life, preferably before marriage. Her skills can be used to supplement the family income and provide some of the "wants" many families couldn't otherwise afford. And in some sad cases, those skills will make the difference between bare existence and living, when divorce occurs.

No one wants to think about losing a spouse, but it happens, and generally speaking, women outlive men. Today, the average widow is fifty-four years old, and she's been out of the job market for at least twenty years. If she has no minor children, Social Security will not be of any help to her for almost a decade. If her husband was wise enough to have life insurance, she'll survive on the benefits for a couple of years, but then she's faced with returning to work and/or changing her lifestyle.

For these reasons, I have tremendous respect for any couple who makes sure that both spouses are involved in managing their personal finances so either one is prepared in case she or he is left alone. Thinking about divorce or the death of a spouse is an unpleasant task, but anticipating problems helps to prevent them.

Whether you're married or single, with or without children, just beginning your marriage or the veteran of one, you'll benefit by pondering these questions:

1. What are your "needs" for living?
2. Is your current lifestyle balanced, or is it excessive?
3. If you found yourself divorced or widowed tomorrow, could you cope?
4. Are you financially prepared for life's potential problems?

If you can't answer these questions satisfactorily, you might want to take a few minutes right now to identify the areas you need to work on. Then take steps to get the information you need.

WHY THE ANSWER TO YOUR PROBLEMS IS NOT SIMPLY INCREASING YOUR INCOME

A popular myth today is that people with financial problems can solve them simply by making more money. Whether you earn $20,000 or $200,000 a year, the only way to get out of debt is to *stop spending more than you earn.* In fact, increasing your income may simply *prolong* your problems.

To prove my point, look to the government for a bad example. Income tax provides income for the federal government. For thirty years, Washington has continued to raise taxes while failing to balance the federal budget. Instead, the government continues to *increase* its spending.

National and personal debt will continue to grow until all of us accept the fact that we shouldn't buy goods and services we can't pay for. The underlying cause of financial problems is not lack of dollars; it's lack of contentment and poor allocation of funds. Once we learn to be thankful for what we have, we can quit worrying about what we want and concentrate on managing what God has already given us. Once we begin to control our spending, we'll reverse our deficits and have the opportunity to deal with surplus.

Chapter 8 will go into more detail on practical aspects of spending. The accompanying checklist (see box on page 36) included here spells out a few basic spending principles that are important to keep in mind.

PRINCIPLE 10—MANAGE YOUR INCREASING INCOME

If you're like most people, income is probably the greatest financial asset you have. Hundreds of thousands of dollars can flow through your hands during your lifetime.

Finances are like our human bodies and minds: They operate on the law of growth or atrophy. Either we have a plan to grow and develop, or we watch as our bodies, minds, and finances dwindle away. If you have no plan, then both time and wealth will slip through your fingers. At the end of the race, you'll have nothing to show for your efforts. But if you commit to a program of developing yourself and your skills, your income will grow beyond the average. And if you have a plan for managing that increased income, the odds of financial success will tip dramatically in your favor.

Unfortunately, however, people don't plan for or respond to gradual changes, and the increase is dissipated. Commit now to using a percentage of your next raise to achieve worthwhile goals and objectives for yourself and your family (see accompanying box on "Potential Savings from Income Growth," page 37). If you do this, time will become your ally.

A CHECKLIST FOR SPENDING CONTROL

If you want to begin to control your spending, eliminate overspending, and retire debt, ask yourself the following questions before you make a purchase.

1. *Is this expenditure motivated by love of things?* "Do not love the world or anything in the world. If anyone loves the world, the love of the Father is not in him" (1 John 2:15).
2. *Have I misused the money God provided to meet this need?* "You want something but don't get it. You kill and covet, but you cannot have what you want. You quarrel and fight. You do not have because you do not ask God. When you ask, you do not receive, because you ask with wrong motives, that you may spend what you get on your pleasures" (James 4:2-3).
3. *Do I have doubts rather than peace about the decision?* "But the man who has doubts is condemned if he eats, because his eating is not from faith; and everything that does not come from faith is sin" (Romans 14:23).
4. *Have I given God an opportunity to meet my need?* "The LORD does not let the righteous go hungry but he thwarts the cravings of the wicked" (Proverbs 10:3).
5. *Will this expenditure be disadvantageous to my spiritual growth?* "'Everything is permissible for me'—but not everything is beneficial. 'Everything is permissible for me'—but I will not be mastered by anything" (1 Corinthians 6:12).
6. *Am I using God's money wisely?* "Store up for yourself treasures in heaven, where moth and rust do not destroy, and where thieves do not break in and steal" (Matthew 6:20).
7. *Will this purchase put me into debt?* "The rich man rules over the poor, and the borrower is servant to the lender" (Proverbs 22:7).
8. *Do I or my family really "need" this, or is the purchase an indulgence?* "Watch out! Be on your guard against all kinds of greed; a man's life does not consist in the abundance of his possessions" (Luke 12:15).

Two characteristics of financially and spiritually mature people are *self-discipline* and *planning ahead*. Spending may be more fun than saving, but saving will provide huge dividends throughout your life. Be encouraged by these words: "No discipline seems pleasant at the time, but painful. Later on, however, it produces a harvest of righteousness and peace for those who have been trained by it" (Hebrews 12:11).

POTENTIAL SAVINGS FROM INCOME GROWTH

If you earn $20,000 per year today, and your income grows by 5 percent each year, here's what your income will look like at several different time intervals:

Year	Income	Savings	Save at 4% Interest
1	$20,000	-0-	-0-
5	$25,526	$2,155	$2,415
10	$32,578	$5,503	$8,417
15	$41,578	$9,789	$15,427
20	$53,066	$14,075	$25,537
30	$86,438	$29,971	$59,631
40	$140,800	$55,840	$121,934

If these figures seem unrealistic, look back ten years ago at what you were earning. Your wages during the past decade have probably grown between 60 and 100 percent, along with the cost of living. If you had allocated just one-half of your annual increases to savings, you would now be saving almost 20 percent of your income in ten years!

Perhaps you are single today, twenty-five years old, and committed to saving half of all raises, bonuses, and gifts. If you continue this process for forty working years, and earn only 4 percent on your savings, you could accumulate as much as $121,934. If you are fifty years old and do the same thing consistently for fifteen years, putting your money in government savings bonds paying 4 percent, you could have a retirement nest egg of $15,427. Small amounts of money properly managed over time yield amazing results, thanks to the power of compound interest.

PRINCIPLE 11—APPLY THE TRANSFORMING POWER OF SCRIPTURE

I encourage you to read this chapter more than once. Write down the principles, along with relevant Scripture passages, that seem most important for your particular circumstances right now. Meditate on these biblical principles. Do you understand them? In what ways are you living by them in your day-to-day attitudes and actions? Where do you want to make changes to apply them more thoroughly?

If you weren't already committed to living a biblically based life, you probably wouldn't have read this far. If you feel either discomfort or eagerness at this point, perhaps it's the convicting work of the Holy Spirit, encouraging you toward change. Remember the apostle's words: "Do not merely listen to the word, and so deceive yourselves. Do what it says" (James 1:22).

The power to change your life and to manage your finances according to God's will is found in the living word of the Bible. As you listen to it, read it, study it, and meditate on it, you can be sure that it will transform your life—because the Bible says this about itself: "For the word of God is living and active. Sharper than any double-edged sword, it penetrates even to dividing soul and spirit, joints and marrow; it judges the thoughts and attitudes of the heart" (Hebrews 4:12).

Just as our physical growth and survival depend upon our intake of food and water, so our spiritual life depends upon our intake, understanding, and application of Scripture. If you aren't consistent in daily study of the Bible, I encourage you to try it for twenty-one days. At the end of that time, you will experience, in a very dramatic way, the benefit of time spent in God's Word each day.

THREE

SAVING

■

Go to the ant, you sluggard, consider its ways and be wise!
It has no commander, no overseer or ruler,
yet it stores its provisions in summer
and gathers its food at harvest.
PROVERBS 6:6-8

■

There is precious treasure and oil in the dwelling of the wise,
But a foolish man swallows it up.
PROVERBS 21:20, NASB

By nature, Americans are a positive, resourceful, optimistic people. We tend to assume that when things are good, they will continue to be good forever, so we spend as much as we earn.

In fact, however, all economic expansions and periods of good times are ultimately followed by periods of economic contraction, recession, or even depression. When we fail to act according to this reality, we find ourselves severely affected when the downturn comes.

The financial hardship accompanying bad economic times can be eased or eliminated if we simply learn to save a percentage of what remains after tithing and requisite expenses. *The Living Bible* says it best: "The wise man saves some of his paycheck but the fool spends whatever he gets" (Proverbs 21:20).

If you look back over our country's two-hundred-plus years, you will find that for one hundred and sixty of those years, the American people followed the biblical principle of saving 10 percent of their incomes. Benjamin Franklin's statement "a penny saved is a penny earned" was, I'm sure, an often-quoted bit of wisdom that most people applied to their lives. However, in the last forty years, the savings rate of the American people has dropped by 80 percent while our debt load has risen 1,000 percent!

The average American worker has no savings and lives paycheck to paycheck. This fact is most significant in light of the increasing number of homeless families on our streets. Many of the homeless failed to prepare themselves for hard economic times; when they lost their jobs, they had no savings to cover their housing payments. Most people could survive missing one paycheck, and many could scrape by if they missed a second one. But for the vast majority of the American population, missing a third paycheck would likely mean having to sell possessions and being foreclosed on or evicted from their home.

Are you saving some of every paycheck that comes your way? If you are, I congratulate you, because you are a member of a wise minority. If you're not saving, I admonish you to begin, because the harvest season does not last forever. If you're a realist, you must understand that the good times will not roll forever. If your beliefs contradict your habits, you need to change your habits.

SAVINGS: A BIBLICAL CONCEPT

The Bible repeatedly teaches the wisdom of consistently saving part of our income. This wisdom is demonstrated in the first verse from Proverbs quoted in the opening of this chapter. The ant, who saves a portion of the food gathered during a good season for use during barren times, is analogous to the wise person. Failure to save means hunger, hardship, and even death during lean times. Through God's Word, we are to learn this behavior (which is instinctive for the ant) and apply it to our lives.

The principle of saving ahead of time occurs in the Bible when Joseph, after interpreting Pharaoh's dream of seven good years followed by seven years of famine, suggested that Pharaoh save a fifth of the produce in the land of Egypt during the coming years of abundance as a reserve for the subsequent seven years of famine. Obviously, the purpose for the reserve (savings) was to protect the people from perishing during the famine. This is the principle expressed in the second passage from Proverbs quoted above.

In the past, I've heard Christians say that saving for the future replaces trust in God to provide. In defense of this position they point to the Bible's teaching in Matthew 6:26—God feeds the birds, who neither sow, nor reap, nor store up reserves. Because we know we're more important to our Creator than birds, this thinking goes, we can adopt a "Don't-worry-God-will-provide" attitude about saving.

The problem with this logic is that it removes responsibility from us and places all the obligation on God. That isn't faith and trust, it's simply presuming on God to do everything so that we can ignore our own responsibility. I like the old saying, "Pray as if it all depends on God, but work as if it all depends on you."

Now I'm going to ask you two questions. Don't just read the questions; put this book down and give them some serious thought. If the answers frighten you, it's time to make some changes in your spending and saving habits. Here goes:

1. If you became ill and couldn't work, if you were laid off, or if your income were reduced, how long could you survive, financially?
2. If you lost all means of financial support tomorrow, how many months would pass before you lost your home?

WHERE AND WHAT TO SAVE

I suggest specific savings accounts for seven different necessities:

1. Big items (cars, appliances, etc.)
2. Reserves (in case you lose your job or are unable to work)
3. Retirement
4. Education
5. Repair and maintenance (on home, automobiles, and appliances)
6. Emergencies (airfares, excessive medical bills not covered by insurance, etc.)
7. Annual events (Christmas, birthdays, etc.)

Later in this chapter, we'll explore the particular principles that apply to each of the above. But first, we'll examine various places to accumulate savings by looking at the pros and cons of different types of accounts.

Places to Save

Today there are more places than ever to save: banks, credit unions, insurance companies, government instruments, brokers, and mutual funds. Each of these places offers different advantages.

Your first concern should be for the safety of your savings. Evaluate this factor by determining whether you can withdraw as much (or more) than you deposited if and when you need the money. If there's any chance of loss, you look for another account that will at least guarantee the return of your deposits.

A second important factor in a savings account is the ability to withdraw money if and when you need it without paying a withdrawal penalty. For example, a one-year Certificate of Deposit (CD) may offer you a higher rate of interest than a savings account, but that comes with a built-in disadvantage: You will pay a substantial penalty for early withdrawal. This is what is meant by a CD becoming "liquid" only upon maturity, and not before. Look for easy accessibility to your funds.

The rate of interest varies with different types of accounts. When you are evaluating interest rates of varying accounts, be careful not to compare apples with oranges. Make sure that safety (liquidity without penalty) and accessibility are identical.

Some people prefer to open a separate savings account for each general category of savings. Others like to keep all their savings in one account. My recommendation would be to use one account in what's called a money market mutual fund. Unlike savings accounts, most money markets have no minimums or service charges and offer free check-writing privileges with a minimum check of $100 or more.

If your bank has established a minimum for opening such a money market account, you may want to use envelopes for each of the separate savings accounts until you're able to save the minimum. That way, you eliminate paying a service charge each month.

Now let's look at the savings principles for each of the seven general areas of savings listed above.

PRINCIPLE 12—SAVE FOR THE BIG ITEMS

I encourage you to save for the major items you buy, such as automobiles, appliances, furniture, or landscaping for your home. Since home and transportation are the two biggest expenses for the average family, I have devoted an entire chapter to each of these two areas (chapters 5 and 6). Here I simply want to emphasize how important it is to save for major expenditures in those areas ahead of time, rather than buying everything at once and financing at high rates of interest over time.

To illustrate the principle of saving for major items, let's assume you want to buy a new dining room set. The set you have selected costs $2,500 total, including tax and delivery.

There are two ways to buy the furniture. The most common (and most expensive) is to buy it now and finance it over forty-eight months, at about 15 percent interest. That would require you to make payments of $69.58 a month. The other way is to buy it later. In the meantime, you make those payments of $69.58 to yourself each month, putting them into a savings account that earns you 6 percent interest. If you choose option number two, you'll have your new furniture in just thirty-four months, saving $974.12 in interest—almost 40 percent the price of the furniture!

PRINCIPLE 13—SAVE FOR REPLACING YOUR INCOME IF DISASTER STRIKES

If you were to experience an illness, accident, layoff, or pay cut, would you have enough reserves to carry you through? Most of us wouldn't, because we prefer to think that those things happen only to other people. But this is an unbiblical and dangerous position.

How much should you keep in savings to protect yourself from disasters that can reduce or eliminate your income? I recommend saving a minimum of three to six months of living expenses. If your after-tax spendable income is two thousand dollars per month, you should keep a minimum of six to twelve thousand dollars in savings as protection against unforeseeable circumstances. It is not excessive to keep twelve to twenty-four months of wages in reserve in case of disaster. In fact, most financial experts consider a one- to two-year reserve (or, on the two-thousand-dollar monthly figure, savings of twenty-four to forty-eight thousand dollars) a conservative guideline.

I'm sure that now you're asking, "How in the world can the average person ever save that much for reserves?" You can find the answer in principle 18 of this chapter.

PRINCIPLE 14—SAVE FOR RETIREMENT

Let's illustrate the principle of saving for the future with three hypothetical people: Buck, Penny, and Rich. Interestingly enough, all three were born on April 15.

Buck began saving early in life. Every year for eight years, starting at the age of twenty-one, he faithfully deposited $2,000 in his IRA account, which earned him 10 percent interest. After his twenty-eighth birthday, Buck quit funding his IRA and simply let the account compound until he reached age sixty-five. During his eight years of following good principles, Buck invested a total of $16,000 for his later years.

Penny, on the other hand, reached twenty-one and put off funding her IRA for eight years. But starting on her twenty-ninth birthday and every year thereafter, she faithfully deposited $2,000 a year into an IRA. Penny continued to invest $2,000 a year for thirty-seven years, saving a total of $74,000 at 10 percent interest in her IRA by the time she reached sixty-five.

Who do you think had the larger IRA at age sixty-five, Buck or Penny?

Year	Age	Buck	Penny	Rich
1	21	$2,200	-0-	$4,722
2	22	$4,620	-0-	$7,394
3	23	$7,282	-0-	$10,333
4	24	$10,210	-0-	$13,566
5	25	$13,431	-0-	$17,123
6	26	$16,974	-0-	$21,035
7	27	$20,871	-0-	$25,339
8	28	$25,158	-0-	$30,073
9	29	$27,674	$2,200	$35,280
10	30	$30,441	$4,620	$41,008
15	35	$49,026	$20,872	$72,475
20	40	$78,957	$47,045	$141,426
25	45	$127,160	$89,198	$241,200
30	50	$204,793	$157,086	$401,886
35	55	$329,821	$266,420	$660,673
40	60	$531,180	$442,503	$1,077,452
45	65	$855,471	$726,087	$1,814,032

You can see from the figures in the accompanying chart that on their sixty-fifth birthdays, Buck had $129,808 more money than Penny did, even though he had invested $58,000 less. The lesson is the younger you begin to save, the greater your benefit.

What about Rich? Well, Rich really understood the value of compound interest. So unlike either Buck or Penny, he didn't wait until his birthday (April 15) to fund his IRA. Rich chose to fund his IRA fifteen months and fifteen days earlier, on January 1 of the year he would reach his twentieth birthday. The earliest you can fund an IRA is January 1, 1990, for example. The longest you can wait to fund an IRA is April 15, 1991. Rich combined the consistency of Buck and

Penny while getting an earlier start. His account balance on his sixty-sixth birthday was $1,814,032—$230,474 greater than Buck and Penny combined ($1,581,558). Rich invested only $4,000 more than Buck and Penny, once at age twenty and again at sixty-five for his sixty-sixth birthday coming fifteen and one-half months later. But because he invested before the tax deadline (which coincidentally was the same as his birthday), his savings yielded him $230,474 more. Rich demonstrates the value of "do it now."

Be Realistic in Your Retirement Planning

After looking at Rich and his $1,814,032 retirement package, you may be thinking that all there is to retirement planning is to start an IRA at age twenty and put two thousand dollars into it every year thereafter. After all, any fool could live on just the interest from almost two million dollars.

But chances are good that you didn't start an IRA at age 20, and may not have one even now. So let's assume that you are age thirty-five today and want to have at least $2,000 per month to retire on at age sixty-five. How much will that investment over the next thirty years yield upon retirement?

Interest rates vary, but let's assume you will earn 10 percent each year for the next thirty years. You will need $240,000 at age sixty-five in order to produce ten years of income at $24,000 per year, or $2,000 per month. Using the compound interest charts (or a calculator), you'll find that all you need to do is save $1,326 per year at 10 percent interest to reach your goal of $240,000 at the age of sixty-five. The following chart shows the amount of required annual savings at varying rates of interest, in order to achieve the equivalent of $2,000 per month retirement income.

Age	10% Interest Rate	8% Interest Rate	6% Interest Rate
21	$334	$778	$1,889
25	$493	$1,072	$2,438
30	$805	$1,612	$3,386
35	$1,326	$2,452	$4,773
40	$2,218	$3,800	$6,878
45	$3,809	$6,070	$10,258
50	$6,867	$10,230	$16,212
55	$13,690	$19,175	$28,629
60	$35,738	$47,349	$66,942
65	$240,000	$300,000	$400,000

If you earn 8 percent instead of 10 percent, your goal would be to have a total of $300,000 in savings by age sixty-five, but an 8-percent interest rate requires a substantially higher annual savings. If you earn only 6 percent, you need $400,000 to yield the same $2,000 per month for your retirement income. Look carefully at your annual required savings. A thirty-five-year-old, earning 6 percent interest, needs to save $4,773 per year every year to have a $2,000 a month retirement income. Depressing, isn't it? And there's more.

When saving for retirement, you must consider what inflation will average during the next thirty years. Of course no one knows with any certainty, and estimates can vary greatly, but the following chart can help you project the rate of inflation. It shows you how many dollars you will need in the future to buy what a dollar buys today.

Years	3% Inflation Rate	5% Inflation Rate	7% Inflation Rate
5	$1.16	$1.28	$1.41
10	$1.34	$1.63	$1.97
15	$1.56	$2.08	$2.76
20	$1.81	$2.65	$3.87
25	$2.09	$3.39	$5.43
30	$2.43	$4.32	$7.61
35	$2.81	$5.52	$10.68
40	$3.26	$7.04	$14.97
45	$3.78	$8.99	$21.00

Examine the last thirty years and you will find that we have experienced about 5 percent annual inflation. Remember Rich's $1,814,032 nest egg? If he had experienced a 5 percent inflation rate over his forty-five years of faithfully funding his IRA, his buying power would have been reduced to $199,385 on the day of his retirement. Still, who couldn't retire on almost $200,000?

You may already be planning for retirement, but are you planning for inflation? A retiring couple at age sixty-five today has a joint life-span of approximately twenty years. During that time, prices will probably continue to rise. Optimists figure that prices will double over the next twenty years, while the pessimists say they will quadruple. Even if you earn 10 percent interest on your savings, the buying power of your income stream will drop 50 to 75 percent over your lifetime. Pretty depressing, isn't it? And there's more. . . .

There will be taxes due on your nest egg. If you're like Rich, lucky enough to have $1,814,032 tucked away, you'll have to pay about 31 percent in taxes when you finally withdraw your IRA to live on. At the risk of seeming really morbid, let's look at what happens to Rich's IRA.

Apparent value	$1,814,032 (invested $92,000)
31% loss to taxes	− $562,350
46-year loss to inflation	− $1,098,696
Real NET money left	$152,986

Remember that Rich earned 10 percent interest each year. What if you earn only 8 or 6 percent? After taxes and inflation, you wouldn't be able to retire, would you?

Now you have a realistic picture of retirement planning. You must diminish the apparent fortune compounded at 10 percent for the effects of inflation and taxes to see what you will *really* need to retire on. Then you can adjust that for rising prices over your retirement years, and decide to liquidate all your principal so you can spend your last dollar the day you die.

That's a true picture of what's required to build a retirement plan. It illustrates why the number-one fear of all retirees is inflation. Here is where we need to examine two critical ideas for biblical retirement planning.

Biblical Retirement Planning

There is only one reference to retirement in the entire Bible (Numbers 8:24, which refers to the retirement of priests at age fifty). Our culture places a very unbiblical emphasis on retirement. Most people look at retirement as a deserved break from hard work, a time to have fun and do what they *want* to do instead of what they *have* to do. Yet biblical guidelines don't encourage us to retire at a set age and live for ourselves. Instead, the Bible steers us away from self-indulgence and encourages us to lead a productive life for God as long as we live.

What are your goals for retirement? When do you want to retire, and why? Spend some time meditating on your answers to these questions. Instead of retiring from work, think about slowing down in your later years. If you are in a physically demanding job, you might not be able to work eight-hour days—but what about four-hour days? What about changing to a less physically demanding job?

There are many alternatives to retirement. Pray about how you should serve the Lord once you finally have some free time on your hands.

As an investment advisor in a retirement community, I have dozens of clients who volunteer to serve others. Some teach or tutor, some visit shut-ins, others help in the hospice program. All of those who serve, do so remembering that "even the Son of Man did not come to be served, but to serve, and to give His life as a ransom for many" (Mark 10:45).

When you formulate a biblical philosophy on retirement, you will see how biblical principles will lead you toward godly goals.

Recently, I gave a seminar in which I covered the material about retirement savings plans that you have just read. A gentleman attending that seminar returned the following day, ready to prove that retirement was not a realistic possibility, given the state of today's economy. He accused me of ignoring the facts, and trying to appease those who had no real possibility of retiring, anyway.

After showing me his careful calculations, which demonstrated the financial impossibility of retiring on an average retirement savings plan, he shouted at me, "Why don't you tell these folks the truth? There's no way, even with Bible principles, to be able to retire unless you inherit money, marry it, or really make the big dollars!"

Then he challenged me: "Try to solve this problem using your Bible bunk!"

The Bible *does* have the answer. It's principle 11, "Manage Your Increasing Income," which we looked at in chapter 2.

Let's say you save 10 percent of your earnings. We'll assume that your earnings never rise in real terms, but they do keep up with inflation, which averages 6 percent per year. If you never earned more than $24,000 per year, look where you would be on the two rates of return:

Year	10% Savings on 0% Earning Increase	10% Savings on 2% Increase
5	$13,529	$14,363
10	$31,634	$35,331
15	$55,925	$65,765
20	$83,147	$103,033
30	$186,602	$257,384
40	$354,899	$546,684

These numbers ignore the fact that by using the principles laid out in the next three chapters (debt, home, and car) during your final ten to twenty working years, you can become debt free, enabling yourself to save 20 to 40 percent of your paycheck for retirement.

Finally, if you shift to a 60 percent workload from age sixty-five to seventy, you'll still be earning a living while your assets continue to compound. If, at age seventy, you combine your $24,000 per year over time with your $354,899 in savings, you'll have enough capital to last an additional fifteen more years. So you see, *following biblical principles does work* if *you apply the principles* now.

If you're like most people, all these dollars, time periods, interest rates, taxes, and inflation numbers give you a headache. To simplify everything, let me tell you that in order to retire, you must save a *percentage, not a dollar amount*, of a rising income. Then you'll be able to retire on 70 percent of your current income, with enough money to last beyond your average life-span plus ten years.

In the following chart, find your age. The corresponding percent is the amount of your income you should save in order to retire, assuming average rates of return, inflation, and taxes.

Age	Percentage of Your Income You Must Save
25	10%
30	14%
35	20%
40	28%
45	41%
50	64%
55	114%

These percentages do not take into account the principles you will learn in the remainder of the book. If you utilize these principles, you can cut the required savings by 50 to 75 percent, or double to triple your retirement dollars. To repeat, *retirement is not a problem if you commit yourself to applying biblical principles to your life, starting NOW.*

PRINCIPLE 15—SAVE FOR YOUR CHILD'S EDUCATION

Most parents feel responsible for providing their children with a college education, but how responsible are you, *really*, for putting your children through college? Experience has shown me, time and again, that those men and women who pay some or all of their own college expenses learn life's lessons earlier and get far more out of their college experience than do those who let their parents pay for everything.

The book of Proverbs challenges parents to get their children into a right relationship with God, teach them a trade, and pray that they marry a godly man or woman. Nowhere is it written that parents are financially responsible for the higher education of their children.

The issue of whether or not to foot the bill for your child's education is a matter of personal choice, which depends on individual circumstances. Higher education is not the right of every child; it is a privilege earned through biblical diligence and hard work.

Hebrew wisdom tells us that the man who doesn't teach his son a trade raises a thief. But there's a big difference between teaching a child a trade and sending him to school for four years to earn a degree. In the world, we're paid for what we can do. We are not paid for what we know. In my opinion, our society overemphasizes grade-point averages and college degrees while underemphasizing learning a trade and developing a godly character, both of which are imperative for children to become successful adults. Regardless of what society tells us, adults *can* succeed in the real world without a college degree, and college is not the best answer for everyone.

As an example, consider Mary, who lost her husband at age thirty and appeared to be stuck. She had no job skills, only a tenth-grade education, and a ten-year-old daughter to raise. Knowing that God had a special place in his heart for widows, she began to pray for guidance. Soon Mary had an idea: she excelled at cleaning homes—after all, she had sixteen years of experience! It was a perfect solution; she could set her own hours and still be home when Alice returned from school. Within a year, Mary was earning over $20,000 a year cleaning homes.

Although Mary was not by any means affluent, she managed to provide quite nicely for herself and her daughter. She even put aside $7.50 per week for her daughter's education. That doesn't seem like much, but $7.50 per week became $375 per year.

At the end of eight years, Mary ended up with $3,760, which Alice used to complete a licensed practical nurse training program in just eighteen months. During the training program, Alice lived with her mother. She got her first job before she reached the age of twenty, starting at $20,000 per year.

During the next five years, Alice's salary rose to $24,000 per year, due to the quality of her work and her exceptional character and people skills. At the same time, she was attending night school. By age twenty-four, Alice was a registered nurse. She was offered a job making $46,000 a year, which she quickly accepted.

Since Alice had learned good money management skills from her mother, she saved the majority of her $24,000 salary while going to school! After taxes, giving, and contributing to her own support, Alice managed to save $13,076 per year. After her graduation ceremony, Alice handed her mother a check for $60,000, which Mary used to pay off her mortgage. She even had enough left over to buy herself a beautiful, two-year-old Honda Accord.

Clearly, Mary didn't have the resources to provide Alice with the

$100,000 education that is so common today. But she did have hours in her day to spend reading and studying the Bible with her daughter. Because Mary took the time to teach her daughter biblical wisdom and followed the Bible's command to get her child into a right relationship with God, Alice is now a godly wife. She married a Christian doctor and today is busy raising three lovely children of her own.

My youngest son, John, was born in 1979. Back then, a year at our state university cost about $2,560, compared to about $7,300 for a year at an Ivy League school. I knew college prices would rise over time, so we did our planning based on that fact.

In the last ten years, the cost of attending college has risen almost 10 percent per year. We figure that by the time John's ready for college, four years at a state university will cost $45,000, while an Ivy League education will be around $122,546. That pretty much eliminates the Harvards of this world, in my view.

My son happens to be academically inclined. He works hard in school, and he excels. Therefore, it's my choice to pay for his college education. So, early on, I began to plan the most efficient way to save for college. I figured that if I saved $4,387 per year for eighteen years, we'd have enough to send John to a four-year state university. By using a little tax planning so the money would grow without paying taxes until withdrawal, I could reduce my investment to $2,829 per year by buying EE bonds. (EE government savings bonds are bought at a discount and mature at par ten or more years later. All the interest is non-taxable if used for education of a child.) And I could go one step further: by using a Clifford trust (an educational trust, designed by a tax attorney), I could reduce the cost to $1,953 per year. By saving $162.75 a month for eighteen years, John's college expenses would be paid for.

Another alternative would be to save 3.5 percent per year of a $24,000 per year rising income. With each raise, more money could go into the college fund. If my income grew by 5.5 percent per year, the fixed savings rate of 3.5 percent would take care of John's college expenses.

All this planning was done thirteen years ago. Since that time, God has guided me and abundantly blessed our investments. John's college fund is worth over $50,000 today, in part because we have netted over 10 percent interest. At that rate, we will have almost $100,000 in his college fund by the time he's old enough to go.

Here's how we plan to use this fund. John will stay at home his first two years of school, and use part of the interest on the account to pay for his tuition, books, and school expenses. We will give him the balance of the earnings to see how he handles it. If he's wise and industrious, he should be able to save $15,000, which he can use to pay for his second two years of school, either on campus at a Christian university or living at home and commuting, if he so chooses. If he's a wise steward, at graduation he'll have enough money left to buy himself a home and a car, all paid for in cash, and still have $20,000.

On the other hand, if John proves to be foolish or acts as a poor steward, we will use his college fund to support a missionary. If he remains foolish, or is still a poor steward by age twenty-five, we will not give him any more help.

If you're facing the dilemma of what to do about a college education for your child, ask yourself three questions:

- How much responsibility do you assume for your child's higher education?
- Would your child do better learning a trade, or having a degree?
- What will you start putting aside *today*, to meet the liability you assume?

Don't worry if you can't find a way to educate your child. God is sovereign. Maybe His plan is for your child to pay his own way. Personally, I did that—-and many others do it, too. The lessons I learned working full time and carrying a full academic load were invaluable. Maybe God's plan for your child is a full or partial scholarship. (It may interest you to learn that every year, over one-third of all scholarship funds go unused because they are never even applied for.) Regardless of your situation, make your child's education a matter of prayer. When you do, you will find that God will supply all your needs.

PRINCIPLE 16—SAVE FOR REPAIR AND MAINTENANCE

If you don't have specific savings set aside for maintenance and repairs, these expenses will ultimately end up on your credit card at 18.96 percent interest—or worse.

A general guideline is to keep $1,000 to $2,000 in savings to cover the repair and maintenance on your home and car. If you save only $10 each week at 6 percent interest, in twelve months you will have saved a total of $592. If you can manage to save $20 per week at 6 percent interest, you'll have $1,184 in your repair and maintenance fund at the end of one year.

The question is, will you start now to save for repair and maintenance, or will you wait until a problem occurs, and then worry about how to pay for it? The choice is yours.

PRINCIPLE 17—SAVE FOR EMERGENCIES

I recommend saving $500 to $1,000 for emergency use. Perhaps one night you get a call from your parents, telling you your father has had a heart attack and is scheduled for surgery in three days. If you have the emergency fund, use it to buy your plane ticket—that's what it's there for. If not, you have no choice but to charge the ticket, or ask your folks if they can pay your fare.

There are plenty of other uses for emergency funds. What about the $500 deductible on your medical insurance, or the medical expense that isn't covered by your insurance carrier? What about the fender-bender that will cost you $467 to repair? Or the television set that dies two days before the Superbowl game? Saving for emergencies is certainly wiser than hoping your luck holds out.

PRINCIPLE 18—SAVE FOR ANNUAL EVENTS

Annual events are those that occur predictably every year: Christmas, birthdays, anniversaries, vacations, etc. There are two ways to handle the expenses that come with these annual events: (1) the American Way, which entices you to "buy now and pay later"; or (2) the Biblical Way, which is to anticipate the occurrence, plan wisely for the expenditures, and save for them so you don't waste God's money paying high interest rates on your charge cards.

If your vacation costs you $900 a year, you can save for it by putting away $16.78 a week for a year. Not only will you have the money for your vacation, you'll have a few extra bucks earned from interest on your savings for a little extra spending money. The same idea works for Christmas. If you'll need $600 at Christmas, save $11.19 per week and you're home free.

By following the savings method, you will also learn to find bargains long before the date, often at 50 to 75 percent off clearance sales prices My wife, Jeanie, shops at the after-Christmas and January sales for items we plan to give eleven or twelve months later. She buys next summer's clothes in September, when clearance sales reduce prices by 40, 50, or even 75 percent. That's being a smart shopper and getting maximum value for minimum cost.

If you aren't blessed to have a bargain-hunter spouse, or to be one yourself, ask around—you'll be surprised to find several in your church or circle of friends. For example, Jeanie does Christmas and birthday shopping for our family and several others. She loves to root out the bargains and has a ball doing it for other people. Being the astute money manager that I am, I tell her she should charge for her service, but she considers it a ministry to others.

SAVE, DON'T HOARD

The Hoarder says coins are flat because they are designed to be stacked up and hoarded like Scrooge's piles. The Spender says coins are round because they are designed to roll. Both extremes are in error. We need to maintain a balanced perspective between save-it-all and spend-it-all.

By now, you should be convinced of the value of saving. But how much savings are enough? Let's recap each of the major savings areas:

- Savings for big items
- Savings to replace income
- Savings for retirement
- Savings for education
- Savings for repair and maintenance
- Savings for emergencies
- Savings for annual events

That looks like a lot of savings responsibilities. To simplify things, let's prioritize them so if you have enough money for only three of the seven areas, you'll be accumulating savings in the most important ones. Don't be discouraged! By the time you finish this book, you should be able to put something into every account *if* you apply the principles set forth.

Circumstances certainly vary, as do the opinions of experts, but generally, most professionals recommend the following priority in savings accounts:

1. Emergencies: $500–$1,000
2. Repair and maintenance: $1,000–$2,000
3. Income replacement: $6,000–$12,000 (three to six months)
4. Annual events: $500–$1,000 per year

5. Big items (car, furniture, etc.): $1,000–$2,000 per year
6. Retirement: $2,000 per year or a percentage of income
7. Education: $750 per year or a percentage of income
TOTAL: $7,500–$15,000, plus a fixed percentage of your income.

It may take a while to build up to these balances, but it's a worthwhile objective. For 70 percent of us, developing good savings habits will take months or even years. For the 15 percent of us who are naturally frugal (the world calls us "cheap"), it will be quick, easy, and natural. The remaining 15 percent of us make enough money to be sloppy, and our problem will be one of discipline, not dollars.

Regardless of the time it takes, our natural tendencies, or the income we make, we all need to be on guard against greed. The difference between a saver and a hoarder is that the hoarder continues to save long after the need and funds necessary for security have been accumulated. (To learn the consequences of hoarding, read the story of the rich man in Luke 16:19-31.) The same principle applies to investing. When you begin investing, decide how much is enough to accumulate. When you reach your goal, stop. Divert your time, energy, and resources to more worthwhile goals.

If you want to avoid the subtle trap of greed and hoarding, you must determine how much money is enough for you, using the guidelines set forth throughout this book. Once you've determined that, don't hoard more—give more!

DEBT

The rich rule over the poor,
and the borrower is servant to the lender.
PROVERBS 22:7

Given the society in which we live, it's safe to say that there are very few persons reading this who haven't either borrowed or lent money. The world tells us that no one can attain wealth without assuming debt. But what does God say? Our goal in this chapter is to decipher exactly what the Bible says about borrowing and lending money—and then learn how to apply it in specific, practical ways.

WHAT IS DEBT, AND WHY IS THERE SO MUCH OF IT?

Quite simply, debt is monies owed to a second party. There are two kinds of debt: secured and unsecured. Unsecured debt is debt incurred through lines of credit, credit cards, or personal loans, which have no specific underlying asset as security for the loan. A secured debt is debt incurred through use of a loan, lien, or mortgage on a specific item, such as your home, car, or furniture. If we wanted to get really technical, we could further define debt as business or personal, long or short term, and open or closed loan. Regardless of the type of debt, when payments are not up to date on the monies borrowed, the loan is called "delinquent debt."

Although dozens of Bible verses deal with the subject of debt, not a single one says, "Do not borrow." On the other hand, not a single verse encourages borrowing, either. Most verses about debt issue warnings about the dangers of debt.

In biblical times, debtors who didn't repay loans were dealt with harshly. Years ago in America, debtors' prisons were established to accommodate those who didn't pay back what they borrowed. Today, delinquent debt is handled by bill collectors, collection agencies, lawyers, and bankruptcy courts. All these are unpleasant alternatives, to say the least, but by most people's standards, our options today are superior to those of the past.

The Rise of Debt in the U.S.

Forty years ago, no one financed cars. The average person either paid cash or used alternative means of transportation, such as riding a bicycle, walking, bumming rides, or using public transportation. Then, in the early sixties, new car financing became a part of the American Way as Detroit convinced the American people that it was perfectly acceptable to go into debt to buy a car. I was young then (and not nearly so smart!), and I took the bait just like everyone else. My 1965 Corvette convertible was financed to what was then the maximum: two years.

By the start of the seventies, automobile prices had risen sharply for two reasons. First, buyers wanted more options included in the basic model. Second, inflation was rising (and finally peaked in the early eighties). So in order to make the average car more affordable, in the early seventies payments were extended to three years. By the end of that decade, as prices had risen even higher, four-year financing became the answer to making the car affordable. Today, if you want to, you can finance your new car or truck for five or six years.

In the forty years since car financing began, the system has trained buyers to finance while making it easier to do so by lengthening the terms of the loans. The net result is that most people look at payments instead of price, and they are more concerned about the amount of the loan payment than the cost of financing. If you look at the history of the housing market, you'll find the same principle: Finance as long as possible so you can reduce the payments to what you can afford.

If you were to look at the balance sheets of our large corporations today, you'd find that over the last fifty years, a huge growth in debt, both long and short term, has occurred. In business schools back in 1940, the guiding principle for American business was Ben Franklin's motto: "Neither a borrower nor a lender be." Twenty years later, the philosophy investors lived by was "OPM," or "Other People's Money." Debt became the standard for corporate America.

This shift occurred as leverage, or borrowing money, became the preferred way to acquire wealth. Investors determined that if you could borrow $1,000 at 12 percent interest with a $100 down payment, buy a business that was earning 20 percent per year, you would make a tenfold profit on the $100 investment. This kind of transaction was termed an "LBO" (leverage buy-out). Suddenly, leverage buy-outs became the rage on Wall Street. Executives in large corporations began to pool their savings, borrowing the balance to buy the companies that employed them. A few years later, the funds those same executives borrowed became know as junk bonds. Remember the collapse of junk and high-yield bonds some years back? The results were catastrophic for both the borrowers and the lenders.

Now, even federal, state, and local governments assume debt as a way of life. Fortunately, all state and local governments are forced to live on a budget—they're not allowed by law to spend more than they collect in taxes, revenues, and fees. But as you well know, this is not the case for our federal government.

Our Gross National Debt

The national deficit (that is, the difference between income and expenses) stands at an unprecedented—almost unimaginable—high. In 1982, the federal debt crossed the one-trillion-dollar line for the first time. Interest rates and inflation rates were at record numbers, and we elected Ronald Reagan to balance the budget.

A decade later, we're approaching the four-trillion-dollar mark for our national debt. That's just our *reported* debt: The figure does not include government commitments to social security, loan or other guarantees, or off-budget items. We are truly leaving our children and grand-children with an inheritance of a gross national debt!

To give you a feel for the size of our national debt, let's focus on a few understandable facts. The interest alone on our national debt now requires 13 percent of all federal income. Fortunately, at this writing, interest rates are at a thirty-year low. If we had interest rates like we did in 1981, the *interest alone* (ignoring any payback of principal) would consume *one-half of all federal income!* The cost our government incurs with this debt is paid by the taxpayer. Corporations do not pay taxes; they collect taxes by raising prices on goods and services bought by the consumer (the same guy who has to pay the taxes).

HOW GROSS IS OUR NATIONAL DEBT?

The following example will help you understand the true nature of our national debt. Right now, your real personal share of the national debt is almost $200,000, and the government is currently spending $2,000 more of your money each year than it takes in.

The dollar bills in your wallet are slightly more than six inches long. If laid end to end, a hundred bills would stretch fifty feet. If stacked on top of each other, a hundred bills would reach about an inch high. Imagine taking $100 bills and stacking a hundred of them on top of each other. That one pile, reaching about an inch high, equals $10,000. Now start laying these $10,000 stacks (each with a hundred bills at $100 each) end to end. In about a mile, you'll have $1 million. In a thousand miles, you'll have $1 billion. And in a *million* miles of $10,000 stacks laid end to end, you'll have $1 trillion. If you'd like to stack up *all* your $100 dollar bills in one grand pile, it would reach $1 trillion when the stack was 1,578 miles high!

The U.S. is the freest, most powerful, and wealthiest nation on the planet. If we don't conquer the problem of balancing the budget soon, however, it won't stay that way. Private citizens, corporations, and government have all ignored the inevitable problems that debt brings because we have all falsely assumed that debt is the normal way of life. Our current economic problems can be rectified only if we begin to follow sound economic principles and immediately address the problems at hand.

On a personal level, however, we can avoid having debt problems in the first place if we follow the biblical guidelines God has given us for borrowing or loaning money.

BIBLICAL WARNINGS ABOUT DEBT
The Bible warns about the dangers of debt and discourages borrowing for five very sound reasons.

Debt Presumes on the Future
Presuming on the future is both risky and unwise. "Now listen, you who say, 'Today or tomorrow we will go to this or that city, spend a year there, carry on business and make money.' Why, you do not even know what will happen tomorrow. What is your life? You are a mist that appears for a little while and then vanishes" (James 4:13-14).

When I counsel people with debt problems, it usually turns out that they incurred their debt by presuming on the future. They assumed that nothing would change (except for the better). Then when adverse changes did occur, they had debt they couldn't repay.

Debt Lowers Your Standard of Living

You may feel you have raised your standard of living when you buy that new car on time. But you have to repay both the principal *and* the interest, don't you? Car payments consume part of your paycheck, leaving you less to spend. In chapter 6, we will discover the true cost of financing a car and you will learn some better, less expensive ways to meet your transportation needs. Remember Proverbs 21:20 (TLB): "The fool spends all his paycheck; the wise man saves some."

Incurring Debt Delays Decision

Borrowing makes it easy to buy without thinking. When you are borrowing money to buy something, stop and ask yourself: "Is this thing a want or a need? If it's a need, could I pay cash for it? Or could I meet this need just as adequately another way?" Borrowing money costs you money in interest, so you aren't really solving a problem. In fact, you are most likely creating one because you limit your means when you borrow. You are also being impatient and short-circuiting God's promise to meet your needs (see Philippians 4:19). Remember also that "the borrower is servant to the lender" (Proverbs 22:7).

Debt Makes Interest Work Against You, Rather Than for You

Back in grade school, my math teacher showed us the tremendous power of compound interest with this example: If you put a penny in a bank that paid you interest equal to your balance every day, how much money do you think you would have at the end of the month? Let's run the numbers.

Day	Bank Balance
1	$.01
2	$.02
3	$.04
4	$.08
5	$.16
6	$.32
7	$.64
8	$1.28
9	$2.56
10	$5.12
11	$10.24
12	$20.48
13	$40.96
14	$81.92
15	$163.84

Day	Bank Balance
16	$327.68
17	$655.36
18	$1,310.72
19	$2,621.44
20	$5,242.88
21	$10,485.76
22	$20,971.52
23	$41,943.04
24	$83,886.08
25	$167,772.16
26	$335,544.32
27	$671,088.64
28	$1,342,177.28
29	$2,684,354.56
30	$5,368,709.12

Compound interest is an awesome force, isn't it? Why not have it working for you by saving, instead of letting it work against you by borrowing?

Debt May Interfere with God's Plan for Your Life

When going into debt, many people don't consult God first, or even consider His will for them before they buy. It always astounds me that far more Christians respond "I need to pray about that" when asked to serve, than Christians who declare "I need to pray about that" when considering a decision to buy something.

If you accept the fact that God owns everything we have, and we are only stewards, then every spending decision you make is also a spiritual decision. At work, you always check with the boss before you spend his or her money. But do you check with the Ultimate Owner of Everything before you spend *His* money? Remember Proverbs 3:5-6: "Trust in the LORD with all your heart and lean not on your own understanding; in all your ways acknowledge him and he will make your paths straight."

Now that we've examined what debt is, why it's so prevalent, and what the Bible has to say about it, we can establish several key principles about debt.

PRINCIPLE 19—IT'S DANGEROUS TO IGNORE THE BIBLE'S WARNING ABOUT DEBT

The Bible warns us that debt is dangerous and therefore should be used carefully. True, we have been programed by the world to accept debt as a way of life. For many people, however, debt is like a narcotic. In some instances, it can be an effective painkiller; but it's extremely addictive and can and does cause (financial) death when used carelessly or illegally.

I believe that warning labels should be printed on all forms of debt contracts and credit cards: "WARNING: This type of transaction is addictive and can lead to financial death and destruction if used frequently, carelessly, or excessively."

So we know debt's dangerous. But where do we go from here? We can't afford to pay cash for everything, especially homes and perhaps cars, so we proceed, but with caution.

PRINCIPLE 20—DON'T USE CREDIT CARDS

The most common source of debt for all Americans is the credit card. I encourage you to commit the following definition to memory, and say it to yourself each time you're tempted to make a purchase with your credit card: "A credit card is a means of buying something I don't need at a price I can't afford, with funds I don't have, from people who aren't polite, so I can impress people I don't know!"

That may make you laugh, but 95 percent of the time it's true. Almost every place of business has pictures on the door of credit cards they accept: VISA, Mastercard, Discovery, Diner's Club, American Express, and so on. Any retail merchant will verify the fact that the credit cards pictured cost him money. Many people don't know this, but if a merchant accepts your credit card for payment of an item, the credit card company charges him from 1 to 7 percent of the total sale for the privilege of offering you the convenience of charging. Percentages vary, depending on the type of card and the volume of business, but none fail to collect from the seller. In truth, we all pay for the privilege of being able to charge, even though many of us do not.

Innumerable surveys conducted by credit card companies have shown that people will spend 20 to 35 percent more when using a credit than when paying by cash or check. The percentage varies with the card, but the average is 27 percent—that's why merchants are willing to take the cards: Profits generated from the increased spending far outweigh the fee the merchant has to pay.

The company issuing the card usually charges an annual fee to the user and also makes a percentage on every dollar charged, plus the interest. You pay for all that.

Now, read my definition of a credit card again, and say it out loud, three times: "A credit card is a means of buying something I don't need at a price I can't afford, with funds I don't have, from people who aren't polite, so I can impress people I don't know!"

If you're the shrewd shopper who gets a no-fee credit card and pays off the balance at the end of each month, you may feel you are way ahead of the average Joe. You are, but on the average you spend the same 27 percent more on unnecessary purchases than you would if you paid by cash or check.

Every year, my business credit card company sends me a statement showing every item I purchased using their card during that year. One January I put my credit card away for a year and chose to pay only by check or cash. I saved 30 percent that year on the total cost of my purchases. I spent 27 percent fewer dollars and asked for (and got!) a cash discount at over half of the businesses I buy from because I paid cash. I've had dozens of people duplicate the process with identical results.

A fishing buddy of mine, who used to live and work in Las Vegas, read this chapter and told me gambling casinos worldwide operate on the same principle. During college, he worked as a cashier for one of the casinos. His job was to convert cash, checks, travelers checks, and even credit cards to plastic chips to be used for gambling in the casino. The casino converted money to chips of varying colors and markings, each representing different values, knowing a person will lose 25 percent more in plastic than they would with cash. No wonder credit cards are made of plastic!

If you currently charge and pay off your balance at the end of the month, switch to cash or checks and let me know what you save. If you currently have a balance on your credit cards, read on.

PRINCIPLE 21—IF YOU HAVE BEEN OVERSPENDING ON CREDIT, REVERSE THAT BEHAVIOR NOW

The average person has 2.4 credit cards. The typical household charges $2,000 per year and makes minimum payments. Over the years, credit limits are raised as consumers make timely monthly minimum payments until the tenth year, when most begin having problems meeting payments. At that point, they seek counsel to solve the problem. The accompanying chart provides an example of how much this credit has truly cost them. Though rates of interest vary from one card to the next, we'll assume an 18 percent interest rate. The national average is 18.96 percent APR (annual percentage rate).

THE COST OF CREDIT

Year	Annual Charge	Card Balance	Interest Paid
1	$2,000	$2,000	$360
2	$2,000	$4,000	$720
3	$2,000	$6,000	$1,080
4	$2,000	$8,000	$1,440
5	$2,000	$10,000	$1,800
6	$2,000	$12,000	$2,160
7	$2,000	$14,000	$2,520
8	$2,000	$16,000	$2,880
9	$2,000	$18,000	$3,240
10	$2,000	$20,000	$3,600
TOTALS	$20,000	$20,000	$19,800

In reality, the chart is a summary of several credit cards, the later ones being obtained in order to make payment on the existing cards because the consumer couldn't keep up with minimum payments in the seventh, eighth, and ninth years. Now the consumer has two problems: First, he must stop his $2,000 per year overspending habit. Second, he must service his debt, meaning he must pay off the balance, including principal and interest.

The $2,000 per year overspending requires him to reduce his monthly outgo by $166.67. Then, to retire the debt over a ten-year period, he must make a payment of $314.29 per month if the interest rate remains at 18 percent. As you can see, the price of the payback is high:

Reduce charging: $166.67 per month for ten years = $20,000
Repay the loan: $314.29 per month for ten years = $37,715
Funds available for living expenses are reduced by $480.96 per month.
TOTAL COST OF PAYBACK = $57,715

Getting into debt is easy, maybe even fun, but the payback can be equivalent to your day of judgment if you let compound interest work against you. During the twenty-year period covered by this example, the interest earned by the credit card company accumulated as follows:

Interest paid during the first ten years: $19,800
Interest paid during the second ten years: $17,715
TOTAL INTEREST PAID = $37,515

These horrific results are typical for people who overspend their income by using credit without being aware of the dangers of playing with plastic. Some people owe more and some owe less after ten years, but without exception consumers are shocked to find that overspending an amount of $167 a month could cost them $37,515 in interest.

To *really* understand what credit costs you, however, let's see where you'd be if instead of *spending* $167 per month and paying 18 percent interest, you *saved* that same amount and earned 6 percent.

After ten years, you would have saved $20,000, and you would have earned $7,943 in interest. Total = $27,943.

During the second ten years, you could save the monthly $314 repayment at 6 percent interest. Savings deposits of $314 per month for ten years, with interest, would net you $51,715. And all the while, the $27,943 you saved during the first ten years is compounding at the same 6 percent for ten more years. Your $27,943 savings has grown to $50,042. Total savings = $101,757!

If you were a saver, you put away $57,680 over time and *earned* $44,077 in interest. If you were a spender, you spent almost the same amount and *paid* $37,515 in interest. The difference between the saver and the charger is $81,592 in interest.

Maybe now you understand why I defined credit cards the way I did.

Get a Guaranteed 18 Percent Return on Your Investment by Paying Off Your Credit Card

The average American pays out 13 percent of every paycheck for consumer-type interest, which is not even deductible on his tax return. Credit cards carry the highest rate of interest—usually 18 to 21 percent. If you make a firm commitment to pay off all debt on your credit cards, you'll automatically earn a guaranteed 18 percent return on your investment. That's my challenge to you, today. Formulate a plan, begin today, and stick with it till you're free of all credit card debt.

I've seen hundreds of people freed from the bondage of debt by vowing to pay off the plastic. It probably won't be easy, and it will involve discipline and sacrifice, but be assured it will be worth the price.

It sure was for my client, Kerry. Kerry was a single man who committed to paying off his credit card debt. I first met Kerry when he was sent to us by his boss—a principal in the public school system where Kerry taught. As a teacher, Kerry earned $25,800 per year. He had nine credit cards with a total balance of $15,500. He committed to a three-year repayment plan in which his monthly payments would be $509.72. That was 30 percent of his net pay every month for thirty-six months.

During the time that Kerry sacrificed and struggled to pay off his debt, I watched him grow spiritually, as God was continually faithful in honoring Kerry's desire to glorify Him by doing the right thing. God rewarded his efforts by allowing Kerry to pay off his debt in just thirty-one months.

Today, Kerry has the freedom of choosing how to use $509 every month—interest free—to serve and honor his Lord. He also has an active ministry to other teachers and singles as he shares the dangers of debt, the paths to freedom, and the benefits of being debt free.

Credit Card Use Is Not a Problem, It's a Symptom

Use of credit cards is not a problem; it's only one *symptom* of a problem. The real problem is spending more than we earn. Most people who do this are not even aware that they are doing so.

Proverbs 27:23-24 cautions us, "Be sure you know the condition of your flocks, give careful attention to your herds; for riches do not endure forever, and a crown is not secure for all generations." As God's stewards, we are responsible for knowing where we stand financially. Most of us don't have flocks and herds, but we do have income and expenses. It's our job to be aware of them and live contentedly within our income.

Although the problem of overspending is sometimes caused by ignorance, it's more often caused by lack of contentment with what we have. Our society's promotion of a "me first" lifestyle persuades us to believe that we can't possibly be content unless we have more or better.

Another, less subtle, cause of overspending is deliberate disobedience and rebellion. John addresses this issue when he tells us, "Do not love the world or anything in the world. If anyone loves the world, the love of the Father is not in him. For everything in the world—the cravings of sinful man, the lust of his eyes and the boasting of what he has and does—comes not from the Father but from the world" (1 John 2:15-16).

We battle against our sin nature and a worldly system set against God. If overspending is a problem in your life, ask yourself whether the desire of your heart is to please God, or yourself. What motivates you? Pride, or love of God?

You are not limited simply to choosing whether or not to use credit cards. You must decide whether or not you will choose to follow godly principles in *all* areas of your life—including your spending habits. Debt or the mismanagement of money is always an indicator of an underlying spiritual problem.

PRINCIPLE 22—DON'T GET CAUGHT IN THE CONSOLIDATION LOAN TRAP

As you learned in the example of overspending given above, most people wait to get financial counsel until they're so far in debt there seems to be no way out. When they finally come in for help, they're almost always looking for symptom solutions, not problem solutions. Frequently, they will ask about consolidating their loans at a lower interest rate so they can manage the payments.

A consolidation loan does about as much good as putting a bandage on a bald spot—it covers the problem but does nothing to change the situation. Again, the problem is overspending.

Consolidating debt does not cure the problem. In fact, it almost always makes it worse. Albert and Dorothy's example will help you see why.

ALBERT AND DOROTHY'S LOAN SUMMARY

Loan	Balance	APR(%)	Monthly Payment	Number of Payments Remaining
(1)	$3,000	18	$68	60
(2)	$2,208	22	$92	24
(3)	$3,560	15	$258	12
(4)	$424	9	$77	6
(5)	$198	12	$78	3
TOTALS	$9,390		$573	

As you can see, Albert and Dorothy owed a total of $9,390, with payments of $573 per month. They had just been approved for a consolidation loan for thirty-six months that would have given them one payment of $345 per month—$228 less per month than they were currently paying. Albert thought the loan was a great deal, but Dorothy, who had attended our finance class for young marrieds, wasn't totally convinced, so they came to see me.

I recommended against the consolidation loan because their problem wasn't payments, it was overspending—a fact confirmed once I learned that two of the loan payments were for prior consolidation loans. If they consolidated again, they would merely end up committing the freed payment of $228 per month to more debt.

When I explained this to Albert and suggested an alternative plan, he reluctantly agreed to try the following, for six months: He would stay with the current debts and devote any excess cash that came to paying off loan 5. Nothing extra came in during the next three months, but the fifth loan was paid off and then, as agreed, he used the $78 surplus to pay off loan 4, forty-five days later. Then they applied all of what used to be payments for loans 4 and 5 ($155/mo.) to pay off loan 3.

Six months later, Albert was almost, but not totally, convinced. So I showed Albert and his wife how they could be totally free of consumer debt if they would commit to follow the same plan with their remaining three loans: Apply all the payments from paid-off loans to retiring the next shortest loan, until all loans are paid off. When Albert saw that he was less than ninety days away from paying off loan number three, he committed to the plan for another three months.

Nine months after our initial meeting, here's how their adjusted loan balances looked:

ALBERT AND DOROTHY'S ADJUSTED LOAN BALANCES

Loan	Balance	APR(%)	Monthly Payment	Number of Payments Remaining
(1)	$2,590	18	$68	51
(2)	$1,218	22	$92	15
(3)	-0-	-0-	-0-	(+$258)
(4)	-0-	-0-	-0-	(+$77)
(5)	-0-	-0-	-0-	(+$78)
TOTALS	$3,808		$160	(+$413)

Compare the totals with the previous chart to see the dramatic difference that just nine months can make. (The balance on loan 2 is lower than you might expect, because the original balance was estimated at $2208, which included interest, not $1805, which was the payoff amount.)

At our meeting during the ninth month, Albert and Dorothy decided to increase their giving, increase their savings, and continue the plan for nine months, after which time both of the remaining loans would be paid off, and they would be consumer-debt free.

By using the do-it-yourself plan of paying off the shortest loan first and using the freed payment on the next loan, Albert and Dorothy saved $921 interest over the consolidation loan. In addition, they increased their giving and built up some savings. Most important, they learned to manage and live within their income, rather than recycle one financial mess after another into the consolidation loan trap, which would have done nothing to address the problem of their overspending.

Three years after our initial meeting, Albert and Dorothy met with me again to discuss their progress and future plans. They had managed to save $6,200 and were still debt free. Further, they estimated they were over $7,000 ahead because they had not consolidated their loans.

Avoid Home Equity Loans

If Albert and Dorothy had taken out a home equity loan for $9,390 in order to pay off their debts, they would have been paying only 10 to 12 percent interest, and the interest would have been tax deductible. They could have refinanced for $309 per month, used the $264 per month of freed payment to pay down the loan, and perhaps have been even better off than they were.

However, I don't recommend home equity loans initially because, again, payments are not the problem; they are only a symptom of the real problem, which is the inability to live within one's means. I've seen dozens of people use home equity loans as a debt consolidation tool, but not one of those people used the freed payment to retire debt. Instead, they used it to make payments on new debt and ended up in worse shape than before. I'm sure there are exceptions, but I have yet to see one.

Generally, home equity loans are financed over seven to ten years. Imagine the temptation of having all that extra cash when your payments are lowered from $573 (like Albert's) to $154 or $124 per month. If you already have a problem with spending, the temptation would probably be too much to resist.

If you've tried to solve your debt problem by bill consolidation, home equity loans, or finding a second job, you've fallen into the trap of trying to increase your income by direct or indirect means. I've never seen this strategy produce lasting results over time. Generally, the freed payment or extra income is committed to yet another purchase—a reward the buyer thinks he owes himself for the extra effort he's expending.

The Bible commands us to be content with what we have and to diligently manage what we're entrusted with. Nowhere does the Bible say that increasing our income or lowering our payments will solve our problems.

PRINCIPLE 23—BEWARE THE DEDUCTIBLE MYTHS

Most of us believe the myth about tax deductions because we hear four logical-sounding arguments:

1. Interest on a home mortgage is tax deductible.
2. Since the interest is deductible, we lower our taxes.
3. Homes appreciate in value, along with incomes, so we pay back the loans with inflated, cheaper dollars.
4. Using Other People's Money (OPM) is a good investment strategy.

Such reasoning entices many people to take on huge mortgages (or a second or third mortgage) so they have extra cash to do the things they couldn't otherwise afford to do.

Let's assume that you're going to buy a home, and the interest of $8,592 per year is tax deductible. If you pay 32.2 percent federal and state taxes, you'll save $2,767 per year as a result of your deduction. If the home is worth $100,000, you're making $1,000 every time prices rise 1 percent. Let's assume you have invested $10,000 in your home; the remaining $90,000 is Other People's Money. You save $2,767 per year in taxes and make 10 percent on your equity with every 1 percent rise in prices. So, why not finance your home to the maximum?

First, not all of the interest is deductible. Our tax system gives every taxpayer the option of itemizing deductions or using the standard deduction. If you're a single taxpayer, your standard deduction at this writing is $3,700. If you're married, you have a standard deduction of $6,200. Only the excess over the standard deduction is deductible, and that's true only if you itemize deductions.

In the example above, including an $8,592 interest deduction, all the married taxpayer really saves is the excess above $6,200: a savings of $2,392. Using the same tax rate of 32.2 percent, the real tax savings is 32.2 percent of $2,392, or $835. On the other hand, if you had no mortgage, you'd have to pay taxes of $770 on $8,592 of income, but you'd have $7,822 left. Compare that to the tax savings of $770, and you'll understand what I mean about the tax deduction myth.

Even if you're well over the standard deduction because of your generous giving, spending a dollar in interest can save you only thirty-one cents in federal taxes. If you didn't spend the deductible dollar but chose to pay thirty-one cents in federal taxes instead, you'd still have sixty-nine cents left over.

Being debt free may cost you some tax dollars, but you're economically ahead of the debtors by twice as much and you don't have your standard of living reduced by the price of the payments.

Also, don't forget that houses don't always go up in price. Housing prices are dependent upon the local and national economy, and sometimes they go down, as occurred during the eighties in many areas of the country. For example, if you bought a $100,000 home in Houston, Texas, in 1982 and sold it in 1987, you would have lost 25 to 50 percent of your money.

The diligent steward thinks of borrowed money like a magnifying glass: If you borrow money to invest and get lucky, you'll magnify your returns. If you borrow money to invest and get unlucky, you'll magnify your losses.

PRINCIPLE 24—NEVER COSIGN A LOAN

Unless you are willing, able, and prepared to make all the payments yourself, never cosign for anyone else's loan. The Bible warns,

> If you have put up security for your neighbor, if you have
> struck hands in pledge for another, if you have been trapped by
> what you said, ensnared by the words of your mouth, then do
> this, my son, to free yourself, since you have fallen into your
> neighbor's hands: Go and humble yourself; press your plea
> with your neighbor! Allow no sleep to your eyes, no slumber
> to your eyelids. Free yourself, like a gazelle from the hand
> of the hunter, like a bird from the snare of the fowler. (Proverbs 6:1-5)

Lenders will confirm this biblical wisdom. They tell us that 85 percent of all cases involving surety, or cosigned loans, end up the responsibility of the cosigner. I could relate dozens of experiences supporting that figure. Cosigned loans almost always end up destroying the relationship between, and the financial condition of, both parties.

If someone asks you to pledge any of your assets as security for a loan, be extremely cautious.

A friend of mine named Jake learned this lesson the hard way. Several years ago, Jake and his two partners bought an office building valued in excess of $1 million. They purchased the building for $150,000 down and mortgaged the $950,000 balance. The office was 100 percent occupied at the time, and the rents exceeded the payments on the mortgage, so each of the three partners got an immediate cash return on their $50,000 investment.

Everything looked great: All the leases ran several years into the future. Had actual rents escalated according to the estimated 5 percent per year (or inflation, whichever was greater), the investment would have proven to be an extremely lucrative one.

However, nine months after the purchase, the major tenant filed for bankruptcy. This created a major problem, because that one tenant's share of the rents had been $65,000 per year, leaving Jake and his partners with that much deficit against the required mortgage payments. They managed to hold on to the property four months before it was surrendered to the lender as a voluntary foreclosure. The lender then sold the property for $750,000 and held the three partners liable for the $200,000 deficit, plus $40,000 in legal, accounting, and other fees.

When faced with an $80,000 judgment each, Jake's two business associates promptly filed bankruptcy, leaving him with a $240,000 bill. Jake had to sell his home, which was free and clear, and his lifetime savings are gone. He and his family of four live in a rented, two-bedroom apartment and struggle as he pays off a $65,000 loan at 10 percent interest over the next ten years.

Don't learn the hard way about pledging other assets for an asset you must borrow money to buy. If you can't purchase an asset without additional collateral, maybe God is trying to tell you something.

SIX IDEAS THAT WILL HELP YOU ELIMINATE DEBT

If you're like most people today, you've accumulated some credit card debt you wish you didn't have. I'm going to give you six ideas that will help you get free of debt, once and for all. If you're reading this book for pleasure, now may be the time to stop. Here goes:

1. *Stop all nonessential spending.* If you'll commit today to read and apply the chapter on Spending Plans (chapter 8) to your life, you'll eliminate 15 percent of nonessential spending from your budget.

2. *Cut up your credit cards if you have outstanding balances.* Don't tempt yourself by saying you'll put them away temporarily.

3. *Plan your way to being debt-free*, just as we illustrated with Albert and Dorothy. Be realistic, set several short-term goals, and reward yourself when you reach them. Once you're debt free, you will have developed a new self-discipline that will pay dividends in every area of your life.

4. *Put half of all extra cash into debt reduction and half into savings.* I realize you could be debt free faster by using all extra cash for debt reduction, but if a problem occurs, you will have no cash reserves with which to pay the expenses. Also, by saving half, you develop the wise habits encouraged by God's Word.

5. *Sell all financed, depreciating items that you can live without.* You'll pay a price to become debt free, and the price may be painful—something as drastic as changing homes. But remember the encouragement in Hebrews 12:11—"No discipline seems pleasant at the time, but painful. Later on, however, it produces a harvest of righteousness and peace for those who have been trained by it."

6. *Convert assets you no longer need to cash by conducting a garage sale.* This will not only produce cash but also reduce clutter, give you more room, and break you of the hoarding habit.

HOW TO SET REALISTIC OBJECTIVES FOR THE FUTURE
Now that you've acquired knowledge, I challenge you to apply it to your life. Following is a suggested plan.

Write Out the Savings Goals You Wish to Achieve
If the accounts for your savings goals total $10,000, and all you can save is five dollars per week, you may want to reevaluate you goals. Once you've thought about it, if you still want to save $10,000, write it down. Who can it hurt? Begin where you can, and give it your best effort.

If you're like most people, by the time you work through your spending plan, you'll probably find at least $100 per month that was committed to nonessentials. That alone gives you an additional $1,200 per year to allocate between debt reduction and savings.

Record All Your Outstanding Bills, Excluding Home Mortgage and Auto Loans
The following chart provides a handy form for this list.

	Lender	Balance Due	Monthly Payment	Interest Rate	Remaining Payments
1					
2					
3					
4					
5					
6					
7					
8					
9					
10					

Let's say you complete the list and find that you owe $5,000, and your payments are $150 per month. Now you must develop a plan to pay off the smallest bill first. When that's paid, apply the freed payment to the next shortest loan until it's paid off. Continue until you have paid off all your loans. If it takes three years, in three years from now you will have freed up $150 per month, or $1,800 per year, to apply to other items. That, added to the $100 per month you can eliminate in unnecessary purchases, increases your discretionary income by $250 per month, or $3,000 per year.

Now let's say you commit to using half of all raises, bonuses, and windfall profits toward debt reduction and savings. If your salary goes up 10 percent in the next three years, you'll have an additional $2,000 to use any way you choose.

Commit Your Plans to the Lord
Give thanks for what you have. Pray for contentment, guidance, wisdom, persistence, and self-discipline daily.

In my experience, it takes most people less than five years to achieve debt-free status, not including house (and sometimes car) payments. By then, they have probably saved $10,000 and have discretionary income of $400 per month, in addition to enjoying consumer debt-free status.

Commit your plans to the Lord and then work hard to apply the Bible's wisdom. If you reach your goal by the time you're thirty-five years old, you'll be fifteen years ahead of the average person. Five years after that, you'll get to the point where you can buy your cars with cash. Ten years after that, you'll be able to pay off your home, and you'll be only fifty years old!

Imagine what you could do at age fifty, with ten to twenty working years left. No bills, no car payments, no house payments, and $10,000 or more in savings! You'd have $800 per month freed up, to use any way you choose. While 85 percent of all Christians live in bondage to debt, you could be part of the 15 percent who are debt free and able to serve, give, and minister to those in need.

The difference between people who are in debt and people who are debt free isn't education or knowledge. It's wisdom. Wisdom is applying what you know. Begin where you are, and move forward one day at a time. The results are well within reach if you make the commitment and begin *now* to apply biblical principles to your financial matters.

BUYING A HOME

The most significant financial decision that most families make is buying a home. A commitment this big requires a great deal of prayer, study, and effort before you sign on the dotted line. By applying the eleven principles in this chapter, you'll see how the purchase of an average home can mean a savings of over $1.4 million during your lifetime.

PRINCIPLE 25—DECIDE WHAT YOU REALLY NEED IN A HOME

As with the purchase of transportation, wise stewards must learn to separate their wants from their needs. If you're like me, born and raised in the richest nation on earth, you start with a lot of preconceived wrong ideas.

For instance, most of us want our first home to be as nice (or nicer) and as well located (or better located) than the home we were raised in. We forget that our parents labored twenty to thirty years in order to achieve their quality of life.

In addition, we tend to shape our desires according to what we perceive to be the "average," rather than learning the national norms. Statistics vary in different areas of the country, but in general the average family occupies about 1,400 square feet of space. Excluding Third-World countries, the average home drops in size from one-half to two-thirds once you leave the U.S. Internationally, people get by quite nicely with much less than most of us are used to.

So your first decision is to determine how much space you need.

Most of us are raised with unrealistic and lofty expectations about the size of home we need and the area of town we think we need to live in. Though any realtor will tell you the three most important principles in selecting a home are location, location, and location, you must remember that the realtor giving that advice is also compensated with a percentage of the selling price; he has a vested interest in selling you the most expensive piece of real estate he can. The greater the price, the greater his commission.

To illustrate the high price of location, consider two homes that are both 1,400 square feet with two bedrooms and one bath. One is located in Oklahoma City and costs $53,000; the other is in Beverly Hills and sells for $843,000. Admittedly, that's a dramatic difference, but it's a real one, nonetheless. In my area (Scottsdale, Arizona), the price of a 1,400-square-foot home will vary depending upon location from $60,000 to upwards of $250,000. So you see, location can be a costly amenity. Be careful when considering location, but be realistic, as well.

Give serious thought to what you need in the area of home furnishings and landscaping. Builders tell me that individuals spend 10 to 25 percent of the price of the home on landscaping and furnishings. By landscaping yourself and buying one- to five-gallon trees and plants, you can save up to 90 percent of the cost of turnkey landscape designers who use mature plants and add 25 percent of the home's price in landscaping. Do you want your home suitable for the cover of *Better Homes and Gardens* the day you move in, or can you wait a few years and save up to 25 percent of the price of your home?

The price of furnishing your home can also be a tremendous variable. For example, if you shop at top-of-the-line "designer" furniture and department stores, you can spend as much on furniture, drapes, and accessories as you did for half of your home. The opposite end of the spectrum is to shop estate sales, garage sales, or used furniture stores where you can buy merchandise for pennies on the dollar.

A friend of mine helped his daughter and son-in-law completely furnish a three-bedroom house for less than two thousand dollars. When they were through shopping, they estimated that the same furniture, purchased new, would have cost over twenty times that amount! The key to their success was patience. It took them six months to understand, find, and buy value. They paid cash instead of buying on a more convenient but expensive five-year finance plan, saving them an additional ten to twelve thousand dollars in interest!

PRINCIPLE 26—DETERMINE WHAT KIND OF FINANCING IS BEST FOR YOU

Most consumers don't calculate the cost of financing; they simply ponder the amount of money they'll be spending in monthly payments. To illustrate the tremendous power of compound interest, examine the following simple chart showing payments for varying interest rates and various time periods financing a $100,000 home.

HOUSE PAYMENTS FOR VARYING TIME PERIODS AND INTEREST RATES

Number of Years	8%	9%	10%	11%	12%
30	$685	$744	$803	$864	$924
25	$723	$778	$835	$891	$949
20	$786	$838	$890	$942	$996
15	$901	$948	$996	$1044	$1092

These are payments for principal and interest only; they do not include taxes and insurance. As an example, let's look at the difference between a thirty-year loan and a fifteen-year loan at 10 percent interest: The thirty-year payment is $803 per month; the same house, financed for fifteen years, has a payment of $996 per month. By financing for fifteen years instead of ten, the buyer raises his monthly payment 24 percent, or $193 per month.

That may not look like a very wise decision, until you consider the savings over the length of the loan: If the buyer pays $803 per month for thirty years (360 payments), he'll repay $289,080 in principal and interest—a total finance charge of $189,000 on his $100,000 home. However, if he chooses the fifteen-year loan, he repays only $179,280, or $79,280 in interest. The higher monthly payment saved the buyer $109,720 in interest, an amount greater than the original purchase price of the home! The shorter the term of your loan, the lower the cost of your financing.

Fred and Sally are opting for a thirty-year loan ($803 a month), while Jim and Jane are financing their home over fifteen years ($996 a month at 10%). At first, it may be a real struggle for Jim and Jane to make those higher payments, but with time their income will rise and their load will get lighter. Fifteen years later, they'll have a mortgage-burning party when their home is free and clear. They'll have plenty to celebrate because they'll have a roof over their heads, free and clear, and discretionary cash flow of $996 per month for the rest of their lives.

While Jim and Jane are starting a nice bonfire with their loan papers, Fred and Sally are sitting at their dining room table, paying bills. With the help of his adding machine, Fred carefully calculates that he and Sally still owe $80,685 on their original mortgage. They've built up $20,000 home equity, but they still have fifteen years remaining on their mortgage, at $803 per month in payments. (Jim and Jane have $100,000 equity, and no house payments!) Close your eyes for a moment, and imagine what it would be like not to have to make house payments every month. . . . That would be freedom, wouldn't it?

And what if, for the next fifteen years, Jim and Jane saved the $803 a month Fred and Sally have to pay on their mortgage? Depending on the amount of interest they made on their monthly savings, let's look at where they could be, financially:

WHAT JIM AND JANE SAVED INSTEAD OF SPENDING ON A MORTGAGE PAYMENT

Number of Years	0%	3%	6%	10%
5	$48,180	$52,041	$56,305	$62,700
10	$96,360	$112,493	$132,253	$165,861
15	$144,540	$182,714	$234,695	$335,593

If Jim and Jane buried their money in tin cans in the back yard and earned no interest, after fifteen years they would have $144,540 saved plus a paid-for home. If they averaged 10 percent on their investments, they'd have over one third of a million dollars. If they decided to splurge and live off the interest, they'd have an income of $33,539—that's $2,795 per month!

These calculations don't consider the fact that you can obtain a lower interest rate on fifteen-year loans than you can on thirty-year loans— about 1.5 percent annually. In real terms, Jim and Jane's payments could have been $972, not $996 as in our example. That $24 difference per month equals $4,320 over the fifteen years of their mortgage, not counting any interest. If they had chosen to apply that $24 per month toward their principal, they would have paid off the mortgage even earlier.

And in our example, Jim and Jane saved $803 per month, not the $996 payment they had actually been making. If they'd added the extra $24 per month from an 8.5 percent loan *and* the $193 payment difference invested at 10 percent, they could have added $134,363 more to their savings account after fifteen years. That's an amazing amount of money—greater than the price of the home, and it illustrates well the advantage of financing everything you buy—including your home, for as short a time as possible if you must finance.

Fixed Versus Variable Rate Loans

With a fixed rate loan, the amount of interest you will pay is set for the life of the loan. However, since interest rates seldom remain fixed over time, lenders created Adjustable Rate Mortgages (ARMs). With ARMs, the interest rate on the mortgage is adjusted at set intervals of time, (every one, three, or five years). An ARM generally has a "cap," or a limit to how much the rate can change at intervals and over the life of the loan. The interest rate charged on ARM (or "variable rate") mortgages is usually based on major published indexes such as the eleventh district cost of funds, treasury note or bond rates, or prime rate, all of which are reported daily in the financial section of the newspaper.

The desirability of either a fixed or variable rate mortgage depends upon what happens to future interest rates during the life of your loan. If you're willing to gamble that rates will either remain level or decline over the next fifteen to thirty years, take the ARM, because the rates are usually better. But if you're not a gambler, secure a fixed rate and limit the risk with a slightly higher initial payment and rate.

Many people choose ARM loans not because they expect level or declining interest rates but because the payments are initially lower, and therefore the ARM enables them to buy more house than they could otherwise afford. Those people never ask themselves the necessary question: Can we handle the payment if interest rates go up?

Most Americans are optimistic; they never look at the negative side of the ledger. Let's say Fred and Sally buy their $100,000 home with an 8 percent ARM, knowing they can afford a payment of $685 per month. But a year later, when interest rates go up, their house payment increases by $118 a month to $803, and they can barely make it. Then, at the end of the second year, rates jump another 2 percent, and their payment goes to $924. Now they have to rob Peter to pay Paul, and they fall behind in all their bills. By the end of the third year, they're financially ruined when the rate goes up another 1 percent, raising their monthly payment to $983. Their home is foreclosed on, they lose their good credit rating, and they forfeit $15,000 in equity. If they're lucky (but the odds are against them), their marriage survives.

In my example, Fred and Sally's house payment increased by $298 per month with a variable rate mortgage. I don't know your particular situation, but since mortgage rates at this writing are at or near a thirty-year low, I generally advise fixed rates and shorter-term loans because it's inevitable that rates will rise. I remember very well when in the late seventies mortgage rates went from 8 to 16 percent, and many people lost their homes. If I'm wrong, and rates decline, you can always refinance your loan.

Principle 27—Weigh the Advantages of a Resale Home Over a New Home

---

The question of whether to buy a new home or a resale home is a matter of economic and personal concern. A resale may save you several thousand dollars, but you probably won't get exactly what you want. On the positive side, you usually get mature landscape with an older home, and carpets, drapes, and other necessities have usually been paid for by the previous owner. If you can live with the seller's taste, you'll save several more thousand dollars. Especially in a depressed economy, you may be lucky enough to find a distressed seller who's willing to sacrifice his property below market value. The money you save may be more than enough to pay for replacing amenities like wallpaper or carpet you think you can't possibly live with.

Regarding such decisions, which are personal, not economical, my counsel is always to pray, asking God to reveal His plan for you.

Economically speaking, you almost always get more house for your money if you purchase a resale. In my forty-seven years, I've owned five homes. Three of them were resales, one was a new custom home, and one was a fix-up special. National statistics tell us that the average family moves about every five years, so I'm pretty typical. Most of us think that when we buy a home we'll stay in it forever, but it usually doesn't turn out that way. Time has a way of altering circumstances, needs, and desires. If I could do it over again, before I bought a home I'd pray more, listen longer, and be more patient. I'm sure I'd make fewer mistakes. If you're in a tight situation economically, consider buying a fix-up special.

In 1978, I had my first and only experience buying a home that needed a lot of repairs. The yard looked like a jungle, most of the good plants and trees appeared to be dead, the paint was peeling inside and out, the carpet was badly worn, and the former occupant had kept two German shepherds in the back room; when you entered the home, the smell knocked you over.

The good news was, the house was in a great location and the construction, electrical work, and plumbing were all in very good shape for a twelve-year-old home. I bought the home for $25,000 under market value, then factored in the $15,000 I estimated it would cost to get the home into saleable condition. The next year, I worked as hard as I've ever worked. My regular job took ten hours a day, and I worked five-and-a half days a week. I spent most of my "free" time restoring the house.

By shopping carefully, we were able to recarpet our home at a bargain price. For $3,000, I had the inside and outside painted. I spent another $5,500 to finish off the back room where the dogs had lived, replaster the pool, and make a few cosmetic changes. I did 90 percent of the landscaping myself: I installed a simple sprinkler system, cleared the one-and-a-half acres of all the weeds, planted new trees, shrubs, and plants, and seeded the lawn. That cost me another $3,500 dollars and a thousand hours of my time. Finally, I spent another $2,000 and had the pool motors and the central cooling system replaced.

Eighteen months later, I sold the home for double what I paid for it, netting a $60,000 profit. I have to be truthful and tell you that the majority of the profit was not the result of my brilliant skills and selling strategy; it was due to a good housing market.

I also have to tell you that at the time I embarked on my "fix-up" endeavor, I was not walking as closely with the Lord as I should have been. My motive for buying a fix-up was not to be a good steward. Greed, profit, and the pride of saying I lived in "the" section of town were the motives driving me to work eighty-hour weeks with no time off. Because my motivation was not based on the sound biblical principle of honoring God, when my hard work was finally over the results included migraines, ulcers, and anxiety attacks.

If you pursue the idea of renovating an older home, first make sure you're right with the Lord. Be realistic regarding the time it will take you, and don't kill yourself.

God used my experience to teach me some valuable lessons, all of which have stuck with me over the years. Psalm 127:2 became a reality to me: "In vain you rise early and stay up late, toiling for food to eat—for he grants sleep to those he loves." My life was clearly out of balance. I had time for everything except prayer, Bible study, church, and family. It wasn't that I didn't know the biblical truth about motivation, it's that I wasn't disciplined enough to apply that truth to my life. It's the discipline to live by biblical truth that yields the fruit of the Spirit in life.

PRINCIPLE 28—KNOW THE FACTS BEFORE YOU BUY

When determining housing costs, most people consider only the payment, but you must look far beyond that and consider all the expenses you will incur when you purchase a home. In addition to principal, interest, taxes, and insurance (PITI) on your home, you must include the price of electricity and gas, water, sanitation, telephone, and maintenance and improvements. The total of all of these elements will constitute your total monthly cost of housing. Sewer fees, telephone, and maintenance and improvements can easily add 15 to 25 percent to your monthly housing cost.

The writer of Proverbs warns us, "The prudent see danger and take refuge, but the simple keep going and suffer for it" (Proverbs 27:12). Good planning demands that you consider the *total* cost, or live a life frazzled by unexpected and unpleasant surprises. If, for example, you don't plan for maintenance costs, when items need repair you could be in a real bind. Over time, houses need repainting, inside and out, and carpet and appliances wear out and need to be fixed or replaced. Central air and heating systems require yearly maintenance, and sometimes major repairs. Roofs usually last fifteen to twenty-five years, but not always.

Inevitably, the day will come when you'll need to repair or replace expensive parts of your home. Ignoring the problem means discomfort and inconvenience for you, and it usually ends up costing you more in the long run. If, on the other hand, you've been a prudent steward and planned ahead for such expenses, your only problem will be deciding whether to fix it yourself or find a professional to do it.

Save regularly, so you have enough reserves to handle home maintenance expenses. Pay for maintenance and replacements with cash rather than charging them at 18 percent interest and putting a further strain on your finances. And don't forget to plan for major items such as furnishings, decorating, and landscaping. These should be a part of your housing expense plan from the very beginning. The bottom line is, if you spend more money than you earn due to lack of planning, you'll bury yourself in debt.

PRINCIPLE 29—DETERMINE HOW MUCH YOU CAN SPEND

Lenders are typically willing to lend up to 28 percent of your paycheck (before taxes) toward buying a home. For example, if you earn $40,000 per year, that translates to a maximum of $11,200 per year, or $933 per month, that you could spend for a house payment.

Two factors are mandatory to remember before you decide how much money you can afford to borrow to buy a home. First, you may earn $40,000 a year, but you don't bring home (or "net") that much. Federal, state, and local taxes are taken off the top. FICA takes another 15.3 percent of your check if you're self-employed; if you work for someone else, your employer splits that with you. If you have a family of four, after deducting the interest on your mortgage and your $4,000 tithe to your church, you will still owe Uncle Sam $2,500 per year in taxes. If you're single, you'll owe more. So, in reality, this is what you have to live on:

Salary	$40,000
Giving	$4,000
FICA	$3,060
Federal tax	$2,500
State tax	− $500
NET SPENDABLE INCOME	$29,940 ($2,495 per month)

Now that you can see what you *really* have, consider your true housing expense:

Expenses	Per Month	Per Year
Payments (PI)	$933	$11,200
Property taxes	$100	$1,200
Homeowners insurance	$25	$300
Electric and gas	$200	$2,400
Water and sewer	$10	$120
Telephone	$50	$600
Maintenance	$50	$600
Improvements	$50	$600
ESTIMATED TOTALS	$1,418	$17,202

Individually, your actual expenses may be higher or lower than in my example, in which 57 percent of the net spendable income was committed to housing. Even if the giving was eliminated (a decision that would shortchange God and raise your taxes), 46 percent is still committed to housing. These expenses are way above what they should be. Although most of the smaller expenditures are, I believe, pretty realistic for the average person, the house payment is way too high for this family's net income. In all my years of counseling, I've never been able to reduce an individual's spending below income if he has committed more than 40 to 45 percent of his net spendable income to housing. Because the estimates for giving, taxes, utilities, and insurance are pretty accurate, there's only one place where this family can cut spending: the monthly house payment.

To find out what you can realistically afford in the way of a monthly house payment, write down all of your expenses (except the house payment) using the above example as a guideline. Then take 40 percent (maximum) of your net spendable income (in my example: .40 × $29,940 = $11,976) and subtract the expenses. Divide the total by twelve, and you will have a realistic dollar amount. Using that amount, if you assume a 9 percent interest rate on a fifteen-year loan, you can finance up to a $49,621 mortgage. If you opt for a thirty-year loan at 9 percent with the same monthly payment (in this example, $503 per month), you can handle a mortgage of $63,169. By working backwards from net spendable income, less estimated expenses, you won't have the problem most people encounter when they try to spend more than they make.

With these guidelines, you may have just discovered that you're living above your means. If you're feeling surprise, disbelief, or anger (or maybe some of each), I'm sure you're not alone. But believe me, my intention is not to make you anything but aware. Knowledge can be a very useful thing, but only if you're wise enough to apply what you learn to your life.

It's not unrealistic to think that you can find a nice home for a price you can afford. If you're currently thinking, "I'm spending more than this guy tells me I should, and I'm getting by, all right," ask yourself the following questions: Do you give God His rightful share? Do you have enough (or any) savings put away? If your washing machine broke down tomorrow, would you have to charge a new one, paying from 18 to 21 percent interest on the money? And, finally, how hefty is your consumer credit debt?

Lest you get totally enraged and hurl this book out the window, let me remind you that the principles set forth in this book come straight out of the Bible. They are not *rules*, they are *guidelines*. If the percentages I suggest need to be increased, then by all means, increase them. But don't forget: The additional dollars will have to come from someplace else. Only one law is certain: *If you spend more than you make, you'll never get out of debt.*

PRINCIPLE 30—DECIDE WHETHER TO RENT, LEASE, OR BUY

There's no right or wrong answer to the question of whether to rent or buy a home, because individual needs and circumstances vary greatly. With that in mind, consider the following.

If you plan to keep the home you are considering for less than five years, leasing or renting is the less expensive answer. Buying or selling a home generally costs the buyer or seller about 10 percent of the price of the home. If you buy *and* sell within a five-year period, costs will consume 20 percent of the price of the home.

If you know your move is temporary and you can't decide whether to rent or buy, remember that selling a home is time consuming, and a qualified buyer may not appear when you need one. If circumstances force you to move again within five years, imagine being stuck with double house payments if you can't sell your home.

Don't think of rent or lease money as wasted. You may not be building equity in a home, but your monthly payment provides you with housing. In many areas of the country today there are more sellers than buyers, and renting is actually a better decision.

A couple in our church recently leased a two-year-old, 1,800-square-foot home for $650 per month. The home would probably sell for $130,000. It has a $65,000 mortgage, with twenty-eight years remaining, at 9 percent interest. The landlord rented the home for enough to cover his mortgage payment, taxes, and insurance on the property, which he plans to reoccupy in three years. Even if the tenants had $65,000 to buy the home for cash, they're far better off renting.

Never borrow a down payment in order to purchase a home. Borrowing money for a down payment only causes problems as you struggle to pay back the loan *and* the mortgage company. People borrow because they just "gotta have" that perfect home. Or they borrow so they can quit paying rent. In most cases, the individual "helped" by the second or third mortgage is headed down a dead-end road because housing ultimately consumes 50 to 70 percent of his net spendable income. Credit ratings are ruined, relationships are traumatized or destroyed, and dreams and hopes are shattered. *If you don't have the required down payment for a home, don't borrow it!*

The main question, however, isn't whether to rent or buy. It's "What can you afford to do?" Again, pray, *examine the total cost of housing,* and then pray some more to determine which is best for you.

HOW TO GET STARTED IN BUYING A HOME
The first step in buying a home is to work through the principles presented so far in this chapter:

■ Decide what you need.
■ Decide what kind of financing is best for you: How long will you finance? Will you get a fixed or variable rate?
■ Decide whether you want to purchase a new home or a resale home.
■ Calculate the true cost of housing.
■ Determine what you can comfortably afford to spend.
■ Weigh the advantages and disadvantages of leasing and buying.

Once you've decided for sure that you want to purchase a home, don't look at anything you can't afford; that only breeds discontent. By avoiding homes priced above your means, you won't fall into the trap of rationalizing that overtime, raises, or a second job will enable you to have something that, by conservative standards, you can't afford.

My first home was a two-bedroom, one-bath townhouse that would sell for $45,000 today. Back then, I earned about $45,000 per year, in today's dollars. I put $5,000 down and assumed an 8 percent mortgage of $40,000, making my monthly payment $480 per month, plus another $50 a month paid to the homeowner's association. My home was less than a thousand square feet, and it was located in a blue-collar, industrial section of town.

Most of the men I worked with who earned the same salary I did had homes two to three times bigger than mine, and they were financed to the max. Rather than spend all of my net spendable income, I chose to save half of it. In less than thirty months, my home was paid for and we traded for one more than twice the size: my "fix-up special." My rule back then was simple: Give 10 percent to God, save 50 percent, and live the best you can on what's left over.

Looking back, I really did cheat God, and I tried to save too much too fast. But the habit has kept me debt-free all my adult life. Today, I train my teenagers to give a dime to God, pay yourself a second dime, invest a nickel in self-development, and live contentedly on what's left.

Another example of getting started was set by Tim and Darcy. Tim was the breadwinner and Darcy stayed at home with their twins. Tim earned about $36,000 per year as a truck driver for the city. Right off the top, they put $75 per week into the offering plate at church on Sunday. After giving and taxes, they knew they had $2,208 per month to spend. Using the 40 percent guideline for housing, that left them $883 per month for housing. After calculating the costs of taxes, insurance, utilities, water, sewer, phone, maintenance, and improvements, they determined that they could afford $526 per month for a house payment.

That payment allowed Tim and Darcy the following financing options:

Amount	Term in Years	Total Interest
$70,550	30	$118,450
$55,353	15	$39,147
$44,070	10	$18,930
$34,562	7	$9,539

Tim and Darcy bought a used, double-wide mobile home in a nice park with $4,000 down. They purchased it for $38,562. (New, a comparable double-wide sold for $50,000, situated on a $10,000 lot.) At the time, Tim and Darcy really wanted a $75,000 home, but they decided to be practical and settle for the less expensive one. Seven years later, their double-wide and lot were completely paid for. They sold it themselves for $40,000 and used that as a down payment on the $75,000 home they wanted to begin with. With over 50 percent down, they easily got a $35,000 mortgage at 8 percent. Their payments were $526 a month, for seven years.

Today, their home is almost paid for, and they're looking forward to their mortgage burning party. The same year Tim and Darcy's mortgage is paid off, they will both turn forty years old. Their twins will be in high school, and unlike most people in their age and income bracket, they'll have $526 a month that will not be committed to mortgage payments. By doing what they did, Tim and Darcy saved $100,339 in finance charges, because that's what it would have cost them to finance the $75,000 home over thirty years—something they'd have had to do in order to afford the home at that time in their lives.

In order to get started yourself, apply the principles you've learned and *buy only what you can afford, and finance for as short a term as possible.* Then you can consider trading up.

How Much Down Payment Is Best?
To figure out how much down payment is best for you, consider the cases of Mary and Beth. Both have $25,000 to put down on a $70,000 home. They will make different decisions regarding how much to put into a down payment.

Mary keeps $20,000 for investment, puts $5,000 down, and secures a $65,000 mortgage financed over thirty years at 10 percent. Her monthly mortgage payment is $574.60. Mary's investment grows at 12 percent per year. Fifteen years later, she uses her investment to pay off her home ahead of schedule. After paying the $52,445 mortgage, her investment account is worth $57,026.

Beth puts the whole $25,000 down on the same home and finances the remaining $45,000 at 9 percent interest over ten years (119 months). Her monthly payments are also $574.60. Once her home is paid for, she continues to save her payment at 12 percent interest. After fifteen years, Beth's investment account is worth $47,971.

It appears that Mary was wiser by putting a minimum down, because she ended up $9,055 ahead of Beth. But this logic can deceive us into thinking that it's best to leverage our homes and invest. If you examine the examples in depth, you will discover that *Beth* really has the financial advantage. Mary's investment may have earned 12 percent, but after she paid tax on the profit she had only $29,658 left at the end of fifteen years. Beth, on the other hand, had $44,238 left after taxes and was ahead $14,580.

To compare further, Mary was able to take $90,873 in deductions on her mortgage interest during the first fifteen years, while Beth only deducted $23,377. So Mary was ahead there, right? That's right ONLY IF you can borrow money at less than you can earn on an investment. The problem is, investments aren't guaranteed, but there's no doubt about repayment of debt. The crisis we have experienced in this country with savings & loans, insurance companies, and banks has resulted from the wrong assumption that investment earnings would exceed the cost of borrowed funds.

If Mary's investment was worth only what she invested fifteen years earlier, she would have a $52,445 mortgage and $20,000 in cash, while Beth would have a paid-for home and $35,051 in cash.

The lesson here is, don't gamble with borrowed money, especially on your home.

Should I Hire a Realtor or Buy (or Sell) It Myself?
There is no correct answer for the question of whether to use the services of a realtor. You might be able to buy a home more cheaply by dealing directly with the seller. It's also possible that you could save thousands of dollars by functioning as your own realtor and advertising, showing, and selling a home yourself. But it's not that simple. Both of these possibilities hold risks and expenses.

A single woman I know sold her home herself, and initially bragged about her savings. Eight months later, she learned the hard way that she was still liable for the underlying mortgage, now six months delinquent. By the time the disaster was over, she had spent double what she would have paid a realtor.

If you're considering selling or buying a home without a professional to guide you, pray for wisdom and guidance. Become as knowledgeable as possible, and hire a professional to review everything prior to closing. Don't be penny-wise and dollar foolish.

Is a Second Home a Good Investment?
If there are any mortgages involved, a second home is definitely not a good investment. You're always better off renting a vacation home because you have neither the expense nor the problems associated with owning two homes.

I'm not judging those who own two homes. If you're living as a faithful steward, then enjoy the blessing you have received. But for every success story of the fabulous investment on the vacation condo, there's a similar story with disastrous results.

If you're thinking of buying a second home, pray first. Ask God for guidance and wisdom, and seek responsible counsel before you act. And be sure to check your motive for investing. As Christians, we're responsible for what God gives us. *Everything* He gives us is in order that we might use it for His glory. If buying a second home will restrict you financially and make it difficult for you to invest in God's work, that surely will not glorify Him.

Is a Time-Share Home a Good Investment?
Many people consider time-share property as a way to decrease the cost of vacations. Despite some pretty fancy sales presentations showing all the advantages, you're thousands of dollars ahead if you put the same money toward retiring your mortgage. Later in this chapter, you will see how paying extra toward the principal of your mortgage can return 66 to 1,787 percent on your money. With the exception of investing in God's work, nothing offers a better return for your money.

PRINCIPLE 31—SHOP AROUND FOR HOMEOWNERS, LIFE, AND DISABILITY INSURANCE

Buying insurance from a lender so that you can make mortgage payments if you're disabled (or ensure that the loan will be paid off if you die) is *the most expensive* way to buy life or disability insurance. You can buy the same coverage at 25 to 75 percent less if you shop around and buy what you need directly from a reliable agent. (For more information on this, study chapter 7, on insurance.)

Before we focus on the purchase of home insurance, let me tell you about Bert. At age fifty-four, Bert found that mortgage life insurance through his lender would cost him $1,128 per year on his $80,000 mortgage. But Bert found that he didn't necessarily need *mortgage* life insurance. By shopping around, he found an $80,000 annually renewable term policy that would accomplish the same thing for just $200 per year—saving him $928 per year. He had the option of reducing the premiums even more if he added $80,000 of coverage to his existing term policy.

Mortgage insurance goes directly to the lender, but Bert's personal insurance will go to his heirs, if anything should happen to him. If the heirs intelligently invest the proceeds, the income from the proceeds will almost cover the mortgage payments and then once the home is paid for, the heirs will still have the $80,000 principal. The same principles work for disability income.

Most homeowners insurance covers your home, other buildings on the property, your personal belongings, and living expenses for temporary relocation. The premiums you pay are related to the number of risks (called "perils") you choose to protect yourself against. The greater number of perils covered, the higher your premium. Although policies come with a vast array of options, you can generally buy basic, broad, or comprehensive policies.

Basic Guidelines for Buying Insurance on Your Home

- Don't buy from your lender; find an independent agent and shop around for prices.
- Stay with basic coverage but eliminate unnecessary, additional coverage, which can reduce your premium by 10 to 20 percent.
- Only buy insurance on the replacement value of your home, not on the cost of the land. If your home is worth $80,000 and the value of the lot it sits on accounts for $20,000 of that, you need a maximum of $60,000 in coverage for fire insurance.
- Buy replacement value, not market value, coverage on your

home and its contents. If your five-year-old, $3,000 big screen television set is stolen, replacement coverage will pay you $3,000 to replace it, while market value coverage will pay only $500 to $600. Surprisingly, replacement value coverage costs only $10 to $20 more per year.

- If you rent, buy a special tenants' policy protecting your personal property.
- If you're a landlord, protect your investment with a landlord and tenants liability policy.
- You can purchase a separate policy (called a "floater") to cover personal, expensive items such as jewelry, furs, or art. But first, determine whether the premium is worth the price.
- Purchase flood or earthquake coverage only if you are in a government-designated flood plain or earthquake zone.
- Videotape or photograph your valuables for insurance records.

If you haven't already done so, pull out your policy and see what you are and are not protected against. The time to plan is *before* you have to file a claim. Consider devoting a few hours of study at your local library to the topic of homeowners' insurance. By doing this, you will save yourself hundreds of dollars in unnecessary premiums.

PRINCIPLE 32—SAVE ON HOUSEHOLD REPAIRS BY LEARNING TO DO IT YOURSELF

There are dozens of books at your local library that teach the basic how-to's of home repairs. Make use of them and you'll save plenty of money.

A doctor friend of mine in Arizona had his air conditioning go out during August, the hottest month of the year in this state. A technician came over, fixed the problem, and charged my friend $170 for ten minutes of work. The repair part cost $9.90, but because it was summer the company had a four-hour minimum charge at $40 per hour for a weekend call.

The doctor complained to the technician that he was charging an hourly fee of $960. He then told the technician that he was a medical doctor and even *he* didn't earn that much! At that, the technician laid down his socket wrench, looked my friend in the eye and said, "Yeah, I know. That's why I quit practicing medicine."

An investment in a basic set of tools will be one of the best you ever make. Doing your own repairs gives you a sense of accomplishment and a significant financial reward. A pastor friend of mine became an expert handyman in his spare time. Now he's retired from professional ministry and uses the skills he learned over the years to supplement his retirement income. He tells me he makes about ten to fifteen thousand dollars per year as a handyman.

If you simply can't fix mechanical things yourself, or if you just plain don't have the desire to, try to find a handyman who moonlights, and put your home on a preventive maintenance program. We have a man come to our home twice a year on one of his days off to service our heating and air conditioning units. That way, we're sure everything's in working order before the peak demand season. The $40 per year we've paid him has been the only expense required on those units, other than a few worn parts we replaced during his visits.

We use this same method on all items in our home to minimize repair cost, lengthen life of the items, and save money. These expenses are built into our monthly spending plan.

Principle 33—Prepay Your Mortgage for a Whopping Return on Your Investment

Compound interest turns the home mortgage into a monster, out to financially destroy the average family by forcing them to pay twice the value of a home in finance charges in their assumption of a standard thirty-year term loan. The worst part is, most finance charges will be paid early, because it will take over twenty-three years to pay off half of a thirty-year mortgage! It's outrageous when you think about it, but every day, home buyers subject themselves to the horrendous mortgage monster without ever attempting to defend themselves against it.

If you're like most people, you're learning information after the fact. If you have not followed the guidelines above with your current mortgage, here's the second-best investment idea you can learn from me: *Prepay your mortgage for the greatest return possible on your investment.*

The following chart is a twelve-month breakdown on a thirty-year home mortgage for $100,000, financed at 10 percent interest. Each monthly payment is the total of principal and interest equaling the mortgage payment of $877.57. Study the chart and you'll see that the payment is level, but over time, the principal gradually increases while the interest gradually decreases:

Payment	Interest	Principal	Balance
1	$833.33	$44.24	$99,955.76
2	$832.96	$44.61	$99,911.15
3	$832.60	$44.97	$99,866.18
4	$832.21	$45.36	$99,820.26
5	$831.84	$45.73	$99,775.09
6	$831.46	$46.11	$99,728.90
7	$831.07	$46.50	$99,682.48
8	$830.69	$46.88	$99,635.60
9	$830.29	$47.28	$99,588.32
10	$829.90	$47.67	$99,540.65
11	$829.51	$48.66	$99,492.59
12	$829.10	$48.47	$99,444.12

In the first year, the buyer has made twelve payments of $877.57 for a total of $10,530.84. At the end of the twelfth payment, he still owes $99,444.12; he's reduced the loan balance by only $555.88. The remaining $9,974.96 of his payments went toward interest.

Your loan may be for a different length or rate, but the amortization schedule (that is, the breakdown of principal and interest for each payment) will be similar. Ask your lender for an amortization schedule of your loan.

Here are four different strategies that will save you thousands of dollars in interest if you apply them now:

1. Make an extra principal payment each month.
2. Make a constant payment each month to your principal.
3. Make bimonthly mortgage payments.
4. Apply 50 percent of all raises, bonuses, and windfall profits to reducing the principal on your mortgage.

I can illustrate the concept of making an extra principal-only payment each month. Look at the chart above for the first twelve months. Note the amount of principal payments for months 2, 4, 6, 8, 10, and 12. If you add $44.61 to the first payment, making the total payment $877.57, you save $832.96 in interest. Spend $44.61, and save $832.96!

Pay the same payment of $877.57 the second month (which is really payment number 3, because you eliminated number 2 and the interest due on it, by paying the $44.61 in principal), plus $45.36, which is the principal due on payment number 4. Your third payment is $46.11 extra, and you've paid up through payment number 6. Continue the process and at the end of six months, you've paid six regular payments of $877.57, for a total of $5265.42, plus six principal payments totaling $279.10. In percentage, you've increased your payments by only $279.10 (or 5.3 percent), but you've eliminated $4,986.32 in interest! Here's how your payment record would look:

Payment	Regular Payment	+	Extra Principal Payment	Balance
1	$877.57	+	$44.61	$99,911.15
2	$877.57	+	$45.36	$99,820.82
3	$877.57	+	$46.11	$99,728.98
4	$877.57	+	$46.88	$99,635.60
5	$877.57	+	$47.67	$99,540.65
6	$877.57	+	$48.47	$99,444.12
TOTALS	$5,265.42		$279.10	

If you continue this strategy, you will pay off a thirty-year mortgage in fifteen years and save yourself $122,496 in interest! Even though the principal payment rises slightly each payment, don't worry because your income will likely continue to grow over time, also. Continue this strategy, and you'll be free and clear of house payments forever in just fifteen years.

The same principle works if you increase your regular payment a constant amount, and apply that amount to principal each month. If you choose to make an extra $100 principal payment on the same $100,000, thirty-year loan at 10 percent, here's what the results would look like:

Payment	Interest	Principal	+	Extra Payment	Balance
1	$833.33	$44.24	+	$100	$99,855.76
2	$832.16	$45.44	+	$100	$99,710.32
3	$830.92	$46.65	+	$100	$99,563.67
4	$829.70	$47.87	+	$100	$99,415.79
5	$828.46	$49.11	+	$100	$99,266.69
6	$827.22	$50.35	+	$100	$99,116.34
7	$825.97	$51.60	+	$100	$98,964.74
8	$824.71	$52.87	+	$100	$98,811.87
9	$823.43	$54.14	+	$100	$98,657.33
10	$822.15	$55.42	+	$100	$98,502.31
(Payments 11 to 228 are not shown in order to conserve space.)					
229	$12.80	$864.77	+	$100	$571.13
230	$4.76	$571.13	+	-0-	-0-

By increasing your regular payment by a constant amount, you save $90,508.42 in interest and the loan will be paid off in seventeen years and three months. That's twelve years and nine months early!

A third use of the same principle is to make mortgage payments every two weeks, instead of once a month. In some cases, you can arrange the mortgage payments to come due every two weeks. You make twenty-six biweekly payments per year rather than a single payment once a month.

If you're paid every two weeks, you know that twice a year, you receive three paychecks in a month instead of two. Rather than spending those two extra checks, apply them toward reducing your principal, and you can save yourself thousands of dollars in interest. In cases where the lender is not willing to accommodate this arrangement, you can simply use those two extra paychecks to reduce your principal.

On a $100,000 mortgage, financed at 10 percent for thirty years, your bimonthly payments amount to $442.29—slightly more than half of the regular payment of $877.57. Your benefit is that you pay $74,971 less in interest, and you pay off your home in twenty years and seven months, instead of thirty.

Still another option is to take 50 percent of all raises, bonuses, and windfall profits to slay the mortgage monster of compound interest. If you commit yourself to this plan, you will save more than the price of your home in interest charges and pay off your home in less than fifteen years. For example, a $100,000 mortgage at 12 percent for thirty years will mean monthly payments of $1,028.51. If you choose to increase the payment 1 percent per year each year, up to a maximum of a 10 percent increase in your payment, you will save $158,770 in interest and pay off your home 17.5 years early.

The earlier you begin to retire the debt on your home, the greater your financial benefit. Even twenty years into your thirty-year mortgage, paying an extra principal payment will yield a 176 percent return on your investment. If you wait twenty-five years, your guaranteed return is still 66 percent. Where else can you find a 66 percent guaranteed return on your investment?

Any way you do it, prepaying your mortgage will give you a whopping return on your investment. Why not start doing it today?

PRINCIPLE 34—CONSIDER REFINANCING YOUR HOME

There are several costs involved in refinancing, but it still makes good economic sense to refinance your home *if* you can reduce your interest rates enough to pay for the transaction in two to three years. There are several costs involved in refinancing.

First, you'll need to have your home appraised. Costs will vary depending on the type of appraisal and the location and type of property you own, but in general, appraisals cost several hundred dollars.

Second, you'll need to buy new title insurance. Title insurance varies with the price of the home, but it will cost you several hundred dollars more.

Third, most lenders require percentage point fees up front in order to make you the loan. Sometimes you can trade the points for a higher rate of interest. For instance, if the lender requires two points on a $100,000 mortgage at 9.5 percent, that means the borrower either pays $2,000 up front or pays no points by agreeing to a higher interest rate of 9.75 percent.

Fourth, the origination fee typically costs .5 to 1 percent of the total amount of the loan.

Finally, you must pay closing costs, which are necessary for paying off the old loan and recording the new one. These will also cost you several hundred dollars.

The total cost of refinancing a $100,000 mortgage will be from two to five thousand dollars. Refinancing makes economic sense only if your savings in interest are greater than your costs of refinancing. If you're not planning to stay in your home for at least two or three years, don't bother to refinance.

The best motivation for refinancing is not in order to lower your payments but in order to reduce interest charges and pay off your home early. Let's say you have a $100,000 mortgage at 12 percent interest for thirty years. The loan is five years old and your payments are $1,028.61 per month. Your principal balance is $97,663.22. If you paid all costs in cash, and financed the $97,663.22 over thirty years at 9.5 percent, your payments would drop to $821.21—a savings of $207.40 per month. That would also save you $12,947.40 in interest. However, if you kept your payments level at $1,028.61 per month, and applied the savings of $207.40 to the principal each month, you'd retire the balance in fourteen years, eight months and save yourself $126,519.03 in interest!

The real savings, as you can see, aren't in finance charges, but in what you choose to do with the difference in the payment. *If you refinance your home and keep your payment the same as it was before refinancing, you can retire your mortgage in half the time.*

When refinancing, you can find the best lenders the same way you find the best values: shop around. Ask a realtor to refer you to sources of refinancing. Remember that rates, quotes, and the best deals change weekly. Very often, you'll find your current lender to be very competitive, but do take the time to shop, compare, and bargain. You might be able to negotiate rates, points, origination, and other fees. You have nothing to lose by trying, so ask for a better deal after you have shopped and compared.

PRINCIPLE 35—FOLLOW THE GUIDELINES FOR HOME FINANCING AND REAP THE BENEFITS

By now, you've considered the kind of home you need. You've seen the savings you can reap by financing your home for less than thirty years, and you've examined the advantages and disadvantages of variable and fixed rate financing. You know that you must look at *all* the facts in order to determine what you can afford before you buy a home, and you possess the knowledge you need to save dollars on home insurance and repairs. Most important, you've learned about the phenomenal return available to those who prepay principal on their mortgages.

The average American moves every five years. Over time, homes generally appreciate in value. Assuming that the average home will rise in value by 5 percent per year for the next forty years (as they have in the past), today's $100,000 home will cost $700,000 forty years from now. To illustrate further, here's a simple chart showing a $100,000 home at various rates of appreciation over the years:

Year	3%	5%	7%
5	$115,927	$127,628	$140,255
10	$134,392	$162,889	$196,715
15	$155,796	$207,892	$275,903
20	$180,611	$265,330	$386,968
25	$209,378	$338,635	$542,743
30	$242,726	$432,194	$761,225
35	$281,386	$551,601	$1,067,658
40	$326,203	$703,999	$1,497,455

The average person finances a home for thirty years and trades every five years. Because of inflation, prices rise for the same home. Let's see how to make it pay.

We'll say our buyer is thirty years old. We'll assume a 5 percent growth in housing prices, and we'll assume he finances 90 percent of the price of each new home at 10 percent interest for thirty years. (Remember: When he buys a new home every five years, he pays more money each time, because prices have risen. Each time, he puts only 10 percent down and finances the balance for thirty years.) If, like the average person, our buyer moves every five years and does not bother to reinvest all of his equity, here's a recap of his payments and equity at five year intervals:

Year	Payment	Equity	Investments
1	$796	$10,000	-0-
5	$1,015	$12,763	-0-
10	$1,296	$16,289	-0-
15	$1,654	$20,789	-0-
20	$2,111	$26,533	-0-
25	$2,694	$33,864	-0-
30	$3,439	$43,219	-0-
35	$4,388	$55,160	-0-

Look at our buyer thirty years later, at age sixty-five: He is now buying a home for $551,601. (That's the same type of home he started out with, thirty-five years ago, when he paid $70,000!) Again, he puts 10 percent down and finances for thirty years at 10 percent interest. His payments are $4,388 per month.

If he'd financed his home for only fifteen years rather than thirty, here's where he'd be: At the end of the first five years, his home is worth $127,628 and his original $90,000 mortgage is paid down to $86,660, making his equity $40,968. Five years later, in order to buy the same priced home as the first one, he pays $127,628. He puts his equity of $40,968 down (which is all of the equity rather than merely 10 percent) and finances the balance of $86,660 for ten years (sticking with his plan of a fifteen-year mortgage term) at 10 percent for payments of $1,175 a month. Five years later, the same home will sell for $162,889. If, instead of moving, he stays in his second home, his mortgage would be paid down to $53,463. Instead, he puts $109,426 down on a $162,889 home and finances it for five years at 10 percent interest. His payments are now $1,175 per month. At the end of this five-year period, his paid-for home is worth $207,892.

For a ten-year period, his payments were slightly higher than those of someone who financed for thirty years, but he has *no* house payments from here on out. If, during the next twenty years, he exercises discipline and saves the average house payment of the thirty-year financier and earns only 5 percent interest, here's how he'd fare:

Year	Savings	Payment	Equity	Investments
	-0-	$796	$10,000	-0-
5	-0-	$1,175	$40,968	-0-
10	-0-	$1,435	$109,426	-0-
15	$1,654	-0-	$207,892	-0-
20	$2,111	-0-	$265,330	$112,482
25	$2,694	-0-	$338,635	$287,120
30	$3,439	-0-	$432,194	$549,653
35	-0-	-0-	$551,601	$935,385

At age sixty-five, the thirty-year financier has $55,160 equity in the same home as our buyer, but our buyer's home is paid for. He lacked the commitment to stay with the plan and reinvest his equity. The thirty-year financier still owes 360 payments of $4,388 per month. But our buyer's $551,601 home is paid for, and he has accumulated a $935,385 nest egg. *The difference in net worth between the average thirty-year financier and the one who is wise enough to finance for fifteen years and stay with that term is $1,431,826!* That difference assumed only 5 percent on his investments. It's possible that he could have earned 6, 8, or even 10 percent!

Even with rising prices, by setting a goal of paying off your home in fifteen years and sticking with it even if you move, you can be $1,431,826 ahead. "By wisdom a house is built, and by understanding it is established; through knowledge its rooms are filled with all precious and pleasant riches" (Proverbs 24:3-4).

SIX

BUYING A CAR

■

Someone once joked that the best way to get back on your feet is to miss a couple of car payments. With the price of cars, most of us are closer to walking than we'd like to think! Except for purchasing a home, buying an automobile is usually a person's biggest expense.

In a previous chapter, we discussed the importance of separating "wants" from "needs." In today's society, we know that transportation qualifies as a definite need. So unless you live and work in a city with a well-running mass-transit system, the question isn't whether or not you need a car, the question is, "What kind of car do you need?"

PRINCIPLE 36—DECIDE WHAT KIND OF CAR YOU NEED

If we're honest, most of us will realize that the type of car we *want* is often quite different from the type of car we actually *need*. A brand-new Infiniti will get you to work on time—but so will a well-maintained ten-year-old Ford. Granted, you may not look as good driving it—or feel as cool—but the need is met just the same!

The price of reliable transportation can range from $1,500 to $150,000 or more. How does a good steward know how much of

103

God's money to invest in a car?

As Christians, the first thing we should do—as we should with all decisions—is to pray, seeking the Lord's guidance for what kind of investment qualifies as good stewardship. We should ask Him to reveal the truth to us: Will we be spending more than we should? Are we being practical, or do we want a particular car in order to impress others? Is a luxury car a matter of pride, something to inflate our ego? What are our motives?

Once you've spent time in prayer over this decision, the type of car you choose to drive becomes a personal matter between you and the Lord.

Six years ago, I stood looking into my garage, convicted by the sight of two brand-new cars: a Porsche 911 convertible, which I drove, and a Datsun 300ZX—a gift to my wife, Jeanie. Suddenly, a harsh reality hit me: *Sixty thousand dollars of God's money was parked in my garage!* Was this God's plan of stewardship for me, I wondered? Or was I simply overindulging myself in an effort to deal with a previously unrecognized mid-life crisis?

After discussing my concern with Jeanie, we decided that these cars weren't doing anything to glorify God. Together, we decided to sell them and reallocate the money. Shortly after our decision was made, I sold my eight-month-old Porsche for exactly what I paid for it, and Jeanie had an accident in which she miraculously escaped without injury but totaled the Datsun. When all the funds from her insurance and the sale of my car were collected, we managed to buy four new cars. I got a Honda Civic, Jeanie got a comparable Datsun, and we gave each of our widowed mothers a new car, too. When all that was done, we still had $25,000 left over, which we both felt led to give to our church.

Now, I know that God blesses obedience, but you can't imagine my surprise when, a few days later, I watched my sixty-four-year-old mother walk down the aisle of that same church and accept Jesus Christ as her Lord and Savior! After several years of witnessing and inviting her to church, my mother had called for no apparent reason and asked to go with us to a mid-week service. God placed a visiting evangelist in the pulpit that night, and something he said touched my mother's heart in a way I hadn't been able to.

I believe the law of sowing and reaping works every time, and although the rewards for obedience are not always so immediate or dramatic, they *will* be granted!

I'm in no way suggesting that everyone who drives a luxury car is a poor steward. Jeanie and I made a personal decision, based on many factors in our lives. God created all of us uniquely and perfectly to fit into His plan for our individual lives. The kind of profession we're in—or the kind of car we're in—makes no difference to God if we are in a right relationship with Him. What *does* make a difference to God is *the way in which we do whatever He's called us to do.* Paul defines it for us in 1 Corinthians 10:31—"So whether you eat or drink or whatever you do, *do it all for the glory of God*" (emphasis added). This Scripture is all-inclusive, and we should remember it when making a purchase of any kind.

PRINCIPLE 37—THINK TWICE BEFORE FINANCING

The automobile industry prides itself on its ability to entice almost anyone into buying a new car. They offer 3 to 6 percent financing if you purchase a new car, and they also lure buyers with huge rebates, offering anywhere from $500 to $1,000 back—money you can put in your pocket, they say, if you just buy a brand-new car!

When my Honda Civic was three years old, one of these ads enticed me to look closer. To satisfy my curiosity, I priced the best-selling car in the U.S. at the time, the Honda Accord. I discovered that it would cost me about $15,000 plus tax, license, and transfer fees. Still curious, I went into a local showroom to see if improvements in automobiles were significant enough over the past three years to merit such an investment.

When I entered the dealership, I parked my three-year-old Civic next to a beautiful aqua blue Accord sedan. Looking over my shoulder, I noticed the car I had driven to the dealership was dirty and the color had lost its luster. Suddenly, the style of that new aqua blue beauty really caught my eye.

The salesperson who greeted me was every sales manager's dream. She was kind, courteous, knowledgeable, and did not use any high-pressure tactics to convince me. She even offered to let me drive the little beauty—at no obligation, of course.

It was hot that day, and I had worn shorts. As I slid behind the wheel, the seats felt like black velvet against my bare legs. Smiling happily, I noticed there were no food stains on the seat, and no french-fries or candy wrappers wedged between them. Caressing the wheel like a teenager on his first date, I put that baby in drive and took off. The new- car smell stimulated my nostrils like fine French perfume.

Suddenly, lust was in my heart! The stereo (an additional $899) sounded fantastic. I knew I *had* to have that car.

When I returned to the showroom, I think I must have looked like a young boy who'd been kissed for the first time. I was in love with that car, and the salesperson knew it. Minutes later, we were in her office and she was telling me I could drive home in that brand-new car for only tax, license, and transfer—a measly $1,798.50 down! Then, she said, I'd own it—for just $330.36 a month! I looked across the desk at that saleslady—the one who was so kind, courteous, knowledgeable, and used no high-pressure tactics to convince me—and considered her family, and her desperate need to eke out a living selling Hondas. Then I considered the amount of time I spend in my car each week—ten long, grueling hours—and I gave the purchase of that new car some serious thought, trying desperately to keep my head, even though I'd lost my heart.

I glanced out the window at my reliable old Civic. It had only 45,000 miles on it. Even though it wasn't as good-looking as the Accord, it definitely met my transportation needs. And I never make decisions based on the amount of a monthly payment; I always consider the total price. I wasn't considering the $330.36 per month payment; I was considering whether or not I wanted to spend $16,798.50 on a new car. And as always, in times of material temptations, I tried to recall Christ's words: "Suppose one of you wants to build a tower [or buy a car]. Will he not first sit down and estimate the cost to see if he has enough money to complete it? For if he lays the foundation and is not able to finish it, everyone who sees it will ridicule him, saying, 'This fellow began to build and was not able to finish'" (Luke 14:28-30).

After calculating the cost, I just couldn't justify buying that car.

Calculating the Cost: Saving Versus Financing
Though the actual sales price of the car I wanted to purchase had been $15,000, the sales tax, license, and transfer fees added an additional $1,798.50. The monthly payment of $330.36 for sixty months, or five years, was financed at only 1 percent interest, but the finance charge still came to $4,821.60 (sixty months of payments for a total of $19,821.60, minus the purchase price of $15,000). The finance charge added 32 percent to the cost of the car. The tax, license, and transfer fees added another 12 percent, increasing the original price of the car by 44 percent!

Instead of financing the car, I calculated the advantage of opening a special bank account to save for it. If I deposited $213.92 per month in an account earning 6 percent interest, in five years I would have $15,000. I would have earned $2,165 in interest on the total amount of $12,835 (sixty payments of $213.92 each) I had saved.

When I added the interest I would earn by putting money in savings to the financing charges I would have paid, I came up with a final figure that represented the difference between saving and financing: $6,986.26.

The disadvantage of financing the car was now quite obvious. Had I financed the car, I would have been making monthly payments of $330.36—*54 percent higher* than the payments I would have been making to my own savings account. Furthermore, the total amount I would save by deferring the purchase in order to save for the car instead of financing it, $6,986.26, equaled 47 percent of the price of the car! The question now became, "Which decision would demonstrate better stewardship in God's eyes—financing the new car, or saving for it?" Calculating the costs had given me the answer. This leads us to the next principle: *save now, buy later.*

PRINCIPLE 38—SAVE NOW, BUY LATER

I advise everyone to maintain a "transportation fund"—a special savings account specifically designated for replacing your means of transportation. As we have already seen, paying cash will save thousands of dollars.

For example, assuming my three-year-old Civic was purchased new for $9,000 in cash, all I would have needed to save was $128.35 per month for sixty months in order to have the $9,000 I needed to purchase the car. (This includes $1,299 accumulated interest on the savings account.)

Let's assume that six years after purchasing my Civic I will be ready to buy another car. Even if I buy the same model, I'll have to spend more because prices will have gone up. Estimating a 6 percent annual increase, I'll need $12,767 in cash (6 percent annual increase multiplied by six years and compounded) to replace the car I bought new six years before. In order to accumulate that cash in savings, I must deposit $147.02 per month in my transportation fund for six years. Those funds will earn $2,181.56 in interest, and so the total amount in my savings account will give me the $12,767 cash I need to replace my old Civic with a new one.

However, I could choose to ignore the ultimate replacement cost and enjoy the $147.02 per month in cash, instead of making payments to a transportation fund. But that also means that I would forfeit the $2,181.56 in interest I'd make over the six-year period. And then I'll have to finance the replacement car. That means my car payments will be $281.18 per month, which is $134.16 higher than paying *myself* through a savings plan. And not only will I lose the $2,181.56 in interest, I'll end up paying the lender $4,104 in interest!

Therefore, the principle of when to buy a new car is clear: *Consider payments, operating cost, insurance premiums, cost of repairs and maintenance, and reserves for replacing the car when it's worn out.*

PRINCIPLE 39—DON'T BE QUICK TO TRADE IN YOUR OLD CAR

As automobile prices have risen drastically, consumers have been driving their cars for longer periods of time. When I bought my first car in 1961, the average new car buyer traded every two years. Now it's every four or five years.

You may have heard the expression "upside down" in some of the ads run by major automobile makers. "Upside down" means that the amount owed on a car is greater than what the car is worth. You can't trade for a new car if you're upside down on the car you're driving, because lenders won't finance negative equity. If you finance a car for sixty months, it will take you almost four years to get "right side up."

Dealers will tell you that by the time a car is paid for, it's probably time to trade for a new one. After all, your paid-for car has about 60,000 miles on it, and once a car is five years old it can be expensive to maintain. Transmissions, engines, air conditioners, back ends, and electrical accessories tend to need repair or replacement by then. So, they reason, instead of throwing good money after bad, you're much wiser simply to buy a new car.

There's no question that we're educated to trade. But is it really the best option?

The High Cost of Trading: A $124,000 Difference
On the average, a twenty-five-year-old man traveling 12,000 miles per year will cover 480,000 miles and buy ten cars by the time he reaches age sixty-five. Based on prices at the time of this writing and figuring an operating cost of fifty-one cents per mile (according to national car rental companies, who tell me that's what it costs to operate a new

vehicle that's traded every three years), *the average person will spend $244,800 on transportation in his or her lifetime.* By contrast, *those who continue to drive each of their vehicles until the end of its mechanical life will save $124,800!* If the price of a new car continues to escalate in the future as it has in the past, you can realistically multiply that $124,000 savings by four and come out $499,200 ahead!

When deciding whether or not to purchase a new car, remember to separate the desire for luxury and status from the need, which is transportation. Pray for guidance and ask God for the wisdom to use the money saved to bring greater glory to Him.

The following chart reveals that the most expensive ride you'll ever take is the one from the showroom in your brand-new car. ("Depreciation" is the loss in value of a car over time. A two- or three-year-old vehicle is usually worth only one-half of what it cost new.) Consider these industry statistics:

Age of Car	Yearly Depreciation	Cumulative Depreciation
1	28%	28%
2	20%	48%*
3	16%	64%*
4	8%	72%
5	6%	78%
6	5%	83%
7	4%	87%
8	3%	90%
9	2%	92%
10	1%	93%

*The best buy on a used car is when it is two or three years old.

The longer you keep your car, the less you'll spend on transportation. When a car is kept to the end of its mechanical life and the engine and back end are rebuilt or replaced as needed, the cost of operating the vehicle is reduced from fifty-one cents per mile to less than twenty-five cents per mile. Trading vehicles is often a costly investment decision.

If you decide that you must get rid of your old car and buy a new one, don't trade it in simply for convenience, because it always costs you more than selling your old car first and using the cash to buy your new car. If convenience is very important to you, be sure you look at the net difference between the price of the new car and the amount you're allowed for the trade-in. Don't be fooled by what seems to be a generous allowance for your old car.

Sell Your Trade Yourself and Save $1,000

On the average, selling your own car will save you about $1,000. But before you advertise your car for sale, have it cleaned and waxed and do any work needed to put it into display condition. Do your homework, and price the car to sell at its real value, which you can estimate from the *NADA Guide* or the *Kelly Blue Book*.

If you think your car's worth more than what's listed in the guides, take it to a dealer who sells the same make and model, and see what he'll offer you in cash. This will help you determine a realistic selling price. If you price the car too high, no one will buy it; if you price it too low, you're giving money away. When you have cash in hand, you're ready to purchase the newer car.

PRINCIPLE 40—CONSIDER THE SAVINGS IN DOING YOUR OWN CAR REPAIR

Any mechanic will tell you that when properly maintained, the average car will need rebuilding after 100,000 to 120,000 miles. He will also tell you that the transmission won't last more than seven years. Cost of repairs to major elements such as the engine, back end, transmission, and air conditioner will vary, depending upon the kind of car you drive and where you have the work done. But generally speaking, you can have all four major elements of your paid-for car replaced or repaired for less than $4,000. Compared to the average $15,000 price of a new car, that's about one-half of what you'd lose in depreciation during the first three years!

It's cheapest to fix your car yourself. Fred Frugal learned to do his own auto repairs in junior college and drives a twenty-five-year-old Chevy with 290,000 miles on it. Because the car's been mechanically rebuilt twice, Fred's cost per mile of operation is less than nine cents. For the past twenty-five years, Fred's used the $154 per month he saves on car payments to support a missionary—$46,400 invested for eternal dividends!

To get started on doing your own car repair, get a good how-to book from your local library and a decent set of tools. Our local college offers courses from minor auto repair and maintenance to major engine and transmission work for $40 per class; you can learn to do it yourself for less than it would cost you to pay a mechanic for one hour of his time. You may be slower than a trained mechanic, and you may need some help (which the staff at the auto supply, where you buy your parts, will happily give you for free), but the concept is a sound money saver.

If you can't do your own repairs, you can always hire a moonlighting mechanic, usually for half of what a repair shop will charge you. There are numerous do-it-yourself automobile parts stores throughout the country. Most of the time, you can buy the parts yourself for 30 to 50 percent less than what a mechanic will charge.

You can find good mechanics by word of mouth or by checking your local newspapers. Sometimes, a barter arrangement makes good sense. A dentist friend of mine swapped services with a mechanic, trading orthodontics for engine and transmission repairs. Both reported and paid taxes on the "income" paid by service from the other, but both spent 50 percent less by seeking an inexpensive way to do repairs.

PRINCIPLE 41—DON'T RULE OUT BUYING A USED CAR

We already know it makes sense to save for a car rather than to finance one. We also know that keeping a car until the end of its mechanical life will cut the cost of owning transportation from fifty-one to twenty-five cents per mile, or less. But what about buying a used car? Is it safe? Is it cost-efficient?

We're conditioned to think that if we buy a used car, we're getting someone else's problems. Society tells us life is short; we deserve the best and we owe it to ourselves to drive a nice, new car. However, purchasing a two- or three-year-old car at half of its new-car price, with the intent to drive it for five or six years, can be a very wise decision.

Remember the $15,000 car I considered buying? If I buy that same car three years later, I will save $7,500. The first owner absorbed the 50 percent loss of value because he chose to drive it off the showroom floor. By buying the car used, I reduce the $1,798.50 for sales tax, license, and transfer to $768.25—an additional savings of $1,030.25 that I can use for other things. Still another consideration is the cost of auto insurance, which is determined by several factors, including *the age, cost, and make* of the car. Usually, buying a two- or three-year-old car will reduce insurance premiums by 20 to 25 percent.

To summarize, if you buy a car that's two or three years old and originally sold for $15,000, you save the $7,500 depreciation, $1,030 in fees, and about $200 per year on your insurance premium. Provided you keep the car five years, you will save a total of $9,530. That amounts to a savings of $1,906 per year, or $158.83 per month! If you keep the car for thirty years (yes, it *can* be done!), you will save $57,180, and that doesn't even include the cost of inflation on new vehicles!

The following example compares the monetary advantage of buying a used car instead of a new one.

Buying a New Car		Buying a Used Car (the same car, now 2-3 years old, using savings)	
Price	$15,000.00	Price	$15,000.00
		Depreciation	– $7,500.00
		Subtotal	$7,500.00
Fees	$1,798.50	Fees	$768.25
Finance charge	$4,821.60	Finance charge	-0-
Cost new	$21,620.10	Cost used	$8,268.25

Over your car-buying lifetime, the decision to buy a good used car instead of a new one can save you $128,655. If you invest the savings in a 6 percent savings account, your balance could be $359,383 or more!

"A simple man believes anything," the Bible tells us, "but a prudent man gives thought to his steps" (Proverbs 14:15). Small amounts of money saved over long periods of time and intelligently invested make a significant difference for God's people.

Buy the Right Used Car "Right"

Once you've selected the right used car, offer a fair but competitive price for it. There are a number of reports that rate the reliability, dependability, and incidence of repairs for the hundreds of available vehicle models. My favorite resource is *Consumer Reports*, although other publications do a good job, too.

It's wise to establish several choices on make and model and then go looking for those specific cars. Before you go shopping, be sure you know what a fair price is for the make and model of car you want. Two good sources for such information are the *NADA Official Used Car Guide* and the *Kelly Blue Book*. You can find either at bookstores or libraries, or you can inquire at your bank or credit union. If you'll spend an hour studying these references, you'll understand what equipment is standard and which is optional, and you'll save yourself hundreds of dollars and loads of aggravation.

A word of caution: Prices in the guides assume that the car is in good mechanical condition, has good tires, unbroken windshield, a decent interior, and no body damage. If the car requires work on any of the above, subtract a fair repair estimate from the published price. These prices can change monthly or bimonthly, and prices will vary from the "trade-in value" (*NADA*) or "wholesale" (*Blue Book*)—the figure you shoot for to buy right.

The most convenient place to find a used car is from a new or used car dealer. Unfortunately for the shopper, dealers usually command the highest prices. For that reason, many people buy directly from individual owners who advertise in newspapers, auto-trader periodicals, at park-and-swaps, on local bulletin boards, or simply by word of mouth. Repossessions by banks, credit unions, and lease companies may also be good sources for bargains. Rental companies are another good source.

Advice on Shopping for a Used Car

Here are some suggestions for the most effective used-car shopping:

1. Regardless of where you buy, avoid surprises by having the car inspected by a trained, knowledgeable mechanic *before* you buy.
2. Make sure the odometer is accurate by having the seller guarantee it in writing. If he refuses, keep shopping.
3. If you're dealing with a private party, verify that the title is not a salvage title, and make sure there are no outstanding liens on it before you write your check.

What to Do When You Can't Even Afford a Three-Year-Old Car

If you can't come up with the average $7,500 to buy a three-year-old car, two options remain.

1. *Have your existing car mechanically rebuilt, assuming the body and interiors are usable for the next seven to ten years.*

A friend of mine who drives 20,000 miles per year was shocked to find that he could have the engine and transmission rebuilt on his six-year-old car for only $2,500, because he was accustomed to spending $12,000 every six years to trade his cars in. Since he wasn't in the habit of saving for his replacement, he was pleased to drive his rebuilt car for nine payments of $316 a month, rather than trade for another car and make forty-eight payments of $316 per month. As soon as the loan for repairs is repaid, he plans to begin making thirty-nine payments to his savings account of $316 each so he can buy his next vehicle in cash. By using this strategy, he's ahead for a total of $12,324!

2. *If you can't afford to buy a newer used car, then buy good, reliable transportation that gets the job done.* After all, what you need

is transportation, not status.

My sixteen-year-old son wanted a red 1965 Mustang convertible. When he found out that one in good condition would cost far more than the $4,000 he had saved, he got realistic. After we studied the *NADA Guide*, we began to ask around, and we searched the newspaper. We soon had three possibilities: a six-year-old Datsun with 28,000 miles on it for $3,100 (from an estate sale); a two-year-old GEO with 8,000 miles on it for $4,132 (from a Christian dealer I know); or a four-year-old Honda Civic with 50,000 miles on it for $3,950.

After driving all three cars, and praying for God's guidance, we bought the GEO. The car, purchased new, would have cost double the price, and we figure it will run through the balance of high school and four years of college with no major expense.

If you need transportation but you're short on funds, tell God about it. He promises to meet our needs. To encourage you, I'll tell you a story of how God showed his faithfulness to a desperate single mother who suddenly found herself with no car.

For two years, Lisa had saved $75 per month for transportation. When her fourteen-year-old car finally died, she knew it would be next to impossible to find transportation for the $1800 she had accumulated. Still, she made her need a priority in prayer. Thirteen days later, an uncle she had neither seen nor heard from for over ten years appeared out of the blue and gave her a six-year-old economy hatchback. God answers prayers when we ask in faith, with patience and persistence, and commit ourselves to trust in Him to meet our needs.

PRINCIPLE 42—COUNT *ALL* THE COSTS BEFORE YOU BUY

When purchasing a car, most people consider only the cost of the monthly payment. They forget to add the costs of gas and oil, insurance, tax and license, and repair and maintenance. Further, most people never consider budgeting a cash reserve to replace the car when necessary—a step that, as we've seen, will save the car buyer thousands of dollars in financing fees. When *all* of these factors have been considered, the prudent buyer is able to calculate accurately the amount of money he should spend on transportation.

Most car buyers take for granted that automobiles are more fuel-efficient today than they were in the past. They rarely take time to calculate the actual savings of a vehicle getting twenty-five miles per gallon (MPG) over one that gets eighteen MPG. Based on 100,000 miles of travel, the car that gets 18 MPG will consume 5,556 gallons of gasoline; the 25 MPG vehicle will use only 4,000. If gasoline costs $1 a gallon, the savings adds up considerably: $1,556 for the life of the car.

You can locate the MPG rating of a particular vehicle by researching it in *Consumer Reports*. This information will help you limit your choices. Look for those reported to have the highest MPG rating, but along with this factor you should consider ratings for the lowest maintenance costs and the greatest estimates of reliability. While you're doing your homework, study the prices published in either the *Kelly Blue Book* or the *NADA Car Guide* to determine fair prices for the models you're considering.

Weigh the Options

Prices for new cars vary tremendously with options added to the base price. In 1958, the Maroney Act forced all car dealers to itemize prices on window stickers so consumers could fairly and intelligently compare deals offered by competing dealers and manufacturers. Unfortunately, the Maroney Act applies only to cars; trucks are exempt. Whether you're buying a car or a truck, be sure to compare option for option when pricing a new vehicle. What appears to be a super deal may be nothing more than a car with fewer options.

The options you select with your vehicle will constitute a significant portion of the money you spend. Power windows, seats, door locks, stereos, sun roofs, tilt steering wheels, cruise control, and luxury interiors can raise the price of a vehicle by thousands of dollars and increase your insurance and maintenance costs as well.

The Honda Accord I wanted so badly came in four models: DX for $12,545, LX for $15,095, EX for $16,795, and the SE for $19,545. I considered the price difference, wondering if the deluxe SE was worth $7,000 more than the DX. The deluxe stereo/tape player would have cost an additional $899 but was worth only $75 in trade value on a four-year-old model. Personally, I couldn't justify paying $824 over four years for a stereo, especially when I could purchase and install a high quality stereo myself for one-quarter of the price. (If you're curious, I drive a Honda Civic DX with two options: factory air and a stereo/tape deck I installed myself for $229.) It's interesting to note that the $7,000 difference between the cheapest and most expensive models was reduced to only $2,100 if the car purchased was two or three years old.

Quite simply, the fewer options you buy, the cheaper the car and the less concern you will have with repair and replacement of them, down the road.

How to Save 60 Percent on Your New Car

There are two ways to save 60 percent on a car. We've already discussed the first: Don't buy the car new; buy it used and you will save 60 percent. If you feel compelled to buy a brand-new car, however, you can still save the 60 percent. Here's how.

1. *Buy the basic model, not the top of the line.* In my almost "gotcha" experience with the Honda Accord, the $7,000 difference between the basic Accord DX model and the top-of-the-line SE model was a substantial 36 percent.

2. *Avoid appealing but expensive options that add little to the value of the car.* This purchasing restraint will save you another 14 to 22 percent.

I did some homework here. I surveyed options on all Honda models and found that the suggested selling price, with options, was $2,736 above the base model price. That adds 14 percent to the top-of-the-line model and 22 percent to the base model. Among the options on the basic model were dealer preparation and handling, which costs the consumer $245. That's pure profit to the dealer and serves to raise the price of the car while nothing at all to add to its value. Another option on the Hondas was a Scotch Guard interior for a mere $125. If you shop at any auto accessory or furniture store, you'll find that you can buy a can of Scotch Guard for $4—and that's all you need to do it yourself: one can. Other options included undercoating ($195) and pinstriping ($245).

Bookstores and libraries offer dozens of books that tell you what a dealer actually has to pay the factory for a vehicle. The difference between sticker price and dealer cost is the dealer's profit margin. The question then becomes one of fair profit. (That varies from $100 to $1,000 on most models.) Learn the difference between suggested retail and dealer cost, then *you* decide what's a fair profit to offer the dealer. If you'll investigate before you invest, you'll save at least another 10 percent.

3. *Do what most Americans hate to do: negotiate.* Remember, it's not your money, it's God's money—you're only His steward. He's entrusted you with a certain number of His dollars, so do your best to protect His assets. Minimize your outlay on everything, especially new cars or trucks.

Extended Warranties: Are They Worth the Investment?
We all fear being stuck with expensive repairs while we're still making car payments, so we're all easy targets for salespeople eager to sell us extended warranties that will pay for such services. In reality, the probability of collecting on these policies is slim, and the premiums are substantial: $300 to $900.

To the selling dealer, extended warranty policies are a good source of revenue that enhances the profits they already make on financing, credit life, and disability insurance. One major retailer makes more profit financing equipment and appliances than it does when selling the same items. Typically, a retailer earns 50 percent of the premium charged on extended warranties and service contracts. Instead of listening to the story of that one person out of ten who profited by having bought the warranty or service contract, save money each month to cover repairs, maintenance, and ultimately replace the vehicle you buy. Ninety percent of the time, you'll come out ahead.

PRINCIPLE 43—CALCULATE HOW MUCH YOU SHOULD SPEND

Approximately 12 to 15 percent of your net spendable income can be appropriately allocated to transportation. "Net spendable income" is your gross pay, less tithes and federal, state, and local taxes.

Let's assume that you earn $40,000 per year and have a family of four. You give $333 per month, or $4,000 per year, to your church. Federal, state, and local taxes will cost you about $7,200 per year. These two amounts, deducted from your $40,000 salary, will leave you $28,800 of spendable income. If you use the 12 to 15 percent guideline, your total transportation expense should be between $3,456 and $4,320 per year. That sounds like a lot of money, but remember, it includes the cost of your vehicle and all expenses incurred as a result of it, such as:

1. Payments (to yourself or to a lender)
2. Gas and oil, which vary in costs depending on your mileage and the type of car you drive
3. Automobile insurance
4. Repairs and maintenance
5. Replacement fund

By way of example, look at the real costs of my 1990 Honda Civic:

Item	Month	Year
Payments to myself	$128.35	$1,540.00
Gas and oil	$45.83	550.00
Insurance (over six years)	$50.00	$600.00
Repairs/maintenance	$25.00	$300.00
Replacement fund*	$18.67	$224.00
TOTALS	$267.85	$3,124.20

*The $18.67 paid to my "replacement fund" supplements the $128.35 payment I already make to myself and accounts for the difference needed in the future, due to inflation.

The 12 to 15 percent guideline is a benchmark for $25,000 to $60,000 per year incomes; if you raise the guidelines, you may put a strain on other areas of required spending. Circumstances may vary, but one thing remains true in all cases: If your outgo exceeds your income, spending will be your financial downfall.

PRINCIPLE 44—IF YOU MUST FINANCE, DO IT WISELY

Before agreeing to finance a car, ask these questions:

1. How long do you want to obligate yourself to payments?
2. Does the car you want satisfy a desire, or meet a real need?
3. Are you being realistic about what you can afford for transportation?
4. What will your total transportation expenses be? (Include payments, gas and oil, insurance, a reserve for repairs and maintenance, and money for savings, so you can buy the next vehicle with cash.)

In other words, look at the total picture. Then, if you still think you really need the car, do everything you can to minimize the total cost of financing the car. Let's take a look at how to shop financing packages.

Compare Interest Rates

Interest rates are confusing because there are many different ways to calculate them. Interest rates may be simple or compounded. For example, if you borrow $10,000 for one year at 10 percent simple interest, you'll repay $11,000. But if the loan is compounded monthly at the same rate, you'll end up repaying $11,047.10. Or, if you borrow $1,000 at an add interest rate of 10 percent for five years, you'll repay $1,500.

Years ago, the Truth in Lending Law was enacted to help consumers compare interest rates simply and easily. You don't need to dig out a calculator in order to determine the difference between simple and compounded interest, add-on or discount rates, or the impact of delaying your first payment for forty-five, sixty, or even ninety days. All you need to do is compare Annual Percentage Rates, now disclosed by law on all installment contracts. (In addition to stating interest rates in APR, contracts must also disclose the costs in dollars so you can compare them.)

Most of us have seen TV ads offering a brand-new car financed at 4 percent or even lower. But before you drop everything and run out to buy one, make sure you get answers to these questions:

1. Are you paying list price for the car in order to get this great interest rate? If so, be sure to compare the list price to the negotiating price. That way, you can check around to see what it would cost you to obtain your own financing for the lesser amount.
2. Why are they offering such a great interest rate? Is the car a slow seller? If so, why?
3. If you trade your existing car, how much are they allowing for your trade? And how much net difference will you be financing? And again, what's the APR (cost in dollars on your loan)?

Sometimes you can find a real bargain in interest rates, but if securing that bargain causes you to buy a new car rather than paying 50 percent less for a three-year-old model, perhaps the deal isn't so good after all.

Generally, financing at a dealership will cost you more than going directly to your bank or credit union. And although using a home equity loan may lower your payments because the life of the loan is extended, in the long run you'll end up paying much more in interest, and your payments will continue long after the car is worn out and traded for a newer one.

The Rule of 78s

Generally, refunds of interest on car loans are calculated by the rule of 78s: If you total the numbers from 1 to 12, you get 78. This applies to calculating time periods over which interest rates are earned.

If you finance a car for four years (or forty-eight months), during the first four months $^{12}/_{78}$ of the interest is earned. During the next four months, another $^{11}/_{78}$ is earned. In the last four months of your first year, $^{10}/_{78}$ of the interest has been earned. Using this calculation, you can see that during the first year of financing, $^{33}/_{78}$ or 42 percent of the entire interest is earned ($12 + 11 + 10 = 33$).

During the first two years, $^{57}/_{78}$, or 73 percent, of the interest is earned. If you paid off the balance of your four-year loan halfway through, you would save only 27 percent of the interest. If you waited until your thirty-sixth payment, you would save only 8 percent of the total finance charges. *The time to learn this is before, not after, financing!* If you have a car loan for which interest is refunded on the rule of 78s, it pays you to make double payments at the beginning rather than the end of the term.

Purchase, Don't Lease

Though leasing a vehicle is more expensive than buying one, leasing appeals to some people because the monthly payments are lower than purchase payments. This is because leases vary in terms and types.

Generally, leases are either "open-end" or "closed-end." An open-end lease allows the lessee to have lower payments, provided he guarantees that at the end of the term of his lease, his vehicle will be worth $5,000. If the car brings $5,000 or more at the end of the lease, the lessee's ahead. If it doesn't, he's liable for the difference. By contrast, a closed-end lease guarantees a $4,300 residual value on the vehicle and frees the lessee from any personal liability.

When you lease a car, you are guaranteed a certain number of payments at a fixed amount, with a balloon or final payment due at the end of the term of the contract. With a lease agreement, the lessee owns nothing at the end of the lease term. By focusing only on the payments, and not on the cost of transportation over time, many people are lured into leasing because it permits them to drive what they can't afford to buy.

I recently counseled a young businessman who learned the hard way about leasing an automobile. He was in sales, and he wanted very much to drive what he called a "successful executive's car"—a BMW. His manager assured him that a good image was worth the investment, and that if he *felt* successful, he'd *be* successful. His sales manager even agreed to reimburse him the $500 per month lease payment for any month in which he met or exceeded his quota.

The problem developed at the end of the first year of his contract, when the economy (and his industry in particular) hit a slump. As promised, the company reimbursed him for the first twelve payments, but he had to make the next six payments himself because he failed to meet quotas. As a result of his failure to produce, he was laid off.

Then, he couldn't believe the fix he was in. The poor guy owed thirty more payments of $500 each (a total of $15,000), but the car was worth only $9,000. That meant that if he didn't continue to make the payments, the vehicle would be repossessed and sold, leaving him liable for the $6,000 deficit. Today, the same young executive lives with his parents and continues to repay the $6,000 deficit at 15 percent APR. He tells me that every time he writes the $171.19 check to his lender, he's reminded that leasing is more expensive than buying.

Decline Credit Life and Disability on All Automobile Loans

Credit life is a very expensive declining term insurance that will pay off an installment loan if you die before the loan is paid in full. Disability insurance, after a period of fifteen to ninety days, will make loan payments for you if you are "totally" disabled during the life of the loan.

The concept is a good one, but in both cases you can cut premiums 50 to 90 percent by buying the policy separately. That way, you avoid paying an 8 to 18 percent finance charge on the insurance. Be aware that *no* lender can make the loan conditional on your purchase of credit life and/or disability insurance.

PRINCIPLE 45—BUY ONLY AS MUCH CAR INSURANCE AS YOU REALLY NEED

There are some very simple, specific things you can do to cut your insurance rates in half.

First, *don't buy what you don't need.* You can save hundreds of dollars on your automobile insurance by eliminating most or all of the coverage listed below. However, a few of these are required in some states. Check with your agent and eliminate those coverages that are already taken care of under other policies you hold.

- No-fault
- Uninsured motorist

- Medical payments
- Emergency road service
- Car rental expense
- Death/dismemberment
- Specialty coverage

Here is the coverage that, in my opinion, you *must* have:

1. Bodily injury (liability) equal to your net worth plus potential legal fees.
2. A minimum of $50,000 property damage (liability) and a maximum of $100,000.
3. A $1 million umbrella policy with a $100,000 deductible. If your net worth is over $100,000, it will cost you less than $150 per year.
4. Deductibles of $500 to $1,000 on collision and comprehensive.

In addition, I recommend the following:

1. Never file a claim for under $500.
2. Check insurance rates on the car you want to buy before you purchase it.
3. Shop around for rates.
4. Decline all unnecessary coverage, such as towing, car rental, and audio equipment.
5. Find out how much a ticket or accident will raise your premium.
6. Ask for all possible discounts, such as multi-car, driver training, good driver, anti-theft equipment, good student, and senior citizen discounts. Each of these discounts can reduce your premium by 5 to 20 percent!
7. Purchase a six-month policy to cover motorcycles, mopeds, and snow-mobiles, instead of paying premiums on the vehicles when you're not using them.
8. Drop death, dismemberment, and loss-of-sight coverage when those perils are already covered through other policies.

Take some time to study your policy and talk to your agent in order to see exactly what these changes will mean to you, individually, in savings. As an aid, I've included a worksheet for you to complete. Completing this worksheet will enable you to cut your car insurance premiums by up to 50 percent. If you study and apply the twelve guidelines and shop around, you'll save another 35 to 40 percent more. It takes time and effort and may require some homework on your part, but the payoff is worth it because you'll reduce your auto insurance premiums by 50 percent or more.

AUTO INSURANCE POLICY WORKSHEET
(Premiums for all cars)

Current Premium	$_____	New Premium	$_____
Current Limit	$_____	Desired Limit	$_____
Current Deductible	$_____	New Deductible	$_____

1. BODILY INJURY

Current Limit	$_____	Desired Limit	$_____
Current Premium	$_____	New Premium	$_____

(Buy enough to cover your net worth, plus legal fees in the event of a mishap.)

2. PROPERTY DAMAGE

Current Limit	$_____	Desired Limit	$_____
Current Premium	$_____	New Premium	$_____

(Buy enough to cover your net worth, plus legal fees in the event of a mishap.)

3. COMPREHENSIVE* ($500 or + deductible)

Current Deductible	$_____	$500 or + deductible	$_____
Current Premium	$_____	New Premium	$_____

4. COLLISION* ($500 or + deductible)

Current Deductible	$_____	$500 or + deductible	$_____
Current Premium	$_____	New Premium	$_____

5. UMBRELLA LIABILITY** (only if needed)

Desired Coverage	$_____	Amount of Premium	$_____

---

* Eliminate these coverages if your car is valued at less than $1,500. The money you'll save can be used for repairs. If the cost of the repairs exceeds the value of the car, you can't collect anything, anyway.

** This insurance covers the same liability as your auto policy, but costs much less. You need $100,00–$300,000 worth, but you can buy $1,000,000 for under $150 per year.

Principle 46—Follow the Guidelines and Reap the Benefits

We can sum up the principles in this chapter with the following six guidelines, all of which are based on biblical wisdom. If you adhere to these guidelines for meeting your transportation needs, you will reap financial and spiritual benefits.

Six Transportation Guidelines to Keep You on the Right Road

1. Buy transportation—not status, ego, or self-indulgence.
2. Don't finance. Save instead, and purchase your vehicle with cash.
3. Keep your car to the end of its mechanical life.
4. Buy two- or three-year-old vehicles and save 50 percent depreciation.
5. Do your homework before you shop for transportation.
6. Buy within your means, not because of your wants and desires.

Benefits of Following Biblical Guidelines

If you . . .	You'll save . . .
Buy function, not status (DX, not SE)	$7,000
Buy with cash instead of financing	$6,986
Drive it until it dies	$15,600
Buy a two- to three-year-old car	$9,530
Do your homework and shop around	$2,100
Your benefit	$41,216*

*Savings over five years based on purchase of a new vehicle at $15,000 purchase price.

Assuming a 6 percent inflation rate, you can multiply your savings accordingly. To calculate the inflation rate, multiply the inflation factor (see following chart) by the apparent benefit to illustrate true benefits over time. To see the startling accumulation of savings over time, study the following chart:

Driver's Age	Apparent Savings	Inflation Factor	True Benefit
18	$387,430	4.17	$1,615,583
25	$329,728	3.63	$1,196,912
35	$247,296	2.47	$610,821
45	$164,864	1.71	$281,917
55	$82,432	1.21	$99,742

Based on these figures, you can see why a motor vehicle is usually the second highest expense after housing. In real dollars adjusted for inflation, *the average thirty-five-year-old person will save $610,821 over his or her car-buying lifetime by using the principles outlined here.* But remember that they're guidelines, not laws.

Apply What You Learn

For a look at how the typical consumer's dollar is allocated, examine the following data from Runzheimer International travel consultants, which appeared in *Medical Economics Magazine*:

WHERE YOUR CAR DOLLAR GOES

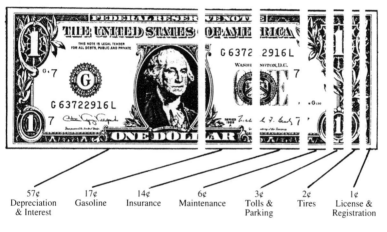

57¢	17¢	14¢	6¢	3¢	2¢	1¢
Depreciation & Interest	Gasoline	Insurance	Maintenance	Tolls & Parking	Tires	License & Registration

Used by permission.

The only truth that will benefit you is the truth that you apply. The question remains, *Are you willing to spend the same amount of time reflecting, meditating, planning, and using what you have learned as you are spending in acquiring this knowledge?* Certainly, knowing the truth is important, but living it is paramount.

As Christians, our difficulty usually is not in *understanding* the Bible's guidelines, but rather in *living* according to them. I pray that you will apply these biblical economic principles to your life, and that as a result of your diligence in doing so, you will begin to see a difference in your finances. As you continue through the material presented in this book, make it your objective to *change your thoughts and habits* regarding money. That is truly the path to making the most of what God has given you.

INSURANCE

No field of personal finance carries more divergent or conflicting information than the area of insurance. Collectively, insurance takes a big bite out of your paycheck, so it's imperative to learn more about the different types.

Financial advisors define insurance as "protection against unpredictable, large losses of a few, with the small, guaranteed loss of many." Statistically speaking, with a group of five hundred men, all age thirty-four, you can count on one of them dying before reaching his next birthday. If each of these five hundred men puts ten dollars into an insurance fund, the fund would be worth $5,000. By contract, the fund would agree to pay that sum to the survivors of the man who died before his thirty-fifth year.

That's the way all insurance works—taking small sums from a lot of people in order to pay out large sums to the few people who will need it. Financially, the only way to win on an insurance policy is to sustain a loss through death, disability, medical emergency, or accident. Since you know you can't win any other way, your goal when purchasing insurance should be to limit the amount you will lose and to optimize your savings.

The best way to limit your insurance losses is to become "self-insured." This means that any loss you incur would be paid out of your assets. Therefore, you would not have to lose money in an insurance fund by paying a regular premium. If each of our five hundred men deposited $5,000 in the bank, they would have enough money for burial and wouldn't need to put ten dollars into a fund to provide burial benefits for themselves in the event of their untimely death. But since the vast majority of us will never accumulate adequate assets to self-insure, the reality is that insurance becomes a necessity.

PRINCIPLE 47—BUY INSURANCE ACCORDING TO STATISTICAL PROBABILITY OF NEED

The first principle in obtaining insurance is to purchase insurance that matches the probability of a claim. For example, in any given year, you are more likely to have a medical claim than to become disabled. And the odds of being disabled are greater than the odds of dying. These facts have been statistically proven. Therefore, I recommend to my clients that they purchase insurance to cover the most likely claim first. If there's money left, insure the second probability, then the third, and so on, until they're fully covered.

Excluding home and automobile coverage, the priorities in buying insurance, according to statistical probability, should be as follows:

- Major medical
- Disability income
- Life insurance
- Nursing home coverage

PRINCIPLE 48—BUY MEDICAL INSURANCE TO COVER POTENTIALLY LARGE CLAIMS WITH MINIMUM PREMIUMS

Most workers obtain medical insurance through their employer. Those who don't will spend several thousand dollars per year for a family of four. If you're forced to buy your own medical insurance, here are some ideas to help you get the most for your money.

Cut Your Premiums by as Much as 40 Percent by Taking a Higher Deductible

Here's a chart showing the annual premiums paid to a large medical insurance company by a thirty-year-old couple with two children:

Deductible	Premium	Savings	Percentage Saved
$250	$4,345	-0-	-0-
$500	$3,229	$1,116	25%
$1,000	$2,329	$2,016	46%
$2,500	$1,729	$2,616	60%

The difference in cost between a $1,000 deductible and a policy carrying a $250 deductible, is $2,016 per year, or $168 per month. If you put that $168 per month into a savings account, you would save $756 in just 4.5 months—enough to pay the increased deductible of $750. For the remaining 7.5 months of the year, you would have $168 per month to allocate to other items. If you saved the $168 for 14 months, you would accumulate $2,352. At that point, you could raise your deductible to $2,500 and lower your premiums even further. Remember: *The goal of insurance is to obtain adequate coverage through spending as few dollars as possible on premiums.*

Reduce Your Costs Further by Selecting a Higher Coinsurance

Besides the direct deductible, there's also a hidden deductible known as "stop-loss" or "coinsurance." This means that whenever you file a claim, you must pay the deductible plus 20 to 50 percent of the next $3,000 to $10,000, depending on the type of policy you have. The insurance company guarantees to pay everything above that amount, up to a lifetime maximum of $250,000 to $1 million or more, depending on your policy.

For example, if you have a $10,000 medical bill and your policy pays 80 percent of the first $5,000 (minus your $1,000 deductible), your cost is the $1,000 deductible plus $1,000 coinsurance. The insurance company pays the remaining $8,000 balance. In other words you have 80/20 coverage: the insurance company pays 80 percent and you pay 20 percent. By increasing your coinsurance from none (100/0) to 80/20, you'll save on premiums because you raise your deductible. The best value is a policy that pays 80 percent of the next $5,000 over your deductible, plus 100 percent of any bill above $6,000.

Maternity Benefits on Your Medical Insurance Are Not Always a Good Buy

If you're planning on having a baby, you have a choice of coverage: pay overpriced insurance premiums that are seldom recovered, or begin a savings plan so you can pay the hospital directly.

Insurance companies limit their losses by setting $3,000 to $5,000 maximum benefits on pregnancies, while charging the insured an extra $200 a month for the coverage. Then, you still have to pay the deductible and the 80/20 coinsurance. Insurance companies don't like people to wait until they decide to have children to take out maternity coverage, so they impose a waiting period of nine to twelve months. This affords you the privilege of paying them premiums while they give you absolutely no coverage whatsoever. If you fall for that, you've wasted $2,400. If the child doesn't come until the second year, you're $4,800 down, plus the interest you would have earned, had you put the $200 a month into a savings account instead.

If there are complications after birth, a baby is automatically covered if the husband's existing policy covers the wife——as long as you follow the company's notification procedure and pay your premiums. If the policy covers the husband alone, arrange coverage for the wife at least six months before the "due" date and follow procedures to add the baby to your policy.

Don't Waste Money Buying Policies that Cover Dental, Accident, or Prescription Drugs

Most Americans overspend 40 to 50 percent on medical premiums because the options are attractive, logical, and the agent convinces them that they need the additional benefits. Dental insurance costs about $450 per year, has a deductible of $50, and covers a maximum of $1,000. If you need dental surgery, it's expensive, but most people are already covered for oral surgery under the surgical section of their medical policy.

Accident coverage is another high-profit, low-risk coverage for the insurance industry. Only one out of six claims is caused by accident, so consider saving the money instead of spending it on accident coverage.

Prescription drug cards also cost much more than self-insuring, unless you have a chronic illness that requires continual medication costing over $40 a month.

Why not pull out your medical policy now, and review it to see how much you can save by buying adequate protection for minimum premiums? From experience, I can tell you that you'll earn well over $200 an hour for the time you invest in restructuring your medical insurance.

PRINCIPLE 49—BE SURE YOU HAVE ADEQUATE DISABILITY INCOME INSURANCE

Statistics tell us that after medical insurance, the second greatest need is disability insurance. Therefore, particularly if you're a breadwinner, you need to protect yourself against a disabling accident, injury, or illness.

Disability insurance (also called income replacement, salary continuation, income protection, or lost income insurance) provides income if you're unable to work. "Actuaries" are statisticians who work for insurance companies, and their findings are frightening: By age twenty-three, the average person is 7.5 times more likely to be disabled than to die. At age thirty-two, it's 6.5 times; at age forty-two, about 4 times; by age fifty-two, 2.5 times. In spite of these facts, most breadwinners do not insure themselves against disability and the subsequent loss of wages. And those who do purchase disability income insurance are usually inadequately covered.

Consider several scenarios:

A manager in her forties is disabled in a car accident. Her $3,000 monthly income is replaced by a $1,200 group salary continuation plan, but her benefits end after just six months. What happens for her then?

A surgeon who earns $175,000 a year is crippled by arthritis. His $2,000 monthly disability income policy will pay him until he reaches age sixty-five. Meanwhile, his fixed monthly expenses total $9,000 per month. What does he do now?

A realtor who earns $50,000 a year suffers a massive heart attack at age fifty. He's no longer able to work, and he has no disability policy because he thought Social Security would take care of him. He was shocked to find that, like 70 percent of all people who apply for Social Security benefits, he was denied coverage. What now?

For all these scenarios, *there's nothing that can be done—after the fact.* The solution lies in planning *before* problems arise. Ask yourself how much money you and your dependents would need each month if you were disabled and your income dropped substantially or stopped altogether.

Let's assume that your family lives well on your income of $30,000 per year. After taxes, you net $25,000 a year, or $2,083 each month. If you become disabled, there are five safety nets between you and disaster:

1. Government disability (a component of Social Security)
2. Workman's compensation (mandatory coverage at work, where 40 percent of all accidents occur)
3. Employer disability income
4. Personal disability insurance
5. Your accumulated savings and assets

I strongly recommend that you have a plan that will provide you with 60 to 70 percent of your monthly pay should you become disabled. If you don't already know, learn what benefits you have from Social Security, workman's compensation, and employer-provided disability income. Cover the deficit with savings and/or personal disability insurance. If your minimum monthly income is $1,750 and Social Security will give you $1,000 per month, you'll need $750 per month more to reach your minimum. This money could come from interest, dividends, and/or disability income.

Like good major medical coverage, good disability income insurance is expensive. The amount of the premium is directly related to six factors:

1. Your age
2. Your health
3. Your occupation
4. The "elimination period"—the time elapsed between your disability and the start of payments from your insurance benefits
5. The size of your monthly benefits
6. The period of time during which your benefits will continue

You can't change your age or the status of your health, and you probably don't want to change your occupation to appease an insurance company. But you can control the elimination period, the size of your benefits, and the duration of your benefit period. To lower your costs, use the following nine guidelines.

1. Choose the longest possible elimination period. The longer you wait for the income benefits to begin following a disability, the lower your premium will be. The following chart shows five possible elimination periods for a healthy male, age thirty-five, who needs $2,000 per month in disability benefits:

Days in Elimination Period	Yearly Cost	Savings Compared to 30-Day Period	Premium Saved, Compared to 30-Day Period
30	$868	-0-	-0-
60	$742	$126	15%
90	$676	$192	22%
180	$594	$274	32%
365	$546	$322	37%

You might not be aware that if you have a qualified retirement plan and withdraw money from it before age 59.5, you'll have to pay a 10 percent penalty over and above your regular income tax. However, if you're disabled, you may take withdrawals at any age, with no penalty. For example, if you needed $2,000 per month income and had $12,000 in a qualified retirement plan, you could use those funds to extend the elimination period on your disability income insurance by six months and save 32 percent on your premium.

2. Study all avenues of existing coverage, then buy only the amount you need. To determine the amount of coverage you actually need, first consider the benefits already available to you from Social Security, workman's comp, employer-provided plans, and other earnings or assets. Perhaps you need only $750 per month in coverage instead of $2,000. *Don't pay for what you don't need.* And don't overlook the earning power of your spouse. If you're a two-income family, you might have to reduce your standard of living, but you could probably get by on one income or greatly reduce the amount of money you would need from disability benefits. Remember the general goal: *adequate protection at minimum cost.*

3. Realistically estimate the time period for benefit payments. If you're realistic in selecting the length of time your benefits run, you can dramatically lower the cost of your premiums. Seventy-five percent of all people who are disabled are out of commission for a period of one to thirty days—not for a lifetime, as the insurance companies would like you to believe. There are always exceptions, of course, but 99 percent of all long-term disability patients either recover or die within a five-year period. For this reason, I suggest that you consider a benefit period of two to five years.

4. Buy a renewable-term disability policy. To get an idea of the savings offered by a renewable-term policy, let's compare two identical policies from the same company for a thirty-year-old male. Both offer $2,500 per month in benefits with a ninety-day elimination period. One offers a level premium of $785 annually, while the other offers premiums that are adjusted upward every fifth year on the renewal date.

Age	Annual Level Premium	5-Year Renewable-Term Policy Premium
30-34	$785	$396
35-39	$785	$464
40-44	$785	$620
45-49	$785	$880
50-54	$785	$1,199

As you can see, for the first fifteen years, the outlay for the term policy is less than the cost of the level-premium policy. If you total the premiums during the twenty-five year period, the level-premium policy would cost $19,625 ($785 × 25 years), while the total of the term policy would be $17,795. Not only do you save $1,830 on the term policy, you have use of the money and adequate coverage during the early years, when the risk of disability and the need for capital is the greatest.

5. Select a policy that cannot be canceled and is guaranteed renewable. Make sure that the policy you buy continues to be in force by virtue of your premium payments only, meaning that the company cannot cancel it or raise your premiums. This guarantees your cost, and if your health declines, you'll have protection when you need it most.

6. Examine the definition of "disability," and pay more for an "own occupation." "Own occupation" means that you're covered as long as you can't work in your regular occupation. Under that definition, you're totally disabled if you can't perform your regular job. Therefore, you can collect benefits even if you're able to earn a supplemental income in a different profession.

7. Look for residual coverage, especially if you're self-employed. "Residual coverage" doesn't penalize you if you return to work on a part-time basis. For example, if as a disabled person you return to work half-time, you can still collect 50 percent of your policy benefits if you have a residual rider on your policy. Without this rider, you would receive benefits only if you did not return to work at all.

8. Look for inflation-adjusted benefits. A cost-of-living adjustment (COLA) rider increases benefits after one year of disability to the same degree that the cost of living increases, according to the Consumer Price Index. In the last twenty years, most items have risen 300 to 400 percent in price. If you were permanently disabled, you would need to protect your income from inflation.

9. Select a policy that won't reduce your payments if you collect additional benefits from other sources. Make sure that your policy won't reduce benefits if you collect additional funds from other insurance such as Social Security, workman's comp, or employer-sponsored plans. Sometimes, insurance companies will deduct the amount of other benefits you receive. But if your policy pays $2,000 per month and your Social Security and workman's comp benefits add another $1,400 to your monthly income, you should be entitled to collect the $2,000 per month you paid premiums for. You can never collect more than you earned, but make sure you get what you paid for.

PERSONALIZE THE GUIDELINES
ON DISABILITY INSURANCE

If you want to personalize this information on disability insurance further, complete the following worksheet.

DISABILITY INCOME INSURANCE WORKSHEET

Method 1

1. If you were disabled tomorrow, what would your family's income be, per month? $ _____

2. What are your fixed monthly expenses? (Mortgage payment, food, utilities, transportation, etc.) $ _____

3. How much monthly disability income do you need? What will you do to compensate for it? $ _____

Method 2

1. Take-home pay, after taxes × 80% $ _____

2. Existing benefits

Social Security	$ _____	
Other government benefits	$ _____	
Workman's Compensation benefits	$ _____	
Group disability benefits	$ _____	
Other income	$ _____	
Investment or retirement plans	$ _____	
TOTAL		$ _____

3. Monthly disability benefits needed $ _____

PRINCIPLE 50—BUY ADEQUATE LIFE INSURANCE AT MINIMAL COST

Premiums on a life insurance contract are divided as follows:

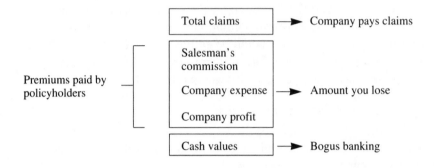

When buying life insurance, you may purchase a policy with or without a savings account attached. Policies with savings accounts attached are deceptive, which is why I refer to them as "Bogus Banking." Contrary to what most people think, policies featuring cash values or savings accounts attached cannot be compared with regular savings accounts at your bank of choice. Most people who buy a life insurance policy with a savings account attached falsely believe that such policies are a good way to save for the future. Here's why.

If you went to "Bogus Bank" (an insurance company) and asked to open a savings account, the following rules would be explained to you: First, to open the account, you'd have to buy term life insurance. In addition to purchasing the insurance, you'd have to deposit a certain number of dollars for each unit of insurance you buy. You would also be told that the bank can keep everything you deposit the first year, and take a 5 to 10 percent fee for each subsequent deposit you make. Later, if you want to borrow from "your savings," you'll be charged 5 to 8 percent interest per year. If you die with an outstanding loan, the amount you owe will be subtracted from the insurance benefit due to your beneficiary. If you refuse to repay the loan on "your savings," the bank will cancel your insurance. If you never borrow from "your savings," once you die the bank will pocket "your savings" and pay your beneficiary only the face amount of your insurance.

Would you take your money to "Bogus Bank"? Millions of Americans do, because it's promoted with clever marketing labels such as "traditional cash-value insurance," "whole life," or "permanent life."

Put Yourself in a Sales Pitch Scenario

To see how policies like this are sold, let's imagine that you're an average, thirty-five-year-old male, listening to a life insurance agent.

"You could buy a ten-thousand-dollar, level-premium, non-participating (no dividends) term policy for only seventy-five dollars a year," the agent says. "But your money will all be gone by the time you hit sixty-five, and so will your coverage. You don't want *that*, do you?"

(Before you say no, realize that by age sixty-five, you either have it made or you'll probably never make it.)

"For only a hundred-fifty dollars a year," the agent offers, "we've got a dynamite policy that never runs out and has great returns on savings that build up. That way, you aren't wasting your money."

(He fails to tell you that you or your beneficiaries must continue paying premiums to age one-hundred!)

"If you want an even better opportunity, take a look at our nice little policy for two-hundred-fifty a year. It's not our top of the line, but after twenty years it's all paid up. After that, no more premiums! Now, if you want our best policy, you pay in only eight thousand dollars over twenty years, and your policy's worth ten thousand! It may sound too good to be true, but it's for real: For just four hundred dollars a year during a limited twenty-year period, you get free insurance and make a two-thousand-dollar profit! Is there any reason why we can't fill out the application right now?"

During his sales pitch, the agent described four different life insurance policies, each valued at $10,000:

1. Term insurance for $75 per year
2. Whole or ordinary life at $150 per year
3. Twenty-pay life for $250 per year
4. Twenty-year endowment for $400 a year

If you die ten years later at age forty-five, the first policy would have cost you $750, and your beneficiary will receive $10,000. The second policy would have cost you twice as much ($1500), but your beneficiary will get the same $10,000. On policies three and four, you will have spent $2,500 and $4,000 respectively, but your beneficiary will *still* receive only $10,000.

If you'd done a little shopping instead of swallowing the sales pitch, you could have found a $10,000 term policy for only $20 per year. If you'd put the $380-per-year savings in premiums ($380 is savings over top of the line endowment contract) into EE savings bonds at 4 percent interest, your beneficiary will receive $4,562 in savings bonds plus the $10,000 insurance. If your invested savings earned 10 percent, your beneficiary would receive a total of $16,056!

The moral of this story is: *Don't combine incompatible things like living and dying*. Instead of building a *dying* plan, build a *living* plan. Saving with an insurance company is bogus banking. It will cost you plenty. Instead, buy term insurance and use the money you save in premiums to build up savings and pay off debts. Only when you're debt-free should you look at the different types of insurance such as single-premium whole-life, universal-life and variable-life, or tax-deferred or variable annuities. (We'll look more closely at those later, in chapter 9 on investing.)

Types of Term Insurance

There are three basic types of term insurance:

- Annual renewable term (ART)
- Decreasing term (DT)
- Level term (LT)

Annual renewable-term insurance has a *fixed amount of coverage* with an *increasing premium* (it rises each year). In most states, you can purchase ART insurance up to age ninety or one-hundred. Companies generally provide two quotes: the guaranteed rate, and the current rate.

The current rate is always lower than the guaranteed rate, but the issuing company reserves the right to charge the guaranteed rate in three to five years if they've had bad claims experience or poor performance in their business. Another feature of ART is "set back" or "reentry," which means that your rate will be lowered if you agree to take a physical at intervals in the future to prove that you're healthy. If you flunk the physical or refuse to take it, you'll pay the guaranteed rate. Most company-provided life insurance is group annual renewable term.

Decreasing term life insurance is the inverse of annual renewable term. Decreasing term has a *fixed premium* with a *decreasing amount of coverage* (it drops each year). You may also purchase a special decreasing term policy (called mortgage insurance) in which the coverage matches the principal payoff on your home mortgage. Other types of

DT insurance decrease coverage over a period of five to thirty years; still others simply decrease the coverage by a fixed percentage each year.

With DT life insurance, you lose the choice of deciding if coverage should decline; with annual renewable-term life insurance, you retain the choice, allowing yourself to adjust your coverage down if needed.

Level term has both a *fixed amount of coverage* as well as a *fixed premium* for a specified amount of time. Common time periods are five, ten, fifteen, and twenty years, and coverage up to age sixty-five. If you choose a five-year LT, the insurance company adds up the ART premiums for five years and averages them so you pay the same premium each year for five years. In effect, you overpay in the first 2.5 years and underpay in the last 2.5 years.

The following charts illustrate various possibilities for term life insurance. Two columns compare ART-type insurance with and without reentry. The last three columns compare five-, ten-, and twenty-year level term insurance. (These scenarios assume a male nonsmoker, beginning at age thirty-five, and offer $100,000 worth of coverage.)

Age	ART	ART*	5 Year	10 Year	20 Year
35	$99	$130	$115	$145	$220
36	$152	$143			
37	$174	$156			
38	$187	$169			
39	$202	$182			
40	$222	$149	$175		
41	$244	$175			
42	$268	$205			
43	$295	$237			
44	$326	$290			
45	$368	$200	$220	$250	
46	$394	$200			
47	$422	$215			
48	$452	$255			
49	$484	$305			
50	$520	$205	$310		
51	$562	$260			
52	$610	$321			
53	$667	$388			
54	$731	$462			
TOTALS	$7,739	$4,647	$4,100	$3,950	$4,400

*With annual reentry every five years (Alexander Hamilton)
5 year = USLICO
10 year = Federal Kemper
20 year = Jackson National

Companies differ and rates change, but the three best options are ART with reentry every three to five years, five-year LT, and ten-year LT. With whole life insurance, premiums would vary between $1,240 and $1,469 per year, with total outlays of $24,800 to $29,380. That's because they include the "Bogus Banking" savings accounts.

Insurance agents will not generally recommend term insurance over whole life. Agents Sam and Dave will illustrate why.

Agent Sam sells term insurance policies worth $150,000 for a monthly premium of $20. Each working day, he sells a policy. At the end of the year, he has sold an adequate life insurance policy to 250 different families. The total amount of insurance he has sold comes to $37.5 million, with total premiums of $60,000. His commission on 250 policies is $45,000.

Agent Dave sells whole life policies worth $2/3$ less ($50,000), but they carry a $50 monthly premium. Each business day, Dave sells a policy. At the end of the year he has matched agent Sam's volume by selling whole life policies to 250 families. The coverage for all families totals only $12.5 million (one-third of Sam's), but Dave's premiums for the year amount to $150,000. His commission on 250 policies is $135,000!

The insurance system is built to reward those who sell the least protection at the greatest possible profit to the company. The lesson is plain: *Buy term insurance and invest the difference!* Term insurance provides the most protection for the lowest cost. Save the difference, or use it to reduce debt or pay down the principal on your home mortgage.

PRINCIPLE 51—MAKE AN INFORMED CHOICE WHEN YOU SELECT AN INSURANCE COMPANY

"Mutual Companies" Versus "Stock Companies"
You have two basic choices among types of insurance companies: (1) "stock companies," which are traded on the stock exchange and owned by shareholders; and (2) "mutual companies," which are owned by the policyholders. Stock companies pay taxable dividends to shareholders, which represent profits in the company, but they don't pay dividends to policyholders. Mutual companies pay nontaxable dividends to policyholders. Dividends paid by mutual companies are not taxed because they're not true dividends; they're a return of overcharge on premiums. Similarly, rebates given when buying a car are not taxed.

Some well-run mutual companies do exist, but generally they charge higher premiums than stock companies. If you examine the following chart, you'll see the difference in premiums between mutual companies (also called "par," implying that policy holders participate in the profits) and stock companies (called "non-par"). The chart shows the cost per thousand to buy a $1,000 whole life policy.

Example: A $100,000 mutual policy would cost $1,981 a year from a mutual company or $1,400 a year from a stock company. Why not save $581 a year with the stock company (a 41 percent overcharge)? Overcharge is the percentage increase over a stock company's policy to buy a mutual policy that pays so-called "dividends," which in reality are rebates cleverly labeled.

Age	Mutual (Par)	Stock (Non-Par)	Overcharge
20	$12.94	$8.98	44%
25	$14.65	$10.00	46%
30	$16.87	$12.00	41%
35	$19.81	$14.00	41%
40	$23.71	$18.00	32%
45	$28.84	$23.00	25%
50	$35.56	$29.00	23%
55	$44.41	$38.00	17%
60	$56.32	$49.00	15%

With a mutual company, you may receive a refund on your overcharge, but the insurance company keeps the earnings on your rebate for an entire year. That's one reason why the life insurance business is the largest financial industry in our country.

You don't have to go directly to an insurance company to buy your policy. You can purchase it from a bank, credit union, insurance agent, stock broker, or financial planner. Wherever you buy it, seek competence and experience first; there's no substitute for either. Next, look for an agent who's capable of doing business with more than one firm so you have options to choose between. Find an agent who puts your wants, needs, and desires first.

Is Your Insurance Company Solvent?

Once you've decided on a company, study its financial health. In years past, several large insurance companies have gone the way of the savings & loans. You can protect yourself and your assets by checking the rating of your insurance company in one or more of the following sources: *A. M. Best, Moody's, Standard and Poors,* or *Duff and*

Phelps. These should be available from your insurance agent, stock broker, or at your library. If you stay with top-rated companies, the likelihood of a default is minuscule. Avoid companies that sell policies direct through the mail, on television, and through slick brochures endorsed by celebrities.

For adequate protection at minimum cost, term insurance from a stock company is your best buy.

PRINCIPLE 52—KNOW WHEN TO BUY INSURANCE AND WHO NEEDS COVERAGE

The time to buy any insurance is when you have a need. It's true that life insurance costs you less when you're young, but the fact that you buy coverage early in life has no bearing on what you'll pay for the coverage when you're older and will probably need less insurance. Certainly, people who buy insurance young are just as apt to die as people who don't buy it.

DEATHS PER 1,000 FOR FOUR MORTALITY TABLES

Age	American Experience	1941	1958	1980
20	7.80	2.43	1.79	1.90
25	8.06	2.88	1.93	1.77
30	8.43	3.56	2.13	1.73
35	8.95	4.59	2.51	2.11
40	9.79	6.18	3.53	3.02
45	11.16	8.60	5.35	4.55
50	13.78	12.32	8.32	6.71
55	18.57	17.98	13.00	10.47
60	26.69	26.59	20.34	16.08

The first column is from the "American Experience Table," based on statistics gathered in 1843 through 1858. Back then, in Abraham Lincoln's day, 8.95 men out of every 1,000 died at age thirty-five during a given year. The second column is from the "1941 Standard Ordinary Table," based on data from 1930 through 1940 (before penicillin). Note that the death rate dropped to 4.59 per 1,000 men for men age thirty-five. By the time of the "1958 Commissioner's Standard Ordinary Table," the death rate had declined to 2.51 per 1,000. The most current table, the "1980 Commissioner's Standard Ordinary Table," shows a death rate of 2.11 per 1,000. The newer the mortality table in your policy, the lower the cost.

Perhaps you have had a life insurance policy in effect for many years. If your agent had told you about the new mortality tables issued after your policy was written, you could have saved hundreds of dollars over the years because the cost of insurance has declined. But because the insurance company's goal is to maximize its profits, it "educates" its agents to look first at the company profit, then at the agent's commission—and, finally, to the client.

Unfortunately, insurance companies aren't forced to lower the premiums of their existing policyholders when a new mortality table comes out. Instead, they continue to charge rates based on the old table. If you have a policy, check to see what mortality table your premium is based upon. If it's an older table, read on, and you'll know how to handle it effectively.

Anyone who provides a necessary economic benefit to your family should be insured. Insurance purchased on children from ages one to seventeen is a waste of money for two reasons. First, children don't contribute to the household income. Second, the odds of death during ages one to eighteen are one in a hundred. Life insurance on singles with no dependents is also a waste of money, as is carrying insurance on retired persons unless they have minor children or dependent spouses. The purpose of life insurance is to replace lost income if the income earner dies before accumulating enough assets to provide for his or her family.

How to Decide Whether to Buy Nursing Home Insurance

Long-term health care for the aging is a serious problem, and it will only worsen as our country's baby boomers approach retirement. Industry statistics tell us that less that 2 percent of all people over age sixty-five have any type of nursing home coverage, because they don't realize that Medicare won't solve the problem.

The cost of nursing home care averages a minimum of $70 per day. I've heard story after story about people who spent their last dollars on nursing home care and left their beneficiaries in debt. Our government won't help families or individuals who own assets. Although some states provide some division of assets to protect a surviving spouse, many do not.

If you're nearing retirement age, or if you have parents who are retired, you'll need to address the question of whether or not you need to purchase nursing home insurance. If you or a loved one is facing a possible stay in a nursing home, here are some ways to help you minimize the cost of nursing home insurance.

1. *Purchase a policy that covers custodial care.* This should cover

care provided either at home or in a facility that provides custodial care, and in non-skilled as well as skilled care facilities.

2. *Don't purchase a policy before you retire.* Even though it's less expensive to buy nursing home protection when you're young, buy it only when it's closer to the probable time of being needed.

3. *As with disability income, take as long an elimination period as possible to reduce your premium cost.*

4. *Purchase enough coverage to pay the cost of care.* For example, if you're a single retiree with $1,000 monthly Social Security income, subtract that income from the average nursing home cost in your area so you don't buy more coverage than you need.

5. *Buy inflation protection on the amount of coverage you purchase if you're concerned with rising prices in the future.*

6. *Realize that the average stay in a nursing home is less than ninety days.* Ninety-five percent of all nursing home patients recover or die within a three-year period.

7. *Consider alternative ways to provide for nursing home costs rather than buying insurance.* A good savings plan, proper asset management, and estate planning with trusts are other options for providing adequate nursing home care.

PRINCIPLE 53—KNOW WHAT KIND OF INSURANCE TO AVOID

Save yourself money by avoiding the following kinds of insurance, which nobody really needs.

1. *"Waiver of premium."* This means that if you remain totally disabled for six months, the company will waive your premiums until you recover or die. Waiver of premium sounds good and is relatively cheap, but you're way ahead using your dollars to buy disability income insurance instead.

2. *Accidental death benefits* (double or triple indemnity). These benefits are cheap, but again, you're dollars ahead if you buy adequate coverage to begin with and use the money elsewhere.

3. *Mortgage insurance.* This is another item to avoid because it's expensive, decreases in value, and the dollars are committed to the lender instead of to your family. Protection to pay off a mortgage can be purchased through other means at significant savings.

4. *All credit life and disability income on installment loans.* You can buy the same protection separately, for one-fifth of the price, and you won't have to pay any finance charges.

Another cost to guard against is individual policy fees. Combine your policies to avoid individual policy fees, and take advantage of decreased premiums with increased face amounts.

A dentist friend of mine had a collection of twenty-six $5,000 policies, purchased over a period of twenty-five years. He was shocked to find that he could reduce his premiums by 60 percent by purchasing a single $130,000 policy from the same company.

Use the economy of scale and, where needed or possible, buy in volume.

PRINCIPLE 54—CALCULATE HOW MUCH INSURANCE YOU SHOULD PURCHASE

There are several ways to determine how much coverage you'll need.

Calculate Salary Replacement

Calculating what you would need to replace your salary is the simplest way of determining how much insurance coverage you need.

To do this, determine 75 percent of your annual salary. If your salary is $30,000, that would be $22,500. That's approximately what you would need to maintain your standard of living, not adjusting for inflation.

In this example, assuming a 5 percent return on your assets, you would need $420,000 worth of coverage to produce $21,000 annual income. If you had accumulated $70,000 in liquid income-producing assets, your need for insurance would drop to $350,000. If your family would be eligible for Social Security benefits of $10,000 per year, your need for insurance would drop to $150,000.

Figure Coverage Against Expenses and Assets

Other ways to determine how much coverage you need involve figuring benefits against your expenses and assets.

To estimate needed coverage against basic expenses, multiply your current before-tax income by five. Add one year's income for each child and the amount of money you still owe on your home mortgage. To that total, add any college costs.

To estimate needed coverage against assets, multiply your income by ten, and then subtract your income-producing assets.

Consider the Factors in Your Personal Circumstances

Here are some other factors to consider when determining the amount of coverage you need:

1. What standard of living does your spouse need?
2. Are there existing debts, installment purchases, mort-gages, liabilities, or commitments that need to be considered?
3. If educational expenditures are expected, what's the cost, time, and your contribution to these expenses?
4. What's the earning capacity of your spouse? Should your spouse work? Starting when?
5. What are your income-producing assets worth? What could be converted to income-producing assets?
6. What Social Security survivors' benefits would your beneficiaries receive? How long would they continue? How long before the Social Security benefits stop and retirement benefits begin? (This is called the "blackout period." After all children are age eighteen, the parents' benefits stop. The child then receives benefits until age twenty, or longer if still in school.)
7. What realistic rate of return can your spouse earn with-out taking investment risks?
8. What do you assume the future rate of inflation will be?
9. What will your final medical and burial expenses amount to?
10. Are there any charitable bequests you desire to make? How about bequests to children or relatives?

Principle 55—Don't Borrow Against the Cash Value of Your Policy

---

Your insurance agent will encourage you to borrow against the cash value of your policy and use the proceeds to buy more insurance, or something else. He'll try to convince you by asking, "Where else can you borrow money at 5 percent interest and still have your insurance coverage?"

Before you fall for that, consider this: If you borrow $10,000, leav-ing $2,500 in your policy as cash value, your interest cost is $500 per year. But you still have to pay the $1,200 premium, and if you died, the face value of your policy would be reduced by the $10,000 loan. There-fore, you end up paying $1,700 per year—$1,200 in premiums, plus $500 interest, for a $90,000 death benefit. That's not a very good plan.

If you currently have cash value policies, consider cashing them in rather than borrowing on them. Then you can minimize your cost for insurance.

PRINCIPLE 56—IF YOU ALREADY HAVE A CASH-VALUE OR WHOLE-LIFE CONTRACT, CONVERT IT TO TERM INSURANCE

If you already have whole life policy and you'd like to switch to term insurance, here's what you can do.

First, determine the cash (or surrender) value of your existing policy. You can usually find the information on your most recent policy statement, or by calling the company directly. If you purchased a $100,000 policy ten years ago, your annual premium is probably around $1,200. If the cash value on your policy is $12,500, your coverage is $87,500.

Ask yourself whether you actually need this coverage at all. If not, drop the policy and put the $12,500 into productive returns (such as retiring credit cards, loans, or your mortgage).

If you do need this coverage, determine the cost per thousand of your existing policy. The cost of coverage is your $1,200 premium, plus whatever you could earn on the $12,500 cash value. If you assume a 6 percent return, your $12,500 would earn you $750, so your cost per thousand of insurance is cost divided by coverage (or $1,950 divided by $87,500, which is $22.29 per thousand). Compare that to what term insurance would cost.

If you're a healthy male, age forty, you can find $100,000 term coverage for $150 to $250 per year, depending on the company and the type of policy you select. Term insurance costs $1.50 to $2.50 per thousand. If you purchase $87,500 in term at $2 per thousand, you will spend $175 for coverage, leaving you $1,775 (compared to the cost of coverage, $1,950, for your former policy) to use more productively.

Of course, your agent will hate the idea, and will argue that by keeping your policy in force and paying the premiums, your cash value will increase to $850. Then ask him, Where does the other $925 ($1,775 minus $850) go?

What About "Universal Life" Insurance?

Many consider "universal life" insurance to be a modern, economic insurance that combines the benefit of cheap term insurance with high, tax-deferred returns.

Universal life has flexible premiums that may vary up or down, within limits. Once policyholders have put enough money in their policy fund, they may choose to skip premium payments without losing coverage. They can raise their insurance coverage at any time, lower it, or keep it level. Some companies even offer the opportunity to withdraw cash values that carry no interest charges.

Universal life appears fair and flexible because the premium is broken down into three parts: insurance, savings, and expenses. It appears to combine term insurance with a tax-sheltered annuity that has variable (rather than a lower, fixed rate) of return. Universal life is offered as a convenient, "single policy" that will meet your every need.

There are five reasons why you're better off buying pure term insurance and using the balance to retire debt.

1. *The high interest rates quoted as being paid on universal life policies are misleading and inaccurate.* These figures fail to disclose what portion of your premium goes to saving and expenses. In reality, you'll have a guaranteed loss on your savings for the first several years. You might break even in the fourth or fifth year, and you might get ahead by the tenth year, but by the time you actually receive the advertised rate quoted, you're generally into the twelfth year. And perhaps you can borrow the accumulated cash value at no interest, but you'll pay the price in lowered rates on the cash that secures your loan. Most times, if you look at the investment performance of the issuing company, you'll wonder how they'll be able to deliver those projected rates.

2. *Commissions are high on universal life.* The average commission paid to the insurance agent is 80 percent of the first year's premium. For a $1,000 premium, a forty-year-old male with a death benefit of $100,000 will pay his agent $800. Compare that to a commission of 60 percent on the same $100,000 of term insurance, which carries a premium of $150 per year. One way, the agent earns $800; the other way, he earns $90. Which policy would your agent recommend?

3. *You can purchase term insurance more cheaply if you buy it separately.* Take the time to shop and compare premiums. Each company is free to charge whatever the traffic will bear. In writing this chapter, I called fifteen different companies, directly out of the yellow pages, for a quote on $100,000 ART for a male, age forty, nonsmoker. The premiums varied from $147 to $354 per year.

4. *You pay high surrender charges on universal life policies.* If you decide to cancel your policy in the early years, your surrender charge can run into the thousands. Surrender charges of up to 100 percent of

the money you've paid in are not uncommon.

5. *There are hidden policy fees, charges, and expenses.*

A CHECKLIST FOR WHETHER TO REPLACE YOUR POLICY

Do replace your policy if you . . .
✔ have more than one policy for the same type of coverage.
✔ have cash value in your policy.
✔ have a policy based on a mortality table prior to 1980.
✔ own a participating or mutual policy.

Don't replace your policy if you . . .
✔ are uninsurable (in other words, don't cancel your old policy and then find out that you are no longer eligible for a new one).
✔ can't lower your costs by converting to a new policy.
✔ are trying to conceal health problems (there's a two-year contestable period), meaning that your benefits could be limited to the return of the amount of premium you paid, or the coverage you would have received had you given accurate information.
✔ value the friend who sold it to you more than the cost you would save.
✔ can't stand the pressure your agent or company will apply to you when you cancel.

How to Avoid Losses in Converting Your Policies

Don't be concerned with what you might lose by dropping a poor policy. Instead, ask yourself how much more you'll have if you replace the poor policies with more efficient ones.

If you decide to change policies, avoid losses by ensuring that you qualify for a new policy *before* you cash in the one you have. Then buy a policy with the same (or adequate) coverage at a lower cost.

Paid-Up Policies Continue to Cost You

If you have an existing policy that is already paid up, you might be thinking that this information on converting your policy doesn't apply to you. But think again.

Let's say you're fifty-five years old and have a paid-up policy worth $10,000 that you bought thirty years ago. You think you have it made! You have $4,500 in cash value if you need it, and $10,000 worth of life insurance that costs you nothing. If that sounds too good to be true, it is.

If you don't need the coverage, surrender the policy and give, invest, or spend the proceeds. Your money can be earning more dividends elsewhere.

If you still need coverage, consider your cost per thousand of insurance. If you cash in your policy and take your $4,500, you forfeit your remaining coverage of $5,500. If you die, the company sends your beneficiary $10,000 but keeps your cash value of $4,500.

Therefore, your true coverage is only $5,500. And it's not free, because in order to keep the coverage, you must give up what you could be earning on the $4,500 in cash value. If you took the money out and invested it in government bonds at 6 percent interest, that $4,500 would pay you $270 per year. If you divide the income of $270 per year by $5,500 worth of coverage, your cost per thousand is $49.09!

If you shop around, you'll find term insurance at less than $5 per thousand. Even if you spend $27.50 per year for term insurance, you're still $242.50 ahead. A paid-up policy may sound like a great deal, and it is—for the insurance company.

Since your goal as a good steward is adequate protection at minimum cost, you're always better off buying term insurance for protection and saving elsewhere than taking your money to Bogus Banks.

SUMMARY
These guidelines summarize the information in this chapter on life insurance policies:

- Buy adequate protection at minimum cost.
- Buy term insurance, preferably ART with reentry, or level term.
- Don't buy whole life, limited payment life, endowment, or universal life. Like all of us, insurance agents work to make money. They're well educated in sales psychology and the technical aspects of insurance, and they know a limitless number of ways to sell you minimum coverage at maximum cost.
- The best way to protect yourself from overpaying is to educate yourself. For every option suggested to you, compare it to term insurance.

This has been a difficult chapter to write, because I know that many agents in the insurance business will argue the facts presented here. I certainly don't wish to offend anyone. My sole purpose has been to encourage you to set priorities and purchase adequate protection in each area at minimum premium cost. Identify your needs in order of importance, define the amount and kind of protection you need, and act on the information here. By applying your knowledge, you could ultimately save thousands of dollars.

If you're lucky, you'll find a knowledgeable, client-centered agent like Ed. Ed came to see me fifteen years ago, after nine months of working with an insurance company whose primary product was whole life. After analyzing life insurance, Ed found that what's best for the customer (term insurance) wasn't best for Ed.

"If I sell term insurance, I can't feed my family, but if I sell whole life, I can't sleep," he explained to me. "What should I do, sell whole life and try to justify it as forced savings?"

My advice was, "Put the customer first, and become excellent in your profession."

Today, Ed is a chartered life underwriter (CLU) and a chartered property and casualty underwriter (CPCU). He handles all types of insurance: medical, disability, life, home, auto, and nursing home. He strives to do what's best for the client, and as a result, he's the agent for almost 90 percent of all insurance purchased by the nine hundred families he serves. Ed sleeps well and eats well because he follows biblical principles in his business and his life.

SPENDING PLANS

■

*"Suppose one of you wants to build a tower.
Will he not first sit down and estimate the cost to see
if he has enough money to complete it? For if he lays
the foundation and is not able to finish it,
everyone who sees it will ridicule him, saying,
'This fellow began to build and was not able to finish.'"*
LUKE 14:28-30

■

*The wise man saves for the future,
but the foolish man spends whatever he gets.*
PROVERBS 21:20, TLB

I have some retired clients who never earned more than $26,000 during their workings years but who today have assets valued at over $1 million. I also have clients who have earned millions but are now merely scraping by on Social Security pensions. *What really determines your ultimate financial destiny is not so much the amount of money you make, but rather the manner in which you plan, control, and manage what you earn.*

How you respond to and apply the material in this chapter will govern your financial future. If you apply the principles here toward planning and controlling your spending, *you will never again be a slave to debt.*

PRINCIPLE 57—PLAN YOUR SPENDING

Proverbs describes those who plan ahead as wise, prudent, and faithful: "A sensible man watches for problems ahead and prepares to meet them. The simpleton never looks, and suffers the consequences" (27:12).

Before you jump to the conclusion that I'm going to try to impose a budget on you, you should know that I don't suggest or create budgets.

Budgets are imposed on people by outsiders (usually lenders, collection agencies, courts, or lawyers) in order to solve problems those people created for themselves.

However, I do help and encourage people to create and use *spending plans*. In contrast to budgets, spending plans are *self-imposed*. They are monitored, managed plans for spending that help people move more closely toward their chosen goals. A spending plan doesn't limit choices; it provides the freedom to make choices within certain guidelines. The guidelines are flexible and set by the designer of the spending plan—you. And *you* retain control.

Boundaries: The Key to Freedom of Choice

Near a house I used to live in, a new elementary school went up. I drove past it twice a day on my way to and from work. There were always children gathered on the playground. At first, I noticed that they always played right next to the building, shying away from two very busy streets that bounded the playground and served as main traffic arteries. Then about two months after the school opened, the school board had the playground fenced. Guess what happened? The children began to use *all* of the playground instead of huddling by the buildings, because they were no longer afraid of the traffic.

Just as a fence around the playground expanded the children's area of play, a spending plan will expand your financial freedom *as long as you stay within its boundaries*. But unlike fences around playgrounds, you have the option of moving the boundaries whenever you choose. Spending plans don't limit freedom of choice; they expand them.

PRINCIPLE 58—PUT GOD FIRST IN YOUR SPENDING PLAN

Throughout the Bible we are told to put God first in our spending. The writer of Proverbs describes the benefits:

> Honor the LORD with your wealth,
>   with the firstfruits of all your crops;
> then your barns will be filled to overflowing,
>   and your vats will brim over with new wine. (3:9-10)

Jesus defined a close relationship of giving and receiving:

"Give, and it will be given to you. A good measure, pressed down, shaken together and running over, will be poured into your lap. For with the measure you use, it will be measured to you." (Luke 6:38)

In his letter to the Galatians, Paul states the law of sowing and reaping: "A man reaps what he sows" (6:9). Giving doesn't guarantee spiritual maturity, but I have yet to meet a spiritually mature Christian who doesn't put God first in everything, including finances. Some Christians will sometimes debate whether or not tithing is binding on Christians today, but I have yet to hear one say that giving is not a principle of Christian living.

Principle 59—Pay Your Taxes

Of all the financial problems I've tried to help people solve over the years, tax problems are the worst. Most of the people who come to me for help don't deliberately try to evade taxes. They simply spend the money that's due Uncle Sam, and then when April 15 comes around and they owe the government money, they don't have the funds to pay what they owe.

Generally, those with the most problems are self-employed business people who either don't know or don't follow federal and state guidelines for paying estimated taxes. If you're self-employed, your FICA withholding tax due is 15 percent of your gross pay. In addition, you'll owe federal taxes, and you may live in a state that imposes additional state and local taxes, as well. In case you doubt it, the tax collector has some hard and fast rules about collecting what's due, and failure to file a tax return is a serious matter.

A couple called me in panic one afternoon when they found that their home, which also housed their business, had been locked up by the IRS (which had also frozen their assets). This couple had foolishly chosen to ignore several letters explaining their tax delinquency and demanding payment. It's no fun to deal with the tax collector, so avoid the problem by paying taxes, off the top.

Paying Taxes Is a Christian Responsibility
People who cheat on their taxes often complain that certain government programs and policies are contrary to the Bible's teachings. They fudge on expenses and fail to report all their cash income. Then they try to

justify their dishonesty by arguing that the government permits and pays for abortions, accepts homosexuality as an alternative lifestyle, spends more than it makes by borrowing, and gives billions of dollars in aid and exemptions to nonbiblical organizations, some of which vehemently oppose biblical teaching.

If you repeat this litany to yourself long enough, you might be able to convince yourself that it sounds like a rational basis for objecting to paying taxes. If so, read what Paul said to Roman Christians during the reign of Nero—a man who not only taxed the people into oblivion but used Christians as human torches:

> Everyone must submit himself to the governing authorities, for there is no authority except that which God has established. . . .
> This is also why you pay taxes, for the authorities are God's servants, who give their full time to governing. Give everyone what you owe him: If you owe taxes, pay taxes; if revenue, then revenue; if respect, then respect; if honor, then honor. (Romans 13:1,6-7)

When Jesus was asked if Jews should pay taxes to their oppressors, He answered: "Give to Caesar what is Caesar's, and to God what is God's" (Matthew 22:21). The Bible makes it clear: Plan, give, and pay your taxes.

Investments to Avoid Paying Taxes Do Not Honor God

The investments I have made that were motivated by an effort to reduce or defer tax payments have been the least successful. The reason is that these investments were motivated by greed and did nothing to glorify God.

A few years ago, billions of dollars were being made by tax-deductible limited partnerships that invested in real estate and leasing. Along with thousands of other investors, I took the bait and made investments I never would have made had it not been for the promised tax benefits.

The results of these investments have been horrendous—for me as well as just about everyone else who was involved in them. For the most part, we all lost God's money: the promised tax deductions were either reduced substantially or disallowed, and we paid taxes, interest, and sometimes penalties—all because we weren't wise or obedient in following the simple advice God gave us in His Word: Pay your taxes.

Taxes are high, and tax law is often confusing and unfair. But our first duty is to obey God and to remember that as Americans, we live in one of the few places in the world where true freedom really exists, and that's worth paying for. We certainly have room for improvement: We should balance the budget, eliminate unnecessary government spending, and privatize. But in spite of the problems we have, ours is still one of the lower tax rates in the world economy.

PRINCIPLE 60—PAY YOURSELF SOMETHING OUT OF EVERY PAYCHECK

Wise Christians maintain three primary financial commitments:

1. Pay God first.
2. Pay your taxes.
3. Pay yourself.

The amount you commit to God is a matter of heart and soul, determined by prayerful consideration of the Bible's teachings. The amount you pay in taxes is predetermined for you by federal, state, and local governments. But the amount you pay to yourself is entirely up to you. If you're a person who finds it difficult to save, you'll have some adjusting to do. The most efficient way to pay yourself is to take a percentage right off the top, before you commit the dollars somewhere else.

The following principle suggests a four-step spending plan. Following it can help you transform your life spiritually as well as financially.

PRINCIPLE 61—CREATE A PERSONALIZED FOUR-STEP SPENDING PLAN

Step 1—Know Where You Are in Your Current Spending

> Be sure you know the condition of your flocks [assets], give
> careful attentions to your herds [spending plan]; for riches
> do not endure forever [bad times happen], and a crown is not
> secure for all generations [planning anticipates and prevents
> problems]. (Proverbs 27:23-24)

Most of us spend more than we realize—for example, by using borrowed funds from credit cards. There's one sure way to find out exactly what you're spending: Record what you spent during the last six months and add up your spending in all categories (see step 3) so you know what you've done. If you've written checks or used credit, you can easily obtain copies of your bank and charge card statements. Subtract from your net pay the checks you wrote and the amounts you charged, and you'll have a figure showing what you spent with cash—things you probably have no records or receipts for. However disheartened you become, remember that this is the beginning of a process that will reward you for your time and effort many times over.

If you have been living on cash and credit, estimate each category of spending on the spending plan as best you can, and record all expenses. During the next three to six months, record and revise your first estimate. If your goal is to be realistic and accurate, remember that it takes an average of three months or longer to learn where you are, financially.

Step 2—Set Realistic Short-Term and Long-Term Goals for Yourself

Planning your spending is a process, not an event. Set several short-term goals that you feel you can achieve within a few months. Setting goals will help you move in the right direction. Achieving them will help you build a momentum of success.

Examples of short-term goals might be:

■ Increase giving by $5 a week.
■ If you aren't already paying yourself something out of every check, commit to saving some amount each month, even if it's only $10.
■ Pick your smallest outstanding debt, and commit to paying it off as soon as possible.
■ Start saving now for birthdays and Christmas giving.

What are your short-term goals? Take time right now (with your spouse, if you're married), and put them in writing.

Long-term goals are a little more difficult. Some examples of long-term goals might be:

■ Increase your giving by a certain percentage.
■ Accumulate six to nine months of income in savings.
■ Pay off all consumer credit card debt.
■ Pay cash for your next car.
■ Pay off your mortgage.

Don't worry about how you'll reach your long-term goals. Simply set them, pray for direction and wisdom, and take one day at a time. Most important: *Put your goals in writing.*

Begin thinking now about how you might accomplish your goals. What is a realistic time frame for achieving your objectives? What obstacles stand between you and your goals? How can you eliminate them? Why are these goals important to you? Do your goals bring glory and honor to God, or are they meant to improve your image or self-esteem? Are they worthy goals that will help you to grow spiritually, or are they self-indulgent ones?

Step 3—Do What You Can to Control Your Spending and Increase Your Surplus

As a guide to help you, Spending Form 1 provides percentage guidelines for eleven categories of spending for a family of four. *Remember that these are guidelines, not laws.* Study the guidelines, and compare your spending to them. Where are you overspending? What steps can you take to reduce your spending in that category?

As you complete this exercise, *you're creating a personalized spending plan.* As you evaluate your position, consider whether your current spending habits are the result of basic needs or the indulgence of wants and desires. If you find that most of your overspending stems from a desire for material possessions, it may be time to take a spiritual inventory, too. Are you content with what God has provided, or are you caught up in the world's addiction to a materialist standard of living?

FORM 1: PERCENTAGE GUIDELINES

Gross Income	$15,000	$25,000	$40,000	$50,000	$100,000
Giving	10%	10%	10%	10%	10%
Taxes	8%	17%	18%	20%	28%
Savings	5%	5%	5%	10%	10%
Net Income	**$11,550**	**$18,000**	**$26,800**	**$30,000**	**$52,000**
1. Housing	38%	41%	35%	35%	32%
2. Transportation	15%	15%	12%	11%	8%
3. Food	15%	12%	11%	10%	6%
4. Insurance	5%	5%	5%	5%	5%
5. Debts	5%	5%	5%	5%	5%
6. Entertainment	5%	5%	6%	6%	7%
7. Clothing	5%	5%	5%	5%	5%
8. Medical	5%	5%	4%	4%	4%
9. School/child care	4%	4%	6%	6%	8%
10. Miscellaneous	3%	3%	4%	4%	5%
11. Surplus	1%	1%	7%	9%	15%

There's only one rule to remember when creating your personalized spending plan: *Spending more than you earn will make your financial situation worse; spending less than you earn will increase your surplus.* With that surplus, you can begin to accomplish your short- and long-term goals.

To help you develop your spending plan, make several copies of Form 2—Monthly Spending Plan, Form 3—Spending Plan Guidelines, and Form 4—Spending Plan Analysis. Forms 3 and 4 help you compare where you are to where you want to be. Remember that this is a process of awareness, management, and control. You won't see any dramatic changes immediately, but you will over time. The important thing is to begin now. Learn where you are, commit to changing your unproductive habits, set new guidelines for yourself, and monitor your progress over the next few months.

FORM 2: MONTHLY SPENDING PLAN

Gross Income	$ _____		**5. Debts**	$_____/___%	
Salary	$ _____		Credit card	$ _____	
Interest	$ _____		Loans, notes	$ _____	
Dividends	$ _____		Other	$ _____	
Other	$ _____				
Less			**6. Entertainment**	$_____/___%	
Giving	$ _____		Eating out	$ _____	
Federal tax	$ _____		Baby-sitters	$ _____	
FICA	$ _____		Other	$ _____	
State tax	$ _____		**7. Clothing**	$_____/___%	
Savings	$ _____				
Net Income	$ _____		**8. Medical**	$_____/___%	
			Doctors	$ _____	
1. Housing	$_____/___%		Medication	$ _____	
Payment/rent	$ _____		Dentist	$ _____	
Telephone	$ _____		Other	$ _____	
Insurance	$ _____				
Taxes	$ _____		**9. School/**		
Electric	$ _____		**child care**	$_____/___%	
Water	$ _____		Tuition	$ _____	
Gas	$ _____		Transportation	$ _____	
Sanitation	$ _____		Materials	$ _____	
Maintenance*	$ _____		Day care	$ _____	
Other*	$ _____		**10. Miscellaneous**	$_____/___%	
2. Auto	$_____/___%		Lunches	$ _____	
Payments	$ _____		Toiletries	$ _____	
Gas/oil	$ _____		Beauty/barber	$ _____	
Insurance	$ _____		Laundry/cleaners	$ _____	
Tax/license*	$ _____		Allowances	$ _____	
Repair/maintain*	$ _____		Gifts*	$ _____	
Replacement*	$ _____		Subscriptions	$ _____	
3. Food	$_____/___%		Other	$ _____	
4. Insurance	$_____/___%		TOTAL EXPENSES	$ _____	
Medical	$ _____		LESS NET INCOME	$ _____	
Disability	$ _____				
Life	$ _____		THE BOTTOM LINE	$ _____	
Other	$ _____				

*Items marked with an asterisk indicate expenses that most people neglect to include in their planning.

FORM 3: SPENDING PLAN GUIDELINES

GROSS INCOME PER YEAR $ _____   PER MONTH $ _____

    Less

         Giving $_____ × _____ %Gross = $ _____

         Taxes $_____ × _____ %Gross = $ _____

         Savings $_____ × _____ %Gross = $ _____

NET INCOME PER YEAR $ _____   PER MONTH $ _____

   1. Housing $ _____ × _____ %Net = $ _____

   2. Auto $ _____ × _____ %Net = $ _____

   3. Food $ _____ × _____ %Net = $ _____

   4. Insurance $ _____ × _____ %Net = $ _____

   5. Debts $ _____ × _____ %Net = $ _____

   6. Entertainment $ _____ × _____ %Net = $ _____

   7. Clothing $ _____ × _____ %Net = $ _____

   8. Medical $ _____ × _____ %Net = $ _____

   9. School/child care $ _____ × _____ %Net = $ _____

  10. Miscellaneous $ _____ × _____ %Net = $ _____

  11. Surplus $ _____ × _____ %Net = $ _____

TOTAL EXPENSES (cannot exceed net income) $ _____

FORM 4: SPENDING PLAN ANALYSIS

GROSS INCOME PER MONTH $ _____

	Guideline	Current Month's Spending	Monthly Difference	New Monthly Plan
Giving	_____	_____	_____	_____
Taxes	_____	_____	_____	_____
Savings	_____	_____	_____	_____
NET INCOME	$ _____	$ _____	$ _____	$ _____
1. Housing	_____	_____	_____	_____
2. Automobile(s)	_____	_____	_____	_____
3. Food	_____	_____	_____	_____
4. Insurance	_____	_____	_____	_____
5. Debts	_____	_____	_____	_____
6. Entertainment	_____	_____	_____	_____
7. Clothing	_____	_____	_____	_____
8. Medical	_____	_____	_____	_____
9. School/child care	_____	_____	_____	_____
10. Miscellaneous	_____	_____	_____	_____
TOTALS (1-10)	$ _____	$ _____	$ _____	$ _____
11. Surplus (deficit)	_____	_____	_____	_____

Beginning to live on a spending plan is like beginning a program to improve your physical fitness. If you joined a health club or spa, your instructor would begin with where you are, physically, by determining your weight, measurements, and eating habits. Then your coach would design a personalized program for you. Perhaps you would commit to an exercise routine of a half hour per day, every other day.

Most likely, you would start out slowly to avoid injuring yourself, because you weren't previously in the habit of exercising. Over time, you would gradually increase the amount and intensity of your exercise, measuring your progress along the way. After a while, if you stuck to your program, everything about your physical body would change: your measurements, weight, overall appearance, health, and well-being.

Financial conditioning like physical conditioning doesn't happen overnight. It requires plenty of effort, time, and discipline to develop physical or financial strength.

Step 4—Reallocate Your Resources Intelligently So You Can Reach Your Short- and Long-Term Goals.

You'll be continually moving toward your goals by taking short-term steps that, when achieved, will lead you closer to your ultimate destination: *financial freedom.* The more steps you take, the stronger and better you'll feel. Eventually, you'll be surprised to find that your entire life will be positively affected by the choices you've made to change your spending habits. When you see benefits such as increased deposits in your savings account and decreased debt, you'll begin to actually enjoy yourself!

When you finally arrive at your goals, you'll be a different person than you were the day you set them. As with physical conditioning, you'll find that you have improved your strength and endurance and developed a positive discipline that will spill over into all areas of your life.

Think of pursuing your financial destination like taking a thousand-mile walk. If you make a mile of progress each day, it will take you a little over three years to reach your destination. If you approach your long-range goals with that kind of realism, you'll have far fewer problems than those with unrealistic expectations. It may take years to reach your long-range goals, but you'll never get out of the place you're in if you don't start taking the first few steps.

In step 4, you choose how you'll allocate the surplus you created in step 3. Because you completed step 2, you have a tentative idea of the direction you want to take. As you eliminate expenses one by one, you'll begin to build your financial momentum. When you get that raise, promotion, or bonus, you'll have the pleasant task of choosing how to allocate the increase. Certainly you'll want to honor God with the increase, but you'll also want to save and spend some of it in other areas. Like Pilgrim in John Bunyan's "Pilgrim's Progress," you're on your way to the celestial city. Enjoy yourself, and remember to give thanks for your daily blessings as you begin your journey to a balanced financial lifestyle.

How to Put Your Spending Plan to Work

Form 2 is the vehicle that will ultimately lead you to accomplishing your goals. After filling it out you may be shocked to see what's left after giving, taxes, and paying yourself first. If you choose not to give anything to God, remember the words of the Old Testament prophet:

> "Will a wise man rob God? Yet you rob me.
> "But you ask, 'How do we rob you?'
> "In tithes and offerings. You are under a curse—the whole nation of you—because you are robbing me. Bring the whole tithe into the storehouse, that there may be food in my house. Test me in this," says the LORD Almighty, "and see if I will not throw open the floodgates of heaven and pour out so much blessing that you will not have room enough for it." (Malachi 3:8-10)

You may choose to give less or more than the guideline, but giving is not an option for a committed, mature Christian.

You're accustomed to taxes coming out of your check, but if you're not used to paying yourself first, that may take some getting used to. The 5 to 10 percent guideline may be too much for you to begin with. Start where you can, and work up to the guideline amounts.

Manage the eleven categories of spending so the total for all is less than your net income after taxes, giving, and saving. A few of you (approximately 15 percent) are already spending less than you earn. For the rest of us, learning to live contentedly within our incomes is a real challenge. If you're among the 15 percent who spend less than you earn, you're also probably debt-free, excluding your home and possibly your vehicle. You should thank your parents (or whoever taught you) for instilling in you such good habits.

Most people who have never determined how much they spend are surprised to find how much of their net income is committed to debt, housing, transportation, and insurance. These categories collectively consume over half your spendable income. That's why I devoted so much time to them earlier and gave you plenty of ideas on how to deal with those obligations.

Look back at the items on Spending Form 2 marked with an asterisk, representing the items that most people omit in their planning. If you haven't planned for maintenance or "other" (such as furniture and appliances) under "housing"; or tax and license, repair, maintenance, and replacement under "auto"; and if you've allocated nothing for gifts for Christmas and special occasions, your spending estimates are unrealistic. These are inevitable expenses that you *will* have to pay when the need arises.

The success of your spending plan depends on your honest and accurate inclusion of what you need to spend. The process of determining and recording expenses often reveals wants and desires that can easily be reallocated to other categories.

A good place to begin with reallocation of funds is category 3, food. If you'll devote some time and energy to planning, you can probably reduce the amount of money you've been spending on food. For example, how much of your food buying is devoted to instant meals, pre-prepared foods, junk food with lots of empty calories, or higher-priced brand names? Do you live on a meal plan for the week and buy what you need, or do you simply go to the market and plan your meals as you wheel your cart down the aisle? Consult any of the dozens of books available on how to get more nutrition for less money.

Clipping coupons is another way to save significantly on your food bill. With the competitive nature of the grocery business, chains sometimes offer double or even triple value on manufacturers' coupons.

Category 6, entertainment is another source of potential savings. Are you in the habit of eating lunch out every day? If you choose to brown bag it instead, you'll save $80 a month or more. Or, treat yourself to lunch out once or twice a week and take your lunch to work the rest of the time.

Is Friday night pizza for the family worth the extra $25 a week, or is there a better place to put $1,300 per year? Why not make homemade pizza and play board games at home with your kids? Better still, take turns preparing special Friday night meals—let your kids do some of the cooking!

What about summer vacations? Do you put them on plastic and

spend more than you should? If family togetherness is the issue, you can take the family camping for a week at a fraction of the cost. As you become aware of your spending, ask yourself if there are better, less expensive ways to achieve the same results. Is your current plan the best way to meet your "needs"?

Clothing is yet another category in which you can probably generate substantial savings. By planning your purchases and buying "needs," not "wants," you can save hundreds of dollars each year. Are the "labels" you've been buying really worth the price you pay? Do you really need brand-name, designer sunglasses when you can buy the same optics for much less? Do brand-name shirts meet the need for covering any better than less expensive ones, or are you caught in the trap of buying status, image, and desires for yourself and your children?

I'm not a status-conscious person. (In fact, people have tactfully asked me if I'm fully sighted. When I tell them I am, I'm often accused of dressing myself in dark closets.) My fashion sense aside, I'm amazed that people will pay multiples in price, just to have a label sewn on the outside of their clothing for everyone to notice. Personally, I think designers ought to pay consumers for advertising if the label is prominently displayed—or at least they ought to give buyers a break on the price, instead of making the item more costly. However, those who sell designer brands have consistently ignored my opinion and continue to charge consumers for the privilege of serving as their billboards.

If you buy clothes on sale, forget your "wants" and purchase your "needs." You'll cut excess spending in this category.

Most optimists omit allocating anything for medical expenses because they figure such expenses happen to others, not to them. Perhaps you're one of the lucky ones, and members of your family seldom get sick. Even so, good planning and preventive medicine (such as vitamins) will pay you dividends. A simple matter like seeing your dentist at least once a year for cleaning and check-up may alert you to problems long before they become critical and expensive.

If you're unfortunate enough to be at the other end of the spectrum, it may seem as if life is one long, unending series of medical bills. Wherever you are, try to be realistic in planning your medical expenses.

For many families, child care and schooling costs are major sources of expense and frustration these days. Day care is expensive, and prices for books and materials increase as your children grow. If your children attend a private school, you may struggle with the cost of tuition.

Category 10, the catch-all "miscellaneous," is full of potential spending reductions. For example, have you taken the time to plan your gift giving, or do you wait until the event and then overspend by paying top dollar or buying impulse items? Do you make gifts if you can? Are you careful not to choose over-priced or nonessential gifts?

Gift-giving is one of the easiest areas to splurge on. Christmas, birthdays, and other special occasions can be truly memorable if you put effort into planning for the occasion, rather than relieving your guilt by overspending because you were too busy to plan.

The gifts that mean the most to me are the ones made by the giver. I still have the pictures, pencil holders, models, and crafts I received from my sons—the best gifts of all, because they represent love, time, energy, and thought from my loved ones. If you can, consider giving handmade gifts for special occasions—they save money and carry special meaning to the receiver.

PRINCIPLE 62—ELIMINATE SURPRISES BY PLANNING AHEAD

Many plans are ruined by unpredictable events. Twice a year, my mail contains a bill for my auto insurance. Since I know the bill is coming, I plan for it by putting reserves aside each of the five months in between so I can pay the bill when it comes. I also anticipate and save for the unpredictable bills for repair and maintenance on my car and home.

If you know expenses are coming but you don't know when they will arrive, you can soften the blow by setting aside some money each month to pay for that contingency. If you'll simply take the time to evaluate, estimate, and complete your spending plan, you'll eliminate most of the problems that take others by surprise.

PRINCIPLE 63—NO PAIN, NO GAIN

There's no quick fix for developing a spending plan. The evolution of a complete and accurate plan takes time, effort, thought, revision, and prayer. There are as many plans for managing money as there are people to make them, but the plans that continue to work all have one thing in common: They're simple to create and use! The more elaborate and complex your plan, the less likely you are to continue with it.

One of the simplest ways to begin a spending plan is with the envelope system: Label one envelope for each category of spending. When you get a paycheck, cash it and divide the money into each of your envelopes. If your net weekly paycheck is $300, put $30 into giving,

$15 into saving, $45 into food, $15 into entertainment, and so on. As you spend the money in your envelopes, record the expenditure on a sheet of paper that you keep in each envelope.

We still use the envelope system at our house as a way of controlling and managing expenses. My wife and I divide our expenses, and each month Jeanie breaks down the funds she manages into a dozen envelopes. The balance goes into our checking account for monthly items we pay for by check: utilities, water, phone, gas, and others. At the end of the month, I merge our expenses into a single record of income and expenses and compare where we are with where we planned to be. The entire process takes less than an hour each month, and we always know where we stand.

The envelope system works very efficiently to prevent running over on expenses: When the "entertainment" envelope is empty, that's it for entertainment. But if you have your checkbook handy, and there's a few dollars left in it, you might not be able to resist the temptation to go out for pizza even though you know you shouldn't. The only real danger in using envelopes is the temptation to borrow from another envelope if the one you need is empty. If you let yourself fall into that trap, the system will get hopelessly complex, and then it will fail.

The number of envelopes you use, and whether you design a manual system or put your plan on a computer, is up to you. Whatever you choose to do, remember: *The simpler your plan, the greater the probability that you will continue to use it.*

PRINCIPLE 64—WATCH OUT FOR THE SIX REASONS WHY PLANS FAIL

Reason 1—Responsibility for Implementation Is Not Clearly Established

The number-one reason why spending plans fail is that no one person takes responsibility for managing and controlling the plan. I've seen plans succeed with husbands as the responsible party, I've seen plans succeed when the wife controls the finances, but I've never seen a plan succeed when no one person is responsible and accountable for the entire task.

Reason 2—Failure to Take the Spending Plan Seriously

If you don't take your spending plan seriously, you are dooming it to failure. The reason for a plan is to help you learn patience, discipline, and ways to control impulse spending. In order for a plan to succeed, you must learn the value of thinking and praying before you spend.

Reason 3—Unrealistic Planning

Over time, unrealistic plans will certainly fail. Sure, for a little while you may be able to get away with it, and perhaps even eliminate a few expenditures for entertainment, clothes, or pocket money, but eventually you'll self-destruct from frustration and despair. Any plan that isn't realistic enough to include "surprises" such as auto insurance premiums and gift-buying is also doomed to failure.

Reason 4—Rigid and Inflexible Approaches

Your plan will fail if you approach it legalistically. Plans are guidelines for spending—they're not inflexible rules that can't be bent. Even the best plan will need adjustment and modification over time. Your needs will change over time, just as your circumstances will. So be flexible enough to adjust your plan with midstream course corrections as they become necessary.

Reason 5—Unfairness to a Spouse

Plans also fail when they're not fair and equitable to both partners. Too many times, spending plans are created to punish one spouse or the other. Spending plans are not meant to be manipulative tools for spouses to wield in nursing a grudge or gaining control.

Early in our marriage, Jeanie and I had trouble agreeing on a fair amount of money to allocate for items she desired in our plan. I thought her figure for clothing, beauty shops, and makeup was excessive. She already had more shoes in the closet than I would buy over a lifetime, and two drawers full of "war paint."

Since neither of us could accept the other's spending estimate, we agreed to consult others to see whose figure was fair and realistic. We ended up allocating Jeanie more than she originally requested. You see, I was way off, realistically, in estimating the cost of her needs. Good plans make good marriages better, because they promote communication, honesty, and understanding—provided the plan is fair to both of you.

Reason 6—Failure to Act on the Plan

The final reason plans fail is because they're not used. A very wealthy friend of mine spent several thousand dollars on a spending, financial, and investment plan created for him by professional advisors. The plan was the most accurate, comprehensive plan I've ever seen (and as a professional advisor, I have seen several thousand).

Today, that leather-bound plan sits on the shelf of his library, collecting dust. It was not, nor will it ever be, used.

"Use it, or lose it" is the law of financial, physical, and spiritual life. If you won't use a spending plan, don't waste the time it will take to create it.

PRINCIPLE 65—DEVELOP BETTER SPENDING HABITS

Lack of patience is a primary cause of financial failure. Today, our entire society is built on what I call the "McDonald's mentality." We want what we want instantly, whether it's a Big Mac at the drive-through or instant weight-reduction pills. We're all conditioned to indulge ourselves and seek instant gratification. We don't expect to wait for anything.

We seldom consider the virtue of patience. There's real excitement in waiting expectantly for God to provide—in His perfect time, and in His perfect way.

Although I hesitate to admit this, I am an impulse buyer who has had to learn to avoid shopping malls and stores. If I go to a store for two new shirts, I end up with two suits, a sport coat, six shirts, a few ties, and a new pair of shoes. I've solved my problem by asking my wife to shop for me, or else I leave my checkbook home, and let Jeanie carry her envelopes. If you're an impulse buyer, don't tempt yourself by shopping—avoid the mall, like an alcoholic would avoid a wine-tasting party.

To avoid wasteful spending, try the "no credit card" philosophy: If an item isn't in your spending plan, don't buy it with plastic. Remember that the average person buys more when shopping on plastic. Using credit makes it more difficult to separate "wants" from "needs." Most important, credit cards cost you money in finance charges.

Create an "I want list." If you find six volumes you just have to have while strolling through the bookstore, put them on your "I want list." Force yourself to wait thirty days before you buy any of them. After thirty days, you'll find that you can live without 95 percent of those items—or you'll find a better buy and be glad you waited.

When I started my "I want list" twenty-one years ago, it ran several pages long by the end of every month. Praise God, He was rightly unwilling to provide me the means to indulge myself, or I would still be buried in debt paying for a warehouse full of items I wanted but didn't really need.

In order to discipline your spending, make it a habit to think and pray before you buy, and learn to separate wants from needs. Over time, you'll learn contentment and self-discipline. A need is something necessary to fulfill God's plan for your life. A want or desire may be nice, but in most cases, it won't help you to grow spiritually. Once you've determined whether the thing you want to buy is a want or a need, think of Jesus shopping with you, and ask Him for His guidance and discernment.

A PRACTICAL EXAMPLE

Jane is a thirty-seven-year-old divorced woman who has full custody of her son, Hugo, age ten. Jane teaches at a public high school during the school year and works part-time during the summer as a leasing agent and tutoring at a learning center. She was referred to me for financial counseling to determine whether or not she could afford a six-week tour of Europe with her son during the summer.

We began by recording her sources and amounts of income.

Teaching salary	$24,800
Tutoring summer	3,800
Real estate commissions	2,100
Child support	4,800
TOTAL YEARLY INCOME	$35,500

By comparison to many single parents, Jane was fortunate. She had good employment and work hours and her ex-husband was faithful to pay her child support.

Next we examined the budget Jane brought with her.

Item	Monthly
Giving ($5/Sunday)	$22.00
Taxes (federal, state, FICA)	422.00
Mortgage payment (PITI)	898.00
Telephone	30.00
Utilities	175.00
Water	30.00
Car payment	256.00
Gas	60.00
Auto insurance	80.00
Food	275.00
Health insurance	25.00
Outstanding debt	400.00
Clothing	100.00
Miscellaneous	100.00
TOTAL	$2,873.00
	($34,476/year)

If Jane was spending $1,000 a year less than she made, why did she owe $400 a month in outstanding bills? How accurate was the budget she prepared? To find out, Jane began to detail her bills from records she had as follows (see page 75 for blank form):

Lender	Balance Due	Monthly Payment	Interest Rate	Remaining Payments
Charge card 1	$2,500	$87	15%	36
Charge card 2	3,500	127	18%	36
Clothing card	1,000	35	15%	36
Department store card	1,500	72	15%	24
School loans	3,500	40	4%	-0-
SUBTOTALS	$11,000	$361		
Loan from parents	6,000	50	-0-	120
SUBTOTALS	$17,000	$411		
Car loan	2,171	256	12%	8
Mortgage balance	100,000	740 PI	8%	360
Home taxes, insurance		158	-0-	360
TOTALS	$130,171	$1,926		

When Jane was divorced three years prior she had $5,000 in savings, a home worth $165,000 with a $100,000 mortgage and no debt except the mortgage. (The payment to the 8-percent, 30-year loan is withheld from Jane's paycheck.) To make ends meet and keep her home, she worked during the summer as a leasing agent for an apartment complex part-time and taught at the learning center. Given this history, do you think she could afford to borrow the $3,500 on a home equity loan to pay for her and Hugo's European exploration?

Here's how Jane completed Form 2.

FORM 2: MONTHLY SPENDING PLAN FOR JANE

Gross Income	$ 2958		**5. Debts**	$ 411/	16%
Salary (teaching)	$ 2067		Credit card	$ 321	
~~Interest~~ (tutoring)	$ 316		Loans, notes	$ 40	
~~Dividends~~ (R.E.)	$ 175		Other (parents)	$ 50	
Other (child support)	$ 400		**6. Entertainment**	$ 260/	10%
Less			Eating out	$ 200	
Giving	$ 22		Baby-sitters	$ 60	
Federal tax	$ 192		Other	$ 0	
FICA	$ 192		**7. Clothing**	$ 150/	6%
State tax	$ 38		**8. Medical**	$ 45/	2%
Savings	$ 0		Doctors	$ 25	
Net Income	$ 2514		Medication	$ 10	
1. Housing	$ 1219/	48%	Dentist	$ 10	
Payment/rent	$ 740		Other	$ 0	
Telephone	$ 30		**9. School/**		
Insurance	$ 40		**child care**	$ 25/	1%
Taxes	$ 118		Tuition	$ 0	
Electricity	$ 175		Transportation	$ 0	
Water	$ 30		Materials	$ 25	
Gas	$ 0		Day care	$ 0	
Sanitation	$ 0		**10. Miscellaneous**	$ 285/	11%
Maintenance*	$ 50		Lunches	$ 25	
Other* (cable)	$ 36		Toiletries	$ 20	
2. Auto	$ 551/	22%	Beauty/barber	$ 35	
Payments	$ 256		Laundry/cleaners	$ 15	
Gas/oil	$ 60		Allowances	$ 80	
Insurance	$ 80		Gifts*	$ 100	
Tax/license*	$ 25		Subscriptions	$ 10	
Repair/maintain*	$ 30		Other	$ 0	
Replacement*	$ 100				
3. Food	$ 275/	11%	TOTAL EXPENSES	$ 3246	
4. Insurance	$ 25/	1%	LESS NET INCOME	$ 2514	
Medical	$ YES				
Disability	$ YES		THE BOTTOM LINE	$ <732>	
Life	$ YES				
Other	$ 0				

*Items marked with an asterisk indicate expenses that most people neglect to include in their planning.

As you can see from Form 2, Jane's actual spending, when all factors were considered, amount to $3,246 a month, which was $732 a month more than she earned! As with most people, Jane's original estimate of $2,873 a month understated expenses. She was enabled to deficit spend by using credit cards and loans from her parents. This accounted for her $17,000 debt and spending the $5,000 she had had in savings after her divorce.

FORM 3: SPENDING PLAN GUIDELINES FOR JANE

GROSS INCOME PER YEAR $ __35,500__   PER MONTH $ __2958__

Less

Giving	$ 2958	×	10 %Gross =	$	296
Taxes	$ 2958	×	18 %Gross =	$	400
Savings	$ 2958	×	5 %Gross =	$	148

NET INCOME PER YEAR $ __25,368__   PER MONTH $ __2114__

1. Housing	$ 2114	×	35 %Net =	$	740
2. Auto	$ 2114	×	12 %Net =	$	254
3. Food	$ 2114	×	11 %Net =	$	232
4. Insurance	$ 2114	×	5 %Net =	$	106
5. Debts	$ 2114	×	5 %Net =	$	106
6. Entertainment	$ 2114	×	6 %Net =	$	127
7. Clothing	$ 2114	×	5 %Net =	$	106
8. Medical	$ 2114	×	4 %Net =	$	85
9. School/child care	$ 2114	×	6 %Net =	$	127
10. Miscellaneous	$ 2114	×	4 %Net =	$	85
11. Surplus	$ 2114	×	7 %Net =	$	146

TOTAL EXPENSES (cannot exceed net income) $ __2114__

As you can see, Form 3 was completed using the percentage guidelines from Form 1. Remember, these are guidelines, not laws, and they are used as input for Form 4 following. In Jane's case we used the third column since her gross income was closer to $40,000 a year than $25,000 a year.

FORM 4: SPENDING PLAN ANALYSIS FOR JANE

GROSS INCOME PER MONTH $ __2958__

	Guideline	Current Month's Spending	Monthly Difference	New Monthly Plan
Giving	296	22	−274	−173
Taxes	400	422	+22	394
Savings	148	0	−148	125
NET INCOME	$ 2114	$ 2514	$ +400	$ 2266
1. Housing	740	1219	+479	1034
2. Automobile(s)	254	551	+297	405
3. Food	232	275	+43	150
4. Insurance	106	25	−81	25
5. Debts	106	411	+305	40
6. Entertainment	127	260	+133	100
7. Clothing	106	150	+44	80
8. Medical	85	45	−40	45
9. School/child care	127	25	−102	25
10. Miscellaneous	85	285	+200	105
TOTALS (1-10)	$ 1968	$ 3246	$ +1278	$ 2009
11. Surplus (deficit)	146	<732>		257

The figures in column 1 (Guideline) are from Form 3.
The figures in column 2 (Current Month's Spending) are from Form 2.
The figures in column 3 (Monthly Difference) show how much the current spending exceeded (+) or fell short of (-) the figures in column 1.
The figures in column 4 (New Monthly Plan) are what seem realistic in light of the facts at present.

When Form 4 was completed, Jane was depressed. She knew she should be giving more and saving something, but the magnitude of her overspending shocked her. The only categories where she didn't exceed the guidelines were insurance (90 percent employer-paid), medical (a very generous medical insurance), and school/child care.

Before you examine the new spending plan, let's see what changes Jane made during the nine months it took to arrive at a balanced plan (labeled New Monthly Plan).

1. She sold her home and used the $55,000 equity to:
   a. pay off $13,500 in debt (everything but her school loan, which remained in her monthly spending plan);
   b. put $12,000 into savings (approximately six months income);
   c. buy a $100,000 home with $29,500 down. She took a $70,500 mortgage for fifteen years at 7 $\frac{1}{2}$ percent. This reduced her payment to $665 a month (principal and interest) and $94 a month taxes and insurance. Her total house payment dropped to $759.
2. She joined the teachers' retirement plan and had $125 a month deducted from her salary, which was matched by an equal contribution from her employer. This reduced her taxes $28 a month.
3. She started to give $40 a week to her church.
4. By creating a meal plan, she reduced her monthly food bill to $150.
5. She cut her entertainment budget to $100 a month by creative planning.
6. She learned to take advantage of sales to reduce her clothing budget to $80 a month.
7. She eliminated the unnecessary "miscellaneous" items and ended up spending $105 a month.
8. Although her car was now paid off and only four years old with 47,000 miles, she committed to save $200 a month toward replacing it, thus leaving her with a monthly automobile expenditure of $405 (including savings of $200).
9. She destroyed all her credit cards and has a bank ID card for cashing checks.
10. She plans to save half of her surplus ($257 a month)

plus 50 percent of all salary increases, bonuses, and gifts for the future, knowing that her $400 a month tax-free child support ends when Hugo is age eighteen, eight years in the future. The other half of her monthly surplus ($128.50) goes into a special account. This will be used for completing her master's degree, which will increase her salary $3,500 a year, helping Hugo with college expenses if needed and making increased giving possible.

Jane's entire life indeed has been transformed. She has resumed the habits she learned early in life from her pastor-father. She has a relationship with the Lord she had not experienced since her teens. She has lost forty unwanted pounds and is currently dating a professor at our local university who is a committed Christian. Praise the Lord for His empowering and guidance of Jane and Hugo.

You, too, can put the process to work. *Start* by completing Forms 2, 3, and 4. Be patient but steadfast. Remember, it took nine painful months of decisions, adjustments, and changes to produce her results. As you work through the process, remember Philippians 2:12-13: "Work out your salvation with fear and trembling, for it is God who works in you to will and to act according to his good purpose."

ENJOY THE BENEFITS OF A SPENDING PLAN

Creating and implementing a spending plan will eliminate habitual, wasteful spending—most likely about 15 percent of your income. If you earn $25,000 per year, a spending plan will save you $3,750 each year.

A spending plan serves as a daily reminder that we are all stewards who want to be found faithful in the management of what has been entrusted to us. A spending plan can be a marvelous tool for learning to be content with what we have, rather than dwelling anxiously on what we want or think we need.

Take Paul's example to heart:

I have learned to be content whatever the circumstances. I know what it is to be in need, and I know what it is to have plenty. I have learned the secret of being content in any and every situation, whether well fed or hungry, whether living in plenty or in want. I can do everything through him who gives me strength. (Philippians 4:11-13)

Contentment is a virtue rarely found in our materialistic culture. But it's an attitude that you can choose to adopt. If you set your eyes on Jesus, and not on the things of this world, you will experience the joy and peace that come from a thankful, contented heart. Remember that God promises to meet all your needs, and God alone is faithful to do what He promised.

The next time you find yourself desiring something outside the realm of your spending plan, reflect on these words:

> Be joyful always; pray continually; give thanks in all circumstances, for this is God's will for you in Christ Jesus.
> (1 Thessalonians 5:16-18)

INVESTING

■

"Do not store up for yourself treasures on earth,
where moth and rust destroy, and where thieves break in and steal.
But store up for yourself treasures in heaven,
where moth and rust do not destroy
and where thieves do not break in and steal.
For where your treasure is, there your heart will be also."
MATTHEW 6:19-21

Do you ever wonder if Jesus realized the tremendous pressure we'd be under, living in the twentieth century, when He made this statement?

Especially in the U.S., we're taught from an early age to compete with the other guy and to pursue wealth. We're taught to seek pleasure, to "go for the gusto," because we owe it to ourselves—we "deserve a break, today!" Understandably, the concept of contentment is difficult to grasp when everywhere we turn, people are telling us that we *need* more, *deserve* more, should *want* more.

Are you content with what you have, or do you feel you would be happier if you had a higher income? Do you desire fame and recognition, influence and position, or do you hunger and thirst for righteousness? How strong is your desire for power over your life, your spouse, your family, your job, or the system that governs you? By contrast, how strong is your desire for a humble and contrite spirit? Is pleasure your motivation, or do these words of Jesus reflect the desires of your heart? "'Love the Lord, your God, with all your heart and with all your soul and with all your mind.' This is the first and greatest commandment. And the second is like it: 'Love your neighbor as yourself'" (Matthew 22:37-39).

PRINCIPLE 66—CHOOSE TODAY WHERE YOU WILL STORE UP TREASURE

Jesus clearly states that "no one can serve two masters" (Matthew 6:24). We cannot serve both God and money. If we're devoted to one, we despise the other.

Especially in our culture today, the decision to store up treasure in Heaven is difficult to make. Most common is the man or woman who chooses to pursue the temporal, earthly treasures of fortune, fame, power, and pleasure.

Although investing God's money wisely should be a priority, as the parable of the talents (Matthew 25:14-30) teaches us, we should never make investments, income, and net worth our top priority. Our first priority, always, should be to live the great commandment: To love God above all things, and to love our neighbors.

PRINCIPLE 67—FOLLOW PROPER GUIDELINES FOR BUILDING AN INVESTMENT PROGRAM

Your first choice with any surplus capital is whether you want a guaranteed account or an investment. A guaranteed account will produce safety and income. If you deposit $5,000 in your bank for six months, the FDIC guarantees that six months later you will receive your $5,000 plus interest—no more but no less. An investment has no guarantee on value or income, but over the long term, investments have usually earned more than guaranteed accounts. If you are willing to watch your investment rise or fall in value and the income go up and down during the holding period, investments are appropriate for you. Otherwise, stay with guaranteed accounts. The amounts you keep in guaranteed accounts and investment accounts depend on your age, time horizon (or holding period), risk tolerance, goals, and other factors that we will examine. The graph on page 183 from Ibbotson Associates illustrates different results based on where $1 was placed in 1975.

When you build an investment program—whether it's a retirement plan, an educational plan, or a plan to improve your lifestyle—keep the following guidelines in mind.

Know the "Why" Behind the "What"

As you consider what investment goals you want to establish, first determine the reason why achieving them is important to you. Look closely at your motives, because you will either be storing up treasures in Heaven or here on earth. It's important to remember, too, that regardless of what you think your motive is, God alone knows the true motive of your heart.

We often make financial decisions before giving any serious thought to our motives. We think we know why we're doing a thing, but frequently our true motive is not apparent to us. God desires to be first in every aspect of our lives—including finances. He is eager to reveal the condition of our hearts to us, if we simply take the time to ask Him to do so. Prayer should be the first step in making any financial decision.

MUTUAL FUND STYLES OF INVESTING

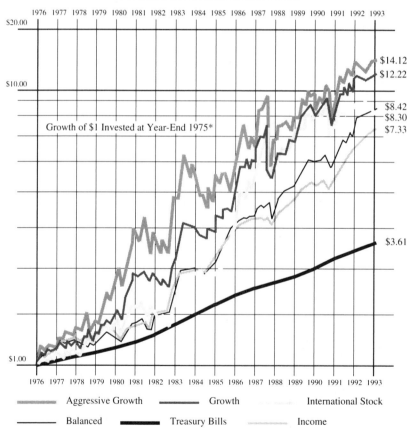

Growth of $1 Invested at Year-End 1975*

Aggressive Growth   Growth   International Stock

Balanced   Treasury Bills   Income

*Based on total return data measured as percentage change in funds N.A.V. plus reinvestment of all income and capital gain distributions.

Source: Ibbotson Associates' I/IDEALS Mutual Fund Equity & Fixed Income Databases: Chicago, IL, 1992. Data from Morningstar, Inc., 53 West Jackson Boulevard, Suite 460, Chicago, Illinois 60604, (800) 876-5005.

Decide How Much Is Enough

How much money do you need each month to live comfortably and maintain a surplus fund for emergencies? Once you have established an amount, be cautious about expanding your goals. For most people, money is extremely addictive. To prevent greed and hoarding, stop when you've reached your goal.

Be Realistic

Be realistic about the time you need to build an investment program and achieve your goals. Also, be realistic about the return you expect to get.

PRINCIPLE 68—USE THE RIGHT INGREDIENTS FOR SUCCESSFUL INVESTING

By definition, all investments involve a certain degree of risk. Therefore, it makes sense to assume risk only if you have adequate reserves in savings and have eliminated all of your liabilities. Simply put, this means, *never invest if you're saving for major purchases*.

The Proper Financial Condition

You should invest only if you have done the following:

- saved six months of living expenses in reserves
- saved enough to pay for repairs and maintenance, emergencies, and other periodic or annual expenses
- paid off all credit cards
- paid off all installment purchases
- paid off all large liabilities, such as your home mortgage

I don't recommend investing before these events, for two reasons. First, if you don't have savings and reserves, circumstances may force you to sell your investment to meet your needs. If you're forced to sell earlier than planned, you could easily end up taking a significant loss on your investment. Second, it doesn't make sense to gamble on a "maybe" return when you have guaranteed liabilities such as consumer debt, car loans, or house payments.

By following these conservative guidelines, you may miss a few investment opportunities, but you'll also eliminate many investments that don't work out, leaving you much further ahead in the long run.

The Appropriate Psychological Prerequisites

These are what I consider the appropriate psychological prerequisites for investing:

- Time
- Temperament
- Training
- Talent

Many investors fail because they don't devote the required *time* to learning how to invest (more about that later in this chapter). A *temperament* suited to investing is able to balance input from both the rational and emotional side (later in this chapter, I'll point out the danger of following your feelings). *Training* is necessary if you want to lose less than you make in your investments. A surprising number of people with years of formal education and/or business experience will invest thousands of dollars simply on tips from a friend, without ever bothering to do some research themselves. Becoming a successful investor requires study, training, and effort—a fact ignored by many, who tragically end up losing their life's savings.

Finally, being a successful investor requires *talent*. Everyone has different gifts and talents. Some people are gifted in the arts or technical fields but simply have no talent for investing. By honestly accessing your natural talent or lack of it, you'll save yourself a lot of pain and suffering. If you have the talent for investing, by all means use it. If not, hire the talent and don't wear yourself out trying to swim upstream.

PRINCIPLE 69—FOLLOW A SIX-STEP METHOD FOR INVESTING

Step 1—Self-Evaluation

The first step in investing is *self-evaluation*. Know exactly where you are, financially, before you begin. Only then are you ready to set your investment objectives.

Step 2—Establish Priorities for Your Objectives

There are thousands of different investments, but they are all designed to accomplish the same five goals: safety, income, growth, tax benefit, and liquidity. Your job is to establish priorities among these objectives.

When you select from various investments, eliminate those that are not suitable for you. Safety, for example, should rank near the top of your priorities in order to minimize or eliminate losses. Will Rogers said, "I am first interested in return *of* my money, then return *on* my money."

After safety, many people invest for income second, others stress growth, and some invest for a combination of both. Regardless of your objective, you need to be aware of your total return—the after-tax total of both income and growth.

Sometimes tax benefits are a priority in investing, especially if the investor is subject to higher marginal tax rates.

The fifth goal, liquidity, varies with the needs of individual investors and time. However you choose to do it, be sure to establish priorities for your investment goals in each of the five areas.

Step 3—Quantify Your Objectives in Order to Measure Performance

After you have established priorities for your investment goals, quantify your objectives so you have a way to measure your performance.

For example, let's assume that you have set your priorities in this order: (1) safety, (2) income, (3) growth, (4) liquidity, and (5) tax benefit. This puts you halfway to setting your investment goals. Now you need to define or quantify levels of safety, amount or percentage of income and/or growth you'd like to see, and what you mean, personally, by "liquidity."

If you say you want more income, you've expressed your desire, but you must quantify it by stating exactly how much income you want. Is 5 percent per year acceptable, or do you expect 7 percent? Answer that question and you will have a precise, measurable standard against which to evaluate where you are and each potential investment you might consider thereafter.

Step 4—Plan Your Methods for Achieving Your Objectives

The fourth step to successful investing is planning your method of achieving your objective.

For example, if you need $100,000 ten years from now, how much will you need to invest to reach that goal? To answer that question, you must know the annual percentage return you'll earn each year on the investment you choose. If you earn 2 percent you'll need monthly savings of $761; if you earn 4 percent you'll need $694 each month;

and so on. Be realistic in estimating the time you'll need to achieve your goal and what you can expect to earn over time.

Step 5—Study the Alternatives

The fifth step requires that you take time to learn about available alternatives. Investors have thousands of options to choose from to help them reach their goals. The greater the number of options, the greater the investor's chance for success.

Educating yourself about the choices can be difficult and time-consuming, but there's no substitute for doing your homework.

Step 6—Stay Alert and Flexible

The final step in investment planning concerns flexibility and your ability to adapt to change. No investment goes up or down forever. Laws, interest and inflation rates, taxes, and the economy are all factors that affect the turbulent arena of investments.

A plan that worked perfectly ten years ago would not be efficient today. Years ago, all you had to do was buy quality investments and hold on to them, and you knew that in time they would make money for you. Today, it's not that easy. Industry leaders, and the investment industry itself, has changed dramatically over the last decade. The price of success is constant effort, diligence, and awareness. You can't simply buy stock in the market and then forget it.

PRINCIPLE 70—EVALUATE RISK AND REWARD CAREFULLY

Perhaps you've heard people say, "The greater the risk, the greater the reward." A more accurate statement would be, "The greater the potential reward, the greater the real risk."

When examining a potential investment, the first decision you make concerns the kind of risk you're willing to take. *No* investment is guaranteed or risk-free. Your first choice is between an "investment" and a "guaranteed investment." But don't be deceived: a "guaranteed investment" is not without risk. Your bank account may be guaranteed by the Federal Deposit Insurance Corporation (FDIC), but it still carries risk. If you don't believe me, ask anyone who survived the Great Depression. Bank accounts, insured savings, insurance contracts, and government securities may all be guaranteed, but they still contain risks such as default of the guarantor, or the risk of having your money destroyed by inflation.

PRINCIPLE 71—ASK THREE QUESTIONS
ABOUT "GUARANTEED" INVESTMENTS

Whenever you hear the word *guaranteed* attached to "investment," ask these three questions: (1) Guaranteed by whom? (2) Guaranteed for what? (3) How well capitalized is the issuer of the guarantee?

Guaranteed by Whom?

In the last ten years, I've seen many investors lose their guaranteed savings because they never asked "guaranteed by whom?" A thrift company advertised that savings at their institution were "insured"—but they never said who was doing the "insuring." It wasn't the FDIC, and today (eight years later), these investors have recovered only fifteen cents on each "insured" dollar.

Guaranteed for What?

Investors in government bonds have sustained losses because they failed to ask "guaranteed for what?" If they had, they would have learned up front that during the holding period of a government bond, the principal is not guaranteed. In times of rising interest rates, the prices of government bonds go down. Today, if you invest $25,000 in a 6-percent, thirty-year government bond and then decide to sell five years from now, when interest rates have gone up, you will receive *less* than the $25,000 you paid. The only way to receive your entire $25,000 back would be to hold the bond to maturity. That's why I encourage you to ask "insured for what?" You may be surprised to find that today, the FDIC has less than one penny available for each dollar guaranteed. Other insurers may have more or less, but you'll have the facts you need to know when you determine the financial health of your guarantor.

How Well Capitalized Is the Issuer of the Guarantee?

A "guaranteed" investment is subject to the risk of inflation. I often hear a client sigh about "the good old days, when I could get 12 percent on my CD." What they fail to realize is that when CDs were yielding double digits, tax brackets were higher, and so was inflation! What they actually kept was much less than 12 percent.

Don't forget: For every dollar of interest you receive, you have to share a portion of it with at least two other entities—the tax collector, who takes the first bite, and then inflation. You get what's left, if anything.

PRINCIPLE 72—LOOK FOR THE REAL RATE OF RETURN

When looking at CDs or other income investments, it's important to look at the "real rate of return." Real rate of return is the amount adjusted for taxes and inflation. In the late seventies and early eighties, investors were getting high rates of current income. Interest rates were high, because the cost of living was out of control and the purchasing power of those income dollars was rapidly eroding. And to add insult to injury, Uncle Sam was taking a bigger share. Remember 1980? The top marginal tax bracket was 59 percent! Ah, yes, how soon we forget. If you were in the highest bracket of CD holders, 59 percent of your return was sent to the IRS. You kept only 41 percent, some of which had to go toward paying state taxes. Take a look at the chart:

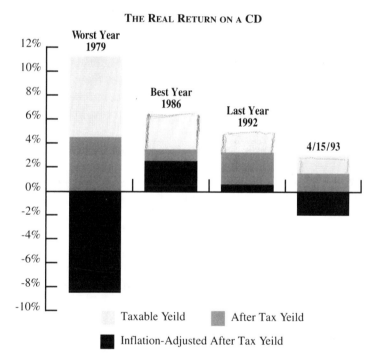

THE REAL RETURN ON A CD

CD rate is 6-month annualized average monthly rate as compiled by Bank Rate Monitor (*Wall Street Journal*). After tax yield is based on federal tax bracket at the 100,000 income level. Inflation based on Federal Reserve CPI.

In 1979, the worst year for the CD investor, six-month CDs yielded 11.44 percent. After taxes, the return was whittled down to 4.69 percent (assuming the investor was in the top 59 percent tax bracket). With inflation running at 13.3 percent, the "inflation-adjusted" return was a *negative*—minus 8.61 percent!

Not all years were that bad, but the returns were not as good as you'd think, at first glance. During the best year, 1986, the real rate of return was under 2.5 percent.

Recently, although inflation has come under control at about 3 percent, six-month CD rates have plummeted to 3.00 percent. But tax brackets have dropped as well. Still, the inflation-adjusted, after-tax return for 1991 was only .37 percent. Studying the real rate of return for CDs over the last twenty years reveals an average of a negative 1.92 percent! Not a great way to hedge inflation or beat taxes, is it?

This is why some people refer to CD investing as a great way to go broke safely. Yet CDs may have a place in your portfolio. Assuming that you stay within the $100,000 FDIC limits, CDs are safe and conservative. But like all investments, they should be examined in the context of your long-term objectives and your tax bracket. So the next time you evaluate an investment, don't forget to pay attention to the real rate of return.

PRINCIPLE 73—KNOW THE RISKS

Investments contain certain risks, and the future value of your asset may be more, less, or the same as what you paid for it.

Market Risk
First, evaluate the market risk of the investment. Even excellent stocks go down with a declining ("bear") market. And average stocks increase in value in a rising ("bull") market. Well over half the value of an investment is due to the direction of the overall market.

Industry Risk
Always evaluate the industry risk. The publication *Value Line*, a common source of investor information, divides the total stock market into ninety-nine different industries, from advertising to trucking. Some industries rise during bear markets, while others decline during bull markets. The sum of all industries constitutes the total market, but the selection of the particular industry determines about 25 percent of the stock's future value.

Financial Risk

Before selecting a specific investment, consider the financial risk involved. Companies and investments are like people: they can and do change over time. Investments are "born" as start-up ventures. Like newborns, some die during the first few days or months. Others survive and prosper during the growth stage, but eventually they mature and the growth curve stops. The final stage may be decline and death. In some cases, companies merge, which may lead to a new birth and regeneration of the cycle.

You might make more on a start-up venture, but you will be assuming a larger risk because most new ventures fail. If you select investments during the growth stage you'll reduce risk, but you'll receive a lower return than in start-up investments. If you are, by nature, a conservative investor, mature ("blue chip") companies offer less risk than growth companies, but the reward is much less in potential growth of your capital.

Timing Risk

The fourth risk investors face is timing. If you bought one hundred shares of General Motors stock in January 1966 at $104 per share, you would have had an investment worth $10,400. But nine years later in 1975, the share price dropped to $30, which would have dropped your investment to only $3,000. After a decline like that, most people sell off and vow to stay out of the market, forever.

But for every seller, there's a buyer. If you invested $10,500 into General Motors in January 1975, you would have owned 350 shares at $30 each. When GM stock went up to $70 a share two years later in January 1977, your investment would have been worth $24,500. In this instance, timing of the market, the industry, and the specific stock made the difference between a 71 percent loss and a 233 percent gain.

There's no way to avoid risk in investing. Your only choice about risk is which ones you'll accept. Investors in general will point out that over long periods of time (fifteen to fifty years), an investor will out-earn a saver or "guaranteed investor" by 3 to 6 percent per year. That's been true in the past. The questions are: Will that be true in the future? Will you be able to hold on during declines, or will you panic and sell? Would you be able to sleep nights if your investment dropped 30 to 70 percent in value after you purchased it?

Before you invest money in guaranteed or non-guaranteed investments, consider carefully your personal level of psychological and emotional tolerance for risk.

PRINCIPLE 74—ESTABLISH PRIORITIES AND LIMIT YOUR RISKS ACCORDINGLY

The following diagram illustrates a suggested priority structure on which to base a plan for limiting risk.

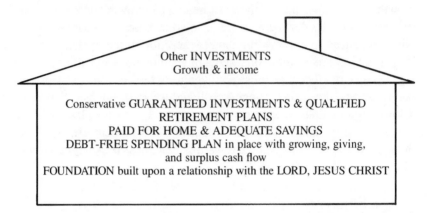

Other INVESTMENTS
Growth & income

Conservative GUARANTEED INVESTMENTS & QUALIFIED
RETIREMENT PLANS
PAID FOR HOME & ADEQUATE SAVINGS
DEBT-FREE SPENDING PLAN in place with growing, giving,
and surplus cash flow
FOUNDATION built upon a relationship with the LORD, JESUS CHRIST

If you can master the first four levels of this structure before you begin investing, you'll have a stable and solid foundation from which to build your financial house. If you turn the triangle upside down and begin with very risky, speculative investments first, your triangle will topple and subject you to many traumatic experiences.

PRINCIPLE 75—KNOW THE SIX ENEMIES OF THE INVESTOR

The investor must be on guard against the following six enemies:

1. Procrastination
2. Inflation
3. Taxes
4. Ignorance
5. No goals
6. No plans

Procrastination

First on the list of potential enemies is *procrastination*: putting off until tomorrow what we can and should do today. Procrastination is deadly because it's so deceptive. Almost everyone agrees that setting goals, planning, education, and financial freedom are solid, logical ideals that we ought to pursue actively. Yet less than 5 percent of us overcome the enemy of procrastination and actually act upon what we know. That's true in the area of finances, spiritual life, family life, and physical well-being.

The following idea was sold to the president of a steel company for $25,000 to help him use the information he already knew:

Take out a sheet of paper and write down the six areas of your life: spiritual, family, physical, personal, social, and financial. Under each category, list the tasks that should be done. When the list is complete, prioritize the items in order of importance from number one, on down.

Then, begin immediately on your most important priority. Work on it alone until it's complete, then move on to item number two, then three, and so on, until all tasks have been completed. At the end of the day, you'll have done the most important things instead of being distracted by urgent, but unimportant matters.

The last task of each day is to create a do-list for tomorrow. List the things you need to do tomorrow, in order of their importance, and begin the day with your list in hand.

That single idea has helped me to overcome procrastination and keep myself on track, moving toward a balanced Christian life—and I got it for free! Try it for yourself, right now write these headings on a sheet of paper:

THINGS TO DO

Spiritual   Family   Physical   Personal   Social   Financial

Inflation

The second enemy of the investor is *inflation*. Remember to consider inflation in your planning—especially on long-term goals. If, for example, your goal is to provide a college education for your newborn daughter, plan what it will cost by adjusting today's prices for the impact of inflation over the next eighteen years. If it costs $8,000 a year for a state university today and you assume 5 percent inflation, your real goal is 4 (years) $\times$ 2.65 = $84,906. The effect of inflation of 5 percent over the years until graduation from college is factored in as 2.65.

Taxes

You must always consider taxes, because all of us have to live on net, not gross, return.

Ignorance

Ignorance is the investor's fourth enemy, but you're conquering that one by mastering the principles in this book. You will need to continue the journey by further study of each area of investing: stocks, bonds, real estate. The more you learn, the better your decision making will become. A good intermediate step would be to read some basic books on financial planning and estate planning. A good public library should have the resources you need.

No Goals

Lack of written, prioritized, quantified goals is enemy number five. We have talked a lot about the need for both short-term and long-term goals throughout this book. Have you taken the time to put your goals in writing yet?

No Plans

Lack of planning is the sixth enemy of the investor. Remember that failing to plan is planning to fail.

P<small>RINCIPLE</small> 76—S<small>EEK AND</small> U<small>SE</small> W<small>ISE</small> C<small>OUNSEL</small>

The best source of counsel is the Bible; it contains everything we need to know in order to live the balanced Christian life. If you have trouble understanding Scripture, consult any of the many books available to help you discern its meaning, or ask a knowledgeable friend to help you.

After you've studied the Bible and prayed, seek godly counsel from men and women. If you're married, your best source of godly counsel may be from your mate. Unfortunately, many men never consider the advice of their wives, because they feel that women are not as knowledgeable or experienced in the areas of finance or business. But God designed husbands and wives to complement each other, so begin by asking your spouse.

Jeanie and I have agreed not to proceed with anything if both of us don't have peace about the decision. My wife has proven to be my best source of counsel, after the Bible and prayer.

If you're single, seek counsel from godly family members, beginning with your parents. In addition, ask your pastors or spiritual leaders.

Usually, a spiritually mature person is a good source of counsel, although spiritual maturity is not necessarily an indicator of financial expertise.

Don't overlook the help of a trusted friend who will be honest with you, give you an opinion, and most important, pray for you. If you need more professional advice, look to attorneys, accountants, financial planners, insurance agents, stock brokers, or investment advisors.

Locate a good advisor by asking for referrals from your friends. If you ask, you'll find Christian and nonChristian advisors whose work, reputation, and skills should serve you well. Look for competence first. But no matter whom you consult, remember that you are solely responsible for your decisions and the results, so temper the advice you receive with your primary source of wisdom: the Bible.

PRINCIPLE 77—DON'T FOLLOW YOUR FEELINGS

One sure way to fail in investing is to follow your feelings. Time and again, I see investors buy at the top of the market when they're excited and motivated by greed, and then sell at the bottom of the market when they're depressed and motivated by fear. They should be doing just the opposite: buying low and selling high.

Following feelings rather than finding facts is a sure formula for disaster. If you want to make money in the stock market, you must have the facts as well as the fortitude to act on them. When the market peaks, there are few bargains to be found. But when it's depressed, there are bargains everywhere.

All markets are cyclical; they go up and they come down. Then they go up again, only to come down again. If you need proof, just examine the stock market, the interest rate cycle, the economic cycle, or even the daily temperature as you progress through the four seasons. Perhaps the following visual aid will help you balance out emotions in your economic decision making:

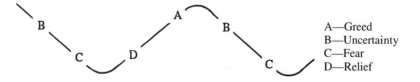

A—Greed
B—Uncertainty
C—Fear
D—Relief

Without exception, people who buy when the market is up are motivated by greed. For days at a time, the market's "new high" is headline news (Point A). But soon after, the news turns negative and disappears, and the greedy investor is left to watch his stock drop in value (Point B). Now the nightly news is full of horror stories: Are we on the verge of another crash, like the one in 1929? Will our currency, government, and country survive? Out of fear and panic, most people sell when there's blood in the streets (Point C), relieved just to recover some of their money. They're not even aware that the market is creeping back up again (Point D). Their feelings of relief continue as the market rises, until suddenly, new market highs are reported again, inciting greed in novice investors once more, and the cycle begins anew.

Don't let feelings dictate your decisions to buy, sell, or hold stocks, because feelings run opposite to the investment cycle.

PRINCIPLE 78—ADOPT A LONG-TERM PERSPECTIVE IN BUYING AND SELLING

Since the stock market is the largest area of investing in our country, let's look at the long-term picture. In 1950, the Dow Jones Industrial average stood at 200. For the next sixteen years, the overall trend of the market was up. There were some dips (1953, 1957, 1960, and 1962), but by 1966 the Dow had reached 1,000. That's a fivefold increase in price over sixteen years, or 10.6 percent per year long-term average.

For the next sixteen-and-a-half years, the stock market went up and down. In 1972, the market broke over 1,000, but by the end of 1974 it was down to 600—40 percent below its 1966 level. By the middle of 1982, the market hit its low, and then began a recovery to its 1966 level of 1,000 by September 1982. During that sixteen-and-a-half-year period (January 1966 to September 1982), investors may have earned dividends, but they saw no growth in share prices.

Then the Dow rose from a low near 800 in the summer of 1982 to its peak—near 3,000—in July of 1987. That's more than triple investors' money back, in less than seven years, or a 20 percent return on their dollar.

Then came 1987. The market soared, beginning its climb at 1,900, and was on its way toward 3,000 until the end of July, when a down draft hit, culminating in a 508-point drop on October 19, 1987: "Black Monday." Stories paralleling those of the great crash of 1929 were commonplace. By the end of the year, however, the market was back where it started: the Dow stood at 2,000 in December 1987 and rose to 3,400 by June of 1992 (that's a 170-percent increase in four-and-a-half years, or a 12.5 percent per year return).

I've shared these facts and figures with you in order to encourage you to look at long-term perspectives before, during, and after you invest. Doing so will improve your decision making.

Twenty-five percent of the performance of your specific investment is directly related to the overall market. Another 15 percent is related to the industry you invest in; the remaining 60 percent of stock performance depends upon the investment itself.

By looking at long-term histories, you'll have the information you need to moderate or delay investing when prices are high. If you bought low, the information will educate you toward knowing when to sell. At the other end of the spectrum, if your stock is at or near a long-term low, you can increase your investing or wait for a recovery when you will sell at a higher price. There are many methods of buying and selling stocks. Again, I encourage you to investigate and study all of them and monitor the stock before, during, and after you buy it.

It's prudent for every investor to know long-term statistics (ten to fifty years) on interest and inflation rates, the Gross National Product, stock markets, price-to-earnings ratios, economic indicators, money supply, and yields on stocks and bonds. If these terms are unfamiliar to you, begin at your library with a basic book on economics and finance. An introductory text on investing will be your next step. From there you can graduate to portfolio selection, composition, management, and timing. Remember, information is your ally against poor choices and significant losses. As I write this (1993), we're near a thirty-year low for interest rates, inflation, and yields on stocks and bonds. We're near thirty-year highs for stock markets, price-to-earning ratios, economic indicators, and money supply.

My estimates are only about 70 percent accurate, but based on the long-term histories of key economic indicators I predict the following: one to three years from today, we'll have higher interest rates (the prime is now 6 percent), higher inflation rates (the Consumer Price Index is now 2.4 percent per year), and higher yields on stocks and bonds (currently 3 percent on Dow Jones Industrials and 8.2 percent on AAA Corporate Bonds, which have the highest rating for safety). I predict lower stock prices and a declining price-to-earnings ratio.

PRINCIPLE 79—STICK WITH THE BASICS

"Basic investing" means cash, guaranteed investments, stocks, and bonds. After you've mastered the basics over a decade of experience, you can graduate to real estate, tangible and global investing, or a myriad of other choices that have at least a decade of investment history behind them to investigate.

Start with a money market fund, and learn to use it as a place for collecting investment dollars. There are over two hundred money market funds available from mutual funds or banks. All of them pool capital from small investors while offering rates comparable to institutions buying the $100,000 CDs. Compare the options at your bank with alternatives available from the government: EE Bonds (savings bonds), HH Bonds (income bonds), treasury bills (government IOUs for zero to one year), treasury notes (government IOUs for one to ten years), or treasury bonds (long-term government debt for ten to thirty years).

If you're thinking of investing today, I don't encourage you to look long-term (ten years or more) because interest rates are near a thirty-year low, and I expect them to rise above today's level. But there will come a time when double-digit returns will be available again, just as they were in the past. When that time comes, consider putting a portion of your capital into long-term, double-digit yielding CDs (like we had in 1981), treasury bonds, or other direct government obligations.

Tax-Deferred Annuities

Other kinds of guaranteed investments are available through the insurance industry. A favorite of many investors is the "tax-deferred annuity" (TDA) offered by most major insurance companies. A "regular" annuity makes an irrevocable transfer of cash to an insurance company in return for a promise to pay income over a set period of time. By contrast, a tax-deferred annuity provides a way for your savings to compound tax-free over time.

There are two kinds of TDAs: *single premium* and *variable premium*. You can start with as little as $2,500 for a single premium and as little as $250 down and $25 a month for a variable premium. The guaranteed interest rate can vary from daily to up to ten years. Before you invest, be sure to compare companies and policies. Contracts can vary substantially from one company to another. The difference can mean thousands of dollars to you, over time.

The following chart illustrates the tax savings available with tax-deferred annuities. It assumes an 8-percent yield and a 30-percent individual tax rate.

Years	$10,000 TDA	$10,000 CD	Savings
5	$14,693	$13,132	$1,561
10	$21,589	$17,244	$4,345
15	$31,722	$22,644	$9,078
20	$46,610	$29,736	$16,874
25	$68,485	$39,048	$29,437

As you can see, the savings over time are substantial. The difference is due to compounded tax savings. If you cashed the $10,000 TDA twenty-five years after purchase, chances are you'd be in a lower tax bracket. But if you leave taxes constant, you'd owe the tax man 30 percent ($17,545) of your $58,485 profit. After taxes on your TDA, you'd have $50,940 left, which is $11,892 more than you would have if you had put your money into a CD. Perhaps the TDA deserves a place in your portfolio.

Stocks

Those of you who want to invest in stocks have two choices: You can purchase individual stocks (such as AT&T, General Motors, IBM, and so forth), or you can buy into a quality mutual fund, which is a portfolio of one hundred or more individual stocks, professionally managed for you.

If you spend the time and make the effort to study, you should be quite pleased with your results. In the long term, stock returns have averaged 10 percent. In some years, your stock or mutual fund may decline in value, but if you hold on, a well-selected and well-managed stock or fund will perform well for you. If you visit your local library or stock broker, you'll find dozens of books, investment services, newsletters, and sources of information to start you on your journey toward becoming a knowledgeable and successful investor. (To determine whether you should enlist investment services or do your own investment, see the following principle, "Decide Whether to Hire an Investment Professional or Do It Yourself.")

If you want guarantees in your mutual fund investing, learn about variable annuities (VAs). Like the TDAs, VAs allow you to compound your capital tax-free inside the contract, and in addition they offer a dual death benefit. Not only are you guaranteed the return of your original investment or the value of the investment (whichever is greater) at death, but unlike the TDA, all accumulated savings in a VA escape taxation at death.

Unlike TDAs, variable annuities are investments, not guaranteed accounts, so your returns depend on the performance of the underlying investments. Several dozen insurance companies offer VAs, and each contract offers a wide array of underlying investment choices, from conservative to very aggressive. To eliminate surprises, investigate before you invest.

To illustrate the benefits, compare the following investments of $1,500 initial capital and $100 per month over time for a mutual fund and a VA, averaging 10 percent per year return at a 30 percent tax rate:

Years	VA	Mutual Fund	Savings
5	$10,160	$9,263	$897
10	$24,376	$20,259	$4,117
15	$47,713	$35,835	$11,878
20	$86,028	$57,898	$28,130
25	$148,935	$89,148	$59,787

As you study and learn more, you'll find that there are over ten thousand options for you to choose from in stocks, bonds, and mutual funds. For most people, who have less than $250,000 to invest, I've found mutual funds to be the best available tools. Today there are over four thousand mutual funds you can invest in to achieve your objectives.

Caution: Regardless of what you've been told, there's no such thing as a "no-load" mutual fund. All funds charge a fee to manage the investor's portfolio, and in addition, every purchase or sale of a stock or bond carries a charge. Some funds have an up-front sales charge; some offer reduced up-front sales charges; some have higher management and expense charges than others; and some charge a fee if you don't leave your investment with them for five or six years.

A good place to get information on all mutual funds is *Morningstar*, a publication providing detailed and comprehensive information on 1,184 mutual funds (write: Morningstar, 53 W. Jackson Blvd., Chicago, IL 60604). In addition to the rating service they offer, *Morningstar* offers a two-day conference around the country that gives sixteen hours of practical information about mutual funds.

PRINCIPLE 80—DECIDE WHETHER TO HIRE AN INVESTMENT PROFESSIONAL OR DO IT YOURSELF

Should you hire a pro, or do it yourself? Let's look at some factors in this decision.

I began in the finance business twenty-five years ago, after three consecutive losing investments from three different professional advisors. That's when I began a search to find the nation's top investors and investment managers.

Several names kept coming up. Over a three-year period, I learned everything I could about these "top guns" in the finance industry, and I decided to copy their proven formulas for investing. One advisor I studied was Sir John Templeton. Since he was the only one who came from a Christian belief system, I ended up buying his mutual fund and comparing its results to my "do-it-myself" method—my synthesis of "the best of the best" available funds.

In retrospect, I would have done better by putting all my investments into his fund. Today, the Templeton Fund has an unsurpassed thirty-eight year history. But remember: hindsight is always 20/20.

Most people prefer to hire a pro because they think it relieves them of the responsibility of educating themselves. In addition, if things don't work out as planned, they have someone to blame.

Both ideas are in error. First, as an investor it's your job to develop your own knowledge, education, wisdom, and experience. Second, you and the professional are both responsible and accountable for the results. Even though you delegate responsibility to another, you are always ultimately responsible for the decision and accountable for the results, good or bad.

I suggest the combination method: *use a professional and become one yourself.* You'll learn a great deal by using this method. The more you know about investing, the greater your chances for success.

If you're a novice investor, here's some advice. Let's say that you earn $25,000 per year, and you're considering investing $10,000. That means you're risking over a thousand hours of your labor. Wouldn't it make good sense to invest at least 10 percent of your time in making yourself a more knowledgeable investor?

You probably have access to dozens of courses offered by local colleges, universities, and private companies that are designed to increase your knowledge. In addition, your local bookstore or library will have hundreds of books on the subject of investing. Organizations such as the Denver-based College for Financial Planning offer correspondence courses leading to the Certified Financial Planner (CFP) designation. The insurance industry offers classroom or correspondence courses that can lead to the Chartered Financial Consultant designation, or you may choose courses offered by the

Society of Financial Analysts.

Reading, studying, and learning take time, effort, and an investment of dollars. But the acquired knowledge will help you eliminate investments that could lose thousands of hard-earned after-tax dollars. Investigate before you invest.

PRINCIPLE 81—DIVERSIFY YOUR PORTFOLIO

The concept of diversification can be stated simply: *Avoid putting all your eggs in one basket and you will limit your losses.*

By spreading your investment dollars over many different investments, you minimize the impact of losses on your entire portfolio. One reason mutual funds are popular is that a $1,000 investment is spread over twenty to twenty-five industries and placed into a hundred or more different stocks or bonds. If one out of the hundred loses half its value, the impact on your investment is only .5 percent, or $5. Had you invested the $1,000 into that one single stock, your loss would have been 50 percent, or $500.

The price you pay for safety is loss of potential gain. If one stock out of your hundred rises 50 percent, it adds only $5 to your $1,000 value. Had you been lucky enough to put all your funds into that single stock, you would have reaped $500.

PRINCIPLE 82—FOLLOW CONSERVATIVE GUIDELINES

Follow a few simple, conservative guidelines before making any investment. If you combine them with common sense, you will substantially reduce your potential losses.

Adopt an Accurate Measurement of Your Success

At set time intervals, measure each asset you have and your overall investment portfolio so you know where you stand. If you do this regularly, your measurement, which I call "buying power" or "real dollar return," will be realistic.

"Buying power" is the equivalent of your total return over time (interest, dividends, capital gains, appreciation, or tax benefit), less taxes (both paid and due), less inflation.

For example: I invest $10,000 in a mutual fund. A year later, my total return is: $10,000, plus my profits: $50 interest, $150 in dividends, $100 in capital gains, and $800 in appreciation. Therefore, my total profit for the year was $1,100. Then I subtract the 30 percent taxes due on my $1,100 profit (or $330) and another $500 if inflation averaged 5 percent during the year. Therefore, my total return, or buying power, was $270. If you prefer a formula, here it is:

Buying Power = Investment + Profit – Taxes – Inflation

If you shoot for a positive total return and achieve it, you'll be in the top 5 percent of all investors and professional managers. That may seem unrealistic, but it's been the case for the last ten to twenty years.

Use Dollar Cost Averaging to Reduce Losses

Consider dollar cost averaging (DCA) in an effort to reduce losses. DCA refers to investing set amounts of money at predetermined time intervals to reduce the chances of purchasing when prices are highest. The result of this method is that you will buy shares at a below-average price. As I've pointed out, most investors have a tendency to buy high and sell low rather than the reverse, so you're usually better off using the discipline of dollar cost averaging.

Here's an example of why you come out ahead with DCA. If you invest in a declining market, you'll buy more in the future because you're spreading your investment dollars over time. As share prices decline, you will have a smaller loss than if you had leaped in. When the market goes up, you'll have more shares and greater profit than those who leaped into the market. The system works, and it doesn't require brilliance or luck—just the discipline to invest consistently.

Recognize that Investment Literature Is Designed to Persuade, Not to Inform

Another conservative investment guideline is to remember that the literature you receive about potential investments is designed to *persuade* you, not *inform* you.

When you ask about potential returns from an investment, you'll hear averages, with the stock's best-ever record dropped in to impress you. But the odds of hitting this average are just 50 percent, and your chances of receiving the "best ever" return are slim at best.

If you base your potential or expected return on worst-case scenarios instead of the announced average return, the majority of the time you'll exceed your projections. If you can't live with the worst-case history, pass up the opportunity and look for another one.

Get a Realistic Picture of Projected Returns

Remember that investment returns are the sum of market returns, industry returns, and the return on your specific stock or mutual fund. Look at the ten-year track record of almost any stock fund between 1974 and 1984, and you'll be impressed. During that period, overall stock prices tripled, so you're looking at performance from a market low to a market high. The overall market grew at 11.6 percent, yielding a 12-percent return. That 12-percent return may look impressive at first glance, but it's only .4 percent better than an unmanaged market average.

To get a realistic picture of expected returns, examine track records during down markets. Does your potential investment still look attractive, or did it lose more than the average in a bear market? Looking at investment histories over time is like looking in the rear-view mirror of your car: You know where you've been, but that's neither a prediction nor a guarantee of where you'll be in the future.

Watch Track Records of Individuals, Not Companies

Remember that individuals, not companies, produce track records, and invest accordingly. Although it's important to look at the history of potential investments, selecting one based on historical returns alone is not a good idea.

If, for example, you invested based on ten-year track records beginning in 1980, you would have bought gold at $800 per ounce, oil at $40 a barrel, and real estate in the Sun Belt at historically high prices. The winners in the nineties are those who sold in the eighties, and for the most part, those who bought in the eighties are proving to be the financial losers of the nineties.

The historical returns for stocks, mutual funds, or any other investment are produced by the people directing the investments. When the people responsible for the results leave, they take their track record with them. If the people directing, controlling, and managing a company change their goals, philosophies, or areas of concentration, you can find yourself in a whole new ball game, with no score.

A good example of this is a mutual fund called "44 Wall Street." In 1980, 44 Wall Street stood at the top of the charts, boasting a ten-year history of 20 percent annual returns. Suddenly, the money that used to come into the fund in wheelbarrows began arriving in ten-ton dump trucks. At the same time, management changed and so did company philosophy, and the track record crashed with the fund.

I hope you know more about investing now than you did when you began this chapter. If so, you should be ready for chapter 10, which describes an investment with not only high, but dual, returns. It offers a 10,000 percent return and carries eternal dividends. In all my years as a financial planner and advisor, I've never met a person who had cause to regret investing in this area. Read on—and you'll educate yourself in one of the most important areas of the field of finance.

GIVING

■

Honor the LORD *with your wealth,*
with the first fruits of all your crops;
then your barns will be filled to overflowing,
and your vats will brim over with new wine.
PROVERBS 3:9-10

Giving is investing with God. Conventional wisdom says that once you give it, it's gone. But the Bible teaches that giving carries rewards that last for all eternity.

The law of sowing and reaping does not say that once you sow your seeds, you'll starve. It says that when seeds are sown properly, your return will be a great harvest. The parable of the soils (Matthew 13:3-23) demonstrates that seeds sown in good soil give returns of thirtyfold, sixtyfold, and one-hundredfold. For those of you into percentages, that's 3,000 percent, 6,000 percent, and 10,000 percent!

The next time you put your offering in the plate or make a donation to a worthy cause, think of yourself as having placed those funds in the hand of God. By giving, you are choosing to invest in Heaven, and your investment will return both temporal and eternal dividends.

WHERE CHRISTIAN GIVING BEGAN

The concept of Christian giving goes back to the days of the Old Testament, when the nation of Israel was a theocracy—a government ruled by God. At that time there were two types of giving: required and free will.

As with our current system, citizens of Israel were required to pay taxes, or "tithes." There were three required tithes for Israelites. First, there was a 10-percent tithe to the Levites, Israel's class of priests. Second, a 10-percent festival tithe provided funds for national feasts and holidays. Third, a 10-percent tithe was given every third year to fund a national welfare system for the poor, widows, and orphans. If you add them up, you'll see that the Israelites paid between 22 and 23.33 percent per year in required giving. As with the taxes we pay today, those tithes were not voluntary.

By contrast, over and above the tithes was a "freewill giving" consisting of various gifts, offerings, and sacrifices. Freewill gifts almost always came from those with willing, loving hearts. This type of giving was not compliance with an officially established formula or percentage, but a heartfelt expression of gratitude for what God had given the giver. This is the kind of attitude or spirit of giving that God wants us to have.

In this chapter, we will explore this important dimension of Christian living by looking at practical ways to develop a rewarding lifestyle of giving in heartfelt gratitude for what the Lord has done.

PRINCIPLE 83—STUDY THE BIBLICAL GUIDELINES FOR GIVING

In the Bible, God has given us some very specific guidelines to encourage us in consistent, generous, and fruitful giving. The following list of guidelines includes the specific Scripture references on which they are based. I encourage you to look up these passages and read them carefully. They will reward the time you spend studying them with rich insights not only into giving financially but in many other areas of Christian living as well.

1. Giving should be both planned and spontaneous, in response to needs. (See 1 John 3:17-18.)
2. Giving should be a demonstration of grace and love, not law. (See 2 Corinthians 8:7-9.)
3. Giving should be done out of cheerful obedience, because giving is commanded. (See 2 Corinthians 9:7.)
4. Giving should be sacrificial. (See Mark 12:41-44, Hebrews 13:16.)
5. Giving affects our spiritual riches. (See Luke 16:10-12.)
6. Giving should be done secretly, and with humility. (See Matthew 6:1-4.)

7. Giving should be voluntary. (See 2 Corinthians 8:13-15.)
8. Giving should be generous. (See 2 Corinthians 8:1-5, 9:6.)
9. Giving does not depend on how much you have to give. (See 2 Corinthians 8:12.)
10. Giving should be personally determined. (See Luke 19:8.)
11. Giving is our way of making God our first priority. (See Proverbs 3:9-10.)
12. Giving honors God and brings Him glory. (See 2 Corinthians 9:13.)
13. Giving acknowledges God's ownership of everything. (See 1 Corinthians 4:7.)
14. Giving bring special blessings to the giver. (See Acts 20:35.)

PRINCIPLE 84—GIVE IN ORDER TO MEET NEEDS

The purpose of giving is to meet needs. Throughout the Bible, God shows His compassion, identification with, and blessing for the poor. We're exhorted to give to others simply because they are in need, in an effort to demonstrate God's love. Remember: Nonbelievers don't read from the Bible, but they do read from our lives and actions. They should be able to see the light of Christ flowing through us from a loving God.

Our giving should not be limited to the poor, however, but should extend into all aspects of Christian endeavor: the church, special ministries and missions, and educational facilities. We're encouraged to give to fellow believers to meet their physical, emotional, and spiritual needs.

Paul's instructions to the Corinthian church to set aside a weekly gift in proportion to individual income were in order that "no collections will have to be made." Proper giving should not be the result of an urgent, emotional plea from the receiver. Proper giving results from the generosity of believers who truly desire to please God. This doesn't mean that the more you give, the more godly you are. However, you will seldom meet a godly person who is not a generous giver.

The Israelites gave so generously to build the tabernacle that the time came when God told them they had given enough:

Then Moses gave an order and sent this word throughout the camp: "No man or woman is to make anything else as an offering for the sanctuary." And so the people were restrained from bringing more, because what they already had was more than enough to do the work. (Exodus 36:6)

Can you imagine how this testimony honored God? Imagine all the people in your congregation reaching for their wallets only to hear your pastor say, "Put your money away, folks; we have more than enough this week to pay all the staff's salaries, maintain the buildings, feed the poor, and provide for the missions!"

Most pastors say that if all believers possessed the heart attitude God longs for us to have and gave according to biblical principles, there would always be plenty of funds for needs, programs, and projects.

To Whom Should We Give?

Most of us are barraged with appeals for donations. With an endless array of options for giving, how do we separate worthy causes from unworthy ones? The important from the urgent? With numerous possibilities for endowments, how does one separate good stewards from poor ones?

The Bible defines several categories of recipients to whom we should give:

1. The first beneficiary of our giving should be *our local church*—not that all our giving must go exclusively to the church, but it should be a top priority.
2. We should support our *pastors, teachers, and leaders.* (See 1 Corinthians 9:11-14, Galatians 6:6.)
3. We should support *evangelists and evangelistic organizations* spreading the gospel.
4. We should give to *disciples and discipleship.*
5. We should support *our families.* (See 1 Timothy 5:8.)
6. We should give to *the poor, widows, and orphans.* (See 1 John 3:17.)
7. We should give to *needy nonbelievers,* in order to provide a witness and testimony.

Use study, prayer, and counsel to determine how to allocate your giving. Your most important investment deserves careful planning, serious thought, and plenty of execution.

Evaluating the Recipients of Your Gifts

In evaluating specific recipients of your gifts among Christian individuals and organizations, look for:

- Willingness to serve.
- Desire to honor God first, foremost, and always.
- Reputation that is above reproach.
- Cooperative attitude toward other churches, ministries, missions, and organizations.

If your potential recipients display these four attributes, you should then evaluate their financial efficiency as stewards by answering these questions:

- How, specifically, will they use your donations?
- Do they need or just desire your gifts?
- What type of lifestyle does their leadership exhibit?

God promises that if we lack wisdom, He will give it to us if we simply ask Him (James 1:5). Before you make a decision to give God's money away, pray and seek His guidance in your giving.

PRINCIPLE 85—GIVE CONSISTENTLY

The timing of our giving is to be systematic and consistent. It can be every week on Sunday, or the first payment out of every check, or once a month—whatever works best, just as long as it's consistent. Consistent giving is imperative because it steadily reminds us that God owns everything, and that we are only stewards.

PRINCIPLE 86—PLAN YOUR GIVING

Giving should be planned. Each of us is commanded to "put aside and save" for God's work and God's people. We must plan to give, acknowledging God as provider of all things by giving back to Him some of what He has given us.

Too often, however, God gets the crumbs—leftovers (or nothing) at the end of the month once all of our needs and desires have been met. Shouldn't the One who gives us the ability to earn and the health to go to work—and life itself—have top priority in our finances?

PRINCIPLE 87—EVERYONE SHOULD GIVE

Scripture says that each of us should set aside a sum of money. This means each and every family member, including children. We should train our children in the fine art of generous stewardship by example.

Let each and every family member experience the joy of giving by allowing him or her to make individual contributions. Once the habit is established, the pattern is set for lifetime stewardship, which will bring great blessing to God and the giver.

PRINCIPLE 88—GIVING SHOULD BE IN PROPORTION TO OUR POSSESSIONS

Giving should be proportional: "On the first day of every week, each of you should set aside a sum of money in keeping with his income" (1 Corinthians 16:2).

I am often asked questions like, "How do I know how much to give?" "Should I give based on my gross or net income?" "Should I tithe?" God's answer to all those questions is found in the law of sowing and reaping, as Paul states it in 2 Corinthians 9:6: "Whoever sows sparingly will also reap sparingly, and whoever sows generously will also reap generously."

For some, the tithe (10 percent) is a reasonable amount. Jesus praised a poor widow who gave a fraction of a penny—but those two cheap coins were 100 percent of what she had to live on, and she gave them graciously (see Mark 12:42-44). God isn't interested in the amount. He's interested in the giver's attitude of heart.

PRINCIPLE 89—GIVING IS A BAROMETER OF SPIRITUAL HEALTH

The nature of our giving is a reasonably accurate indicator of our spiritual maturity. The statistics are not encouraging: of all those who attend church regularly, less than one-fifth give 10 percent or more. The average giving at conservative evangelical churches is 2 to 3 percent of personal income, with only $6 per person per year going to missions. On the average, "Christian Americans" spend more on pet food and chewing gum each year than they give to Christian work.

Our country is spiritually weakened because there's not enough money for evangelizing, discipleship, and meeting the physical and spiritual needs of God's people. Giving extends to time and talent as well as money. Time spent in Bible study, prayer, and sacrificial Christian service is also part of a regular offering to God.

Our attitudes and actions regarding giving are of utmost importance to God. Of the two thousand Scripture verses pertaining to finance, almost two-thirds deal with our attitude toward money.

Throughout the Bible, we're taught that the reason for everything we do in life, including giving, is to glorify God. Giving that results in praise, honor, and thanksgiving to God is part of robust spiritual health. When we try to hold on to the financial rewards and seek recognition for ourselves, the barometer shows a weak spiritual condition.

Our goal should be as Paul instructs in 1 Corinthians 10:31: "Whether you eat or drink or whatever you do, do it all for the glory of God." We are, after all, God's couriers, carrying His valuables from one destination to another. And if we're making the most of every opportunity, as God commands us to do, we're delivering the gospel message along with the goods.

PRINCIPLE 90—LEARN THE FOUR TRUTHS OF SOWING AND REAPING

Jesus states the law of sowing and reaping in Luke 6:38—"Give, and it will be given to you. A good measure, pressed down, shaken together and running over, will be poured into your lap. For with the measure you use, it will be measured to you." Let's explore four important truths based on this law.

Truth 1: You Can't Reap Until You Sow

This truth relates to stewardship of time, talent, and money. If you're short on time, sow time in God's work. In return, you'll reap time. If you're short of money, sow money in God's work—and watch God work for you. These results are promised in the only passage in the Bible where God says, in effect, "If you doubt, test Me—and learn the truth firsthand." It's the passage we looked at in chapter 8, in which God explains through the prophet Malachi that withholding tithes and offerings is equivalent to robbing God. Then God declares:

"Bring the whole tithe into the storehouse, that there may be food in my house. Test me in this way," says the LORD

Almighty, "and see if I will not throw open the floodgates of heaven and pour out so much blessing that you will not have room enough for it." (Malachi 3:10)

Truth 2: There's a Time Lag Between Sowing and Reaping

Just as it takes time for seeds to germinate, it takes time for us to see fruit, or results, when we sow the time, money, and talents that God has given us for His Kingdom. Sometimes the results are immediate, but more often there is a delay before you reap what you sow. Don't think that by giving $100 to your church you have obligated God to credit your account $1,000. The $100 was His all along, so don't think of giving as a cosmic slot machine.

Truth 3: You Reap in Proportion to What You've Sown

The more seeds you toss out into the world, the greater your harvest will be; it's impossible to out-give God. The more generous your giving, the more generous will be your return. If, however, you give with the motive of getting more, you have nullified your return. God is interested in your attitude, not the amount you give.

Truth 4: You'll Reap a Multiple Return on Your Sowing

There's an old saying, "Any fool can count the seeds in an apple, but only God can count the apples in a seed."

Jesus explains the concept of giving as investing in the Sermon on the Mount (Matthew 6), when He tells the multitudes not to collect and hoard treasures on earth because they'll only be destroyed or stolen. Instead, He encourages them to invest in "treasures in Heaven," which can't ever be lost or stolen. The reason, He explains, is because wherever they invest their treasure, that's where their heart will be, too.

Returns are guaranteed by God, regardless of whether we will receive them on earth or in Heaven. Examine your motives for giving—and then rest on the certainty that any investment with God pays eternal dividends.

Principle 91—Remove the Roadblocks to Giving

Selfishness

Four major obstacles stand in the way of giving, and selfishness tops the list. The Bible tells us we are born in sin, and that's the truth. Selfishness is one of our worst inborn traits.

Quite frankly, we prefer a new car to a new sanctuary or education building. We'd rather get some new clothing for ourselves than back-to-school shoes for underprivileged children. We'd rather go out for dinner at a nice restaurant than use the money to buy books for missionaries.

Spiritual maturity comes from sacrifice. Giving is not God's way of raising money, it's His way of raising His children. If we want God's Kingdom to grow, we have to move away from selfishness and toward the image of Christ.

Procrastination

Procrastination, one of life's deadliest sins, also hinders our giving. "I know I should be giving more, and I will . . . right after this debt is paid off . . . right after I get my raise . . . as soon as the kids are on their own" on and on and on.

Those who make $100,000 per year find giving just as difficult as those who make $15,000 a year. In fact, statistics show that those with over $100,000 annual income give a lower percentage than those who make far less.

No matter where you are now, financially, you can choose to honor and obey God right now. If you aren't currently giving, you must resign yourself to accepting that it will not happen in the future if you do not begin today.

Excuses

Another roadblock to giving is the "I'm an exception" sign we often hang on ourselves. Though excuses for not giving (or not giving more) vary across the board, all of them revolve around the fact that most of us prefer to be served, rather than to serve.

Overspending

Overspending is also an obstacle. When we overcommit our resources by spending more than we should, giving is usually the first area we cut back on or eliminate. However, though government, business, and personal overspending has become an accepted way of life, it's not God's way.

Working without a spending plan also keeps us from giving to God what is rightfully His. Without a plan, giving will either be absent or a fraction of what it could be with a careful plan.

If you say that God is number one in your life, your actions should reflect that priority. If they don't, then perhaps God really isn't your first priority after all. The words you say certainly don't determine the reality behind them. If the Lord is really number one in your life, put your money where your mouth is, or quit kidding yourself.

I encourage you to ask God to search your heart and to point out any selfishness or sin regarding your giving. Decide what steps you will take to remove those roadblocks from your path so that you may move forward toward a balanced financial life.

PRINCIPLE 92—GIVE THROUGH YOUR WILL OR TRUST

Unfortunately, most faithful givers forget all about giving to the Lord's work in their wills, trusts, or estate plans (dying plans). Why not consider leaving a percentage of your estate to your church, your favorite mission or seminary, or any worthwhile Christian organization? Treat the Lord's work as an equal heir, along with your children and/or grandchildren. If your children are already well established and successful, you might consider leaving your gift in memory of them, or in their names.

Most people's first tendency is to leave everything to their children, but remember: It's not your money to give away—it's God's. Are your children responsible enough to handle an inheritance, or would they be likely to blow it? Ninety-five percent of the people who inherit sums of $100,000 to $1 million have nothing left five years later. If you're planning on leaving large sums of money to your children, you may want to consider spreading the inheritance over ten years or more, rather than giving them all of it in one lump sum.

The Greatest Inheritance

The word *inheritance* probably triggers thoughts of financial, personal, and tangible assets, but if that is all you leave behind, I pity your heirs.

I once had a wealthy client whose son quoted her the following Scripture: "After all, children should not have to save up for their parents, but parents for their children" (2 Corinthians 12:14). He was upset because she was leaving so much to the church and "only eight hundred thousand" to him.

The greatest inheritance any parent can leave a child is love for God and an education in the gospel. If you leave your children spiritually rich, everything else will seem unimportant by comparison. Our heart's desire should be to leave behind heirs who are faithful stewards, committed Christians, and people of godly character who give and live to honor God. If your children don't know the Lord, keep praying, trying, and reaching out. Don't give up.

Give It Twice

The most popular idea I've found in planning an inheritance is a concept I call "give it twice." It works like this: If you're leaving $100,000 after your death, you create an estate plan that will pay $8,000 per year to your beneficiary for a period of 12.5 years. At the end of that period, your heir will have received the full $100,000. But because of the interest your estate has earned over time, there will still be money left over to give elsewhere.

For example, if the $100,000 is invested at 8 percent the first year, it will earn $8,000—so the $8,000 the beneficiary receives is 100 percent interest. At the end of the first year, the full $100,000 remains in your fund. By the end of the 12.5 years, your fund will *still* be worth $100,000! At that time, your estate plan can direct, let's say, one-third of the balance to your church, one-third to a worthwhile seminary, and another third to a ministry that meets human needs.

With this plan, in reality you have given your estate *twice*: once to your beneficiary, and again—12.5 years later—to the Lord's work. You've provided for your beneficiary, and you've given generously to God's work.

PRINCIPLE 93—GIVE TO THE LORD'S WORK
INSTEAD OF LETTING TAXES CONSUME IT

Although few people give primarily for the tax benefit, giving is tax-deductible for those taxpayers who itemize deductions. If you itemize, give by writing checks, or save your receipts, and you can generally deduct gifts of up to half your adjusted gross income.

A method of giving with tremendous tax benefit is what I call the "Special Trust." I use this to label a variety of different trusts designed to meet special needs in individual estate planning. I'll illustrate by sharing the story of my best friend, Faithful Steward.

Faithful was the widow of a retired government official who lived quite modestly, although her pensions and Social Security totaled over $50,000 per year. She had three children: Samuel, an overseas missionary; David, a successful physician; and Deborah, Faithful's adopted daughter who was afflicted with Down's Syndrome.

Faithful had three substantial assets. The first was a piece of land inherited from her father, worth approximately $1 million. The second was her home—a modest dwelling, but because it was located on ten acres of prime land it was worth another $1 million. Faithful's third asset was stock her husband had bought in 1932 for $8,000, now worth yet another $1 million.

Because I was helping Faithful with her dying plan, I had shown her that if she sold the land, her home, and the stock, her tax bill would have been $1.2 million. In addition, upon her death, federal death taxes would amount to another $500,000. If Faithful were not diligent in planning her estate, the tax collector would get away with $1.7 million, leaving the children the remaining $1.3 million to divide among themselves.

As Faithful developed her plan, she carefully considered the needs and wants of her children. Samuel didn't want the money, but he was concerned about how he would be able to retire in five years on a missionary's pension of only $500 per month. David neither wanted or needed an inheritance, but he was concerned about being able to care for his sister, Deborah, because he was preparing to donate the next five years as a medical missionary overseas with his brother.

On her eighty-fourth birthday, Faithful explained to her children the IRS-approved plan she had created: $1.5 million would be given to them to provide for Samuel's retirement, Deborah's special care, and a nice cushion for David; and $1.5 million would be given to the Lord's work. The tax man would get nothing, and every penny received by Faithful's children would be completely free of federal, state, local, estate, and inheritance taxes.

If, by planning, you could leave assets to the Lord's work instead of the tax man, would you take the time and spend the effort to create a dying plan? If your answer is yes, there are more plans like Faithful's available for you to create. For specific information about this means of giving and estate planning, as well as tax and investment planning, you could do some basic reading and research at your local library.

A MODEL TO EMULATE

John Wesley, the revivalist preacher and founder of Methodism, sparked a radical renewal in eighteenth-century England with his call to "scriptural holiness." This spiritual giant has much to teach all of us about managing personal finances and giving to the Lord's work. To make the following snapshot from his life more meaningful to you, I have adjusted the dollar amounts for inflation.

John Wesley took his first job as pastor of a small church for a salary of $15,000 a year. As a faithful steward, he calculated that he would need $13,000 annually to meet his basic needs. (Note that today, $13,000 is a very modest salary.) He set aside money from each of his checks, giving $2,000 a year back to God. As you may know, Wesley was a marvelous pastor, and in a year's time his congregation had doubled in size. As a reward to their pastor, the church voted to double his salary to $30,000 per year.

Again, Wesley examined his needs and estimated that despite his raise, he could still live comfortably on $13,000 a year. So he invested $17,000 with God the second year. By the end of his second year, the church had again doubled in size and, amazingly, the church again voted to double Wesley's salary. Now, he was making $60,000 a year—a considerable sum.

How would you handle the situation if your salary was doubled twice in two years? Would you upgrade your home? Buy a new car? Improve your lifestyle? Or would you do what John Wesley did and continue to live on $13,000 a year, investing $47,000 in God's Kingdom?

The truth is, most Christians try to keep up with the Joneses when they should be emulating the Wesleys. John Wesley was not a spiritual giant because of how he handled his finances; he was a spiritual giant because his top priority was his spiritual life and he handled his finances accordingly.

Think now about how you will allocate your next raise, promotion, profit, or windfall. If you have no plan for handling an increase, there's a 99-percent probability that you won't handle it God's way. I pray that you will make it your heart's desire to hear the Lord say when you stand before Him, "Well done, My good and faithful servant."

ELEVEN

CHARTING A COURSE

■

*"Do not let this Book of the Law depart from your mouth; meditate
on it day and night, so that you may be careful to do everything
written in it. Then you will be prosperous and successful.
Have I not commanded you? Be strong and courageous.
Do not be terrified, do not be discouraged, for the LORD your God
will be with you wherever you go."*
JOSHUA 1:8-10

I congratulate you for your persistence in studying this material. It's no small accomplishment to read ten chapters packed with principles, Scripture, and practical applications.

When I first began to study everything the Bible says about our attitudes and actions regarding money, my reactions varied from anger to conviction, from hopelessness to hope . . . and, finally, confusion to clarity. If this is your first trip through material like this, you may feel as if you tried to get a drink from a fire hydrant! This is the beginning of your journey to a biblically based, balanced financial life. Now, you have the information necessary to begin charting the course from where you are to where you need to be.

PRINCIPLE 94—PRESS ON TOWARD THE GOAL

I remember well my first course at seminary, with Dr. Earl Radmacher. It was in hermeneutics: the art and science of interpreting the Bible. Fifty-six hours of lecture, two thousand pages of difficult reading, exposure to more material and information than you can imagine, and above all, the godly character example of a master theologian—I was blown away! It was intimidating to open "the Book" for fear that I might mishandle the material.

Maybe you can relate to how I felt, since you have now completed what may have been your first comprehensive course in what the Bible has to say about money and material things. In my first course, Dr. Radmacher made me aware of the complexity and importance of accurately handling the Word of God. I pray that you are now aware of the complexity and importance of handling your finances and are well started on your way to learning even more about managing God's money God's way, for His glory and your benefit.

Even after twenty years of Bible study and financial planning, I'm still struck by how much I need to know, and how much God continues to teach me. Just when I tend to get cocky and self-assured, thinking that I've really mastered becoming financially and spiritually mature, God has a loving, wonderfully effective way of pulling the plug on me with His loving hand of discipline.

However hopeless your finances may look to you, I encourage you not to be overwhelmed by the scope and size of the project laid out before you. And on the flip side, if you're feeling proud of what you know and pumped up by what you've learned, remember that no one lives 100 percent of the truth they know. No matter where you are in your grasp of these issues, keep a balanced view of yourself before God and work diligently at applying to your life the principles and Scriptures given in this book. Only then will you see change.

Change may come more quickly or slowly than you expected, but in either case, *don't give up!* Developing sound financial health is a process. When you get discouraged, reflect on the apostle Paul's example:

> I do not consider myself yet to have taken hold of it. But one
> thing I do: Forgetting what is behind and straining toward
> what is ahead, I press on toward the goal to win the prize
> for which God has called me heavenward in Christ Jesus.
> (Philippians 3:13)

How relevant Paul's statement is for us today! We never quite arrive, but we can always be moving steadily toward the goal of balanced spiritual and financial lives. Individually, we set our priorities. We decide where we'll store our treasure. We alone choose whom we will serve with our life. Paul had a singleness of focus that I have always loved and admired. Becoming like Christ was Paul's goal in life.

PRINCIPLE 95—COMMIT YOURSELF TO THE LORD

"Choose for yourselves this day whom you will serve . . . as for me and my household, we will serve the LORD" (Joshua 24:15). The Bible is clear: We are to serve the Lord, and Him only. But the word from the world is, "Compromise. To get along, you have to go along." Sometime it's very difficult to live in a society that proclaims, "Everything goes." But we're under the rule of a Holy God who says, "Go with Me!"

That's why commitment is so important—once you commit to following the Lord, your focus is narrowed to one thing: *doing everything God's way.* If you rely on the power of the Holy Spirit, you will no longer have to struggle with the impossible task of serving two masters. Once you decide whom you will serve, each financial decision you have to make will be easier, because there's only one way to do a thing: God's way.

Paul wisely advises us to forget what's behind. No one is without fault or failures in his or her financial life. While you're on the journey toward financial freedom, don't get sidetracked by guilt. All of us would make some different choices if we could do them over again. You can't change the past, but you can resolve to make better and different choices in the future.

PRINCIPLE 96—REMEMBER THAT GOD IS AT WORK IN YOUR LIFE

Along with your commitment and resolve, you are assured of the very presence and power of God Himself: "Being confident of this, that he who began a good work in you will carry it on to completion until the day of Christ Jesus" (Philippians 1:6).

God began a good work in you when He put the desire in your heart to read this book and adjust your attitudes toward material things. He's not going to abandon you. Now, you must trust Him for the power to do what He says, so you can become what He calls you to be—holy.

Acquire, absorb, and apply these principles to your life. Your goal should be "repetition of truth over time." Repetition solidifies the principles in your mind so they become an integral part of your attitude, thinking, and actions.

If you've ever watched a pile driver sink a post permanently into the ground, you know that after many repetitions, the post is permanently planted and able to withstand the forces of nature and time. Once you've fully committed yourself to a godly financial life, you'll be pleased to see how quickly your attitudes and actions conform themselves to God's truth.

PRINCIPLE 97—SEARCH YOUR HEART

Begin your new financial life by searching your heart for anything you need to confess to God regarding your handling of money. Have you wasted it? Squandered it? Hoarded it? Have you ignored someone in need? Have you failed to live up to your financial obligations? Have you left any debt unpaid? Have you put money—or your job, so that you could earn more of it—before God? Has money come between you and a friend? Have you ignored what God has laid on your conscience? Do you yearn for things you can't afford, and feel sorry for yourself because you don't have them?

If you feel conviction over anything having to do with money, I urge you to confess it to God, ask His forgiveness, and begin, immediately, to right yourself with God concerning the matter.

PRINCIPLE 98—REVIEW AND REFLECT

Once you've cleared the slate regarding past wrongs and are ready to focus on doing what's right, begin reviewing and reflecting on the material in this book.

If there is a particular area that you know you need to work on immediately, go back and work on that chapter or section first. Otherwise, start with chapter 1.

To review the material, reread it and write down the principles and supporting Scriptures on index cards you can carry around with you wherever you go. Whenever you have a few spare minutes, take out the cards and review them. Pray about them. Write down any specific steps of action you want to take.

After a week with the same cards, spend another week with a new set of cards you create from chapter 2, or the next area you want to focus on. Then repeat the process, one chapter per week, until you have gone as far as you can.

So the first item on your new spending plan should be a pack of index cards!

PRINCIPLE 99—START SAVING TODAY

Don't wait until tomorrow to begin saving. Regardless of the amount you save, take the first step, today. Even if you can put away only $5, go to the bank and make the deposit.

Once these simple steps become a habit, increase your savings over time. When you get a tax refund, gift, bonus, or raise, commit yourself to saving 10 percent of it instead of spending it all. Now you understand the impact of managing an increase over time. Let yourself begin experiencing the rewards.

The important thing is to begin where you are and move toward your goal. A year from now, you can look back, adjust your target, and proceed, reinforced by your accomplishments in year one.

PRINCIPLE 100—ATTACK THE ENEMY: DEBT

The success of moving forward in your savings plan will help strengthen you to attack your greatest financial enemy—debt. Using the principles in chapter 4, develop a plan to become debt-free over time. Determine to pay off every bill. You'll have more discretionary cash flow to reallocate.

Honor the Lord with a slice of what used to be a payment. Save some of the freed payment, and use part of it to accelerate repayment of your remaining debts. Can you feel the momentum you will develop? It's incredible!

Sow a thought and reap a habit. Sow a habit and reap character. Sow character and reap the reward when the Lord says to you, "Well done, good and faithful servant! You have been faithful with a few things; I will put you in charge of many things. Come and share your master's happiness!" (Matthew 25:21).

PRINCIPLE 101—BEGIN REDUCING EXPENDITURES FOR HOME AND TRANSPORTATION

I hope that chapter 5 helped you change your thinking about paying off your home mortgage. Perhaps you noticed ideas in chapter 6 about your transportation needs that you want to begin applying right now.

Remember that you have been learning principles, not laws. Some of these ideas will fit into your financial plan immediately, and others may apply later on when you've grown and matured. No one will use every idea, but you can probably identify several to apply right away for

226 CHARTING A COURSE

reducing expenditures for both housing and transportation. The journey to financial balance is a long-distance run, not a sprint.

PRINCIPLE 102—ACQUIRE ADEQUATE INSURANCE AT MINIMUM COST

Chapter 7 probably cost me a few friends in the insurance business, but that's all right. My goal is to help you acquire adequate protection at minimum cost, not to create more revenues for the industry's companies and agents.

You may end up trading in your insurance agent for a new one, but unlike other areas, your payments will go down and you'll have more discretionary cash flow to allocate sensibly to more worthwhile things. Learning about things like insurance isn't easy or fun. But the information you now have will save you money. And you'll gain peace of mind in knowing that you're providing protection for your family while being a wise steward of your finances.

PRINCIPLE 103—CREATE YOUR SPENDING PLAN

This is the most important principle. If you apply only one idea, make it this one. A spending plan you actually use will stretch your paycheck at least 15 percent further. Creating your own plan will help you to see and eliminate unnecessary expenditures while giving you an accurate picture of what it costs to live.

In your plan, put God first. Paying yourself second is a must; otherwise there will be nothing left at the end of the month to commit to savings. Planning eliminates the unpleasant surprises that used to ruin your day, and looking at the big picture will improve your decision making.

In effect, you're learning to be financially accountable and responsible to God for what He's entrusted to you, and to be content and give thanks for what He's given. To refresh your memory, go back to chapter 8. Copy a set of the forms and study the example. Do your plan, revise it as necessary, and stick to it. Remember, not planning is planning to fail, and not using your plan leads to failure.

PRINCIPLE 104—TAKE THE LONG VIEW OF INVESTMENT

Chapter 9 on investing might not have been what you were expecting or hoping for. We have been conditioned to expect a "quick fix." After learning the steps to becoming debt-free (including your home) and having adequate reserves before you invest, you may feel you'll never be in a position to try your hand in the investment market.

But you probably will, and possibly much sooner than you think. All you have to do is keep moving toward your goal of a biblically balanced financial life. The closer you get, the easier it becomes. If you learn nothing else from the chapter on investing, learn to select counsel carefully, beware of following your feelings, and keep a long-term perspective.

PRINCIPLE 105—BE PREPARED FOR DISABILITY AND DEATH

Do you know that 80 percent of the people whose names appear in the obituaries every day died without a will? A will is a written document that tells how you wish your assets to be distributed at your death. A will is especially important if you have minor children. You, not the courts, should decide who would raise them in your absence. If you don't have a will, put that on your short-term list of goals.

Ninety-eight percent of our population has not planned for disability. If you were totally disabled suddenly, would you have a power of attorney, naming someone to make medical and/or financial decisions for you? If not, protect yourself by choosing the person you want to act for you rather than letting the courts appoint someone. The chances of experiencing a long-term disability before you reach age sixty-five are one in three.

What if an accident leaves you with no chance of improvement or recovery? Would you choose to continue living in some supported condition, or would you choose to die with dignity? You can express your choice in writing by using a document called a living will. If you choose not to plan, you may leave an awesome burden for your family. Act now and execute a living will.

PRINCIPLE 106—LAY UP TREASURES IN HEAVEN

My favorite chapter to write was chapter 10 on giving because it reminded me of the truth that we are each accountable for *100 percent* of our income. Our responsibility doesn't end with giving 10 percent and doing what we please with the rest.

I hope you can see clearly through the "give it and it's gone" lie to the truth: *Giving is investing with God.* Giving that brings glory to God is the only way to lay up treasures in Heaven. Though I placed this subject last in the main text of this book, I consider giving to God the top priority in anyone's financial plan. I pray that you will use the information in that chapter as a barometer to measure and increase your giving.

PRINCIPLE 107—RECOGNIZE THE DECEPTIVE POWER OF WEALTH

Though all the principles in this book are focused on finance, the same principles will work in every area of your life. Remember: as Christians we have no financial problems, because God has already promised to meet our every need. But some of us have spiritual problems that disguise themselves in dollar signs.

Recently, I attended a church program featuring the illusionist André Kole. Mr. Kole performs illusions in order to present the message of the gospel in a unique way, and his performances attract thousands. The illusions he creates of objects appearing, disappearing, and defying gravity are powerful because of how real Mr. Kole makes them appear. The illusions wouldn't be so entertaining if Mr. Kole revealed the truth behind them.

We live in a world that clings to the illusions it creates and consistently defies the truth in the Bible. Our adversary, the devil, is the master of illusion, deception, and doubt.

Of all the illusions our adversary uses to deceive us, wealth is probably the most powerful. We are asked to accept as truth the illusion that wealth will meet our needs to be loved, to belong, and to feel important. So we evaluate people based on their income, their profession, and what they own. That leads to the illusion that these are the people who really count. Associating with them makes us feel more important. It takes no effort to buy into the illusion that money and possessions give us status, power, prestige, and honor—and it's easy to believe the world's deception that we're entitled to these things.

But this is just the opposite of what God wants us to be:

> My brothers, as believers in our glorious Lord Jesus Christ,
> don't show favoritism. Suppose a man comes into your meeting
> wearing a gold ring and fine clothes, and a poor man in shabby
> clothes also comes in. If you show special attention to the man
> wearing fine clothes and say, "Here's a good seat for you," but
> say to the poor man, "You stand there" or "Sit on the floor by my
> feet," have you not discriminated among yourselves and become
> judges with evil thoughts? (James 2:1-4)

If you think greater wealth, more possessions, or increased wages will reduce the stress, worry, and financial pressure in your life, you've bought the devil's lie and doomed yourself to disappointment and financial destruction.

Society attacks our contentment with fifty-thousand advertisements a year, all carrying the message that our lives are incomplete without some new product or service. American advertising is so effective that advertisers fight to spend a million dollars for a sixty-second spot during the Superbowl.

A biblical definition of sin is "meeting true needs in an inappropriate manner." The needs to be loved, to feel important, and to belong are real. There's nothing wrong with feeling these needs. What's wrong is trying to meet them with possessions, position, or pleasure. The only genuine way to meet our deepest, most heartfelt needs is to live in a personal relationship with Jesus Christ, our living Lord.

PRINCIPLE 108—LEARN DISCERNMENT

How can we know whether the thing we're pursuing is an illusion or the truth? "Discernment" is the Bible's term for the ability to separate illusion from reality, error from truth, and evil from good.

When Solomon became king, God appeared to him during the night and said, "Ask for whatever you want me to give you" (1 Kings 3:5). If God were to appear to you and make the same offer, what would you ask for? I encourage you to take a sheet of paper and record your thoughts. Don't censure yourself; record, honestly, whatever comes to mind.

Solomon's response was to request a "discerning heart . . . to distinguish between right and wrong." God granted his wish and gave Solomon riches, honor, and no equal among kings—blessings he didn't even ask for!

Discernment is important to God. We know from Solomon's story that discernment comes through prayer—by asking God for it. As we continually handle the truth, which we can recognize because of the discernment God gives us, the illusions of the world will become more obvious to us. Bank tellers are trained to spot counterfeit money not by studying counterfeit bills, but by repeated and prolonged handling of real currency. Likewise, once we're acclimated to the feel, sound, and logical ring of truth, we will see through deceptive illusions more quickly.

TWO STORIES OF CHANGE

In Hebrews 5, the author refers to elementary truth as "milk" and intermediate or advanced truth as "solid food." The chapter ends, "But solid food is for the mature, who by constant use have trained themselves to distinguish [discern] good from evil" (Hebrews 5:14). Does the phrase "constant use" sound familiar? It's the path to learning and applying truth. The following two stories illustrate the results of "repetition of truth over time."

Mary, Bob, and the Power of Unmasking Illusions

I met with Bob and Mary, both fifty-eight years old, just as they were approaching retirement. They asked me to help them evaluate their plans for retirement; they had relocated to Arizona after disastrous financial ruin.

After we had met during the course of a year, Bob and Mary began to realize that it wasn't bad investments in oil and real estate that had caused them to go under—those were the symptoms. They recognized that one of the real causes was idolatry: of their net worth and Bob's professional status as a cardiologist.

Once they achieved this understanding, their panic about the future began to subside. They started on a new path by honoring God first. They committed 2 percent of Bob's salary to giving, agreed to study the Bible for one year, and each began to look for a place and a way to serve.

It took two months for Bob and Mary to understand that they were spending all their income. They knew they were supposed to be controlling their spending, but they really struggled with arriving at a balanced plan. After all, for the last thirty years they'd been accustomed to living in a 5,000-square-foot home, driving the right cars, and entertaining at the country club. Even though Bob's earnings were way above average, their perceived "needs" were unrealistic.

Mary initially refused to consider trading their luxury residence for a smaller home that would meet their needs more economically. Bob was closed to any idea of withdrawal from their country club or giving up the Mercedes for more reasonably priced transportation. "Physicians have an image to maintain. With our investments gone, the symbols of success are all I have left," he mourned.

My job isn't to tell others how to live their lives, but to expose people to the truth and encourage them to assimilate and apply it to their lives. After twelve weeks in a home Bible study on the principles of finance, Bob and Mary's attitudes, habits, and awareness began to change. They recognized that many of the ideals they had lived by were illusions, not truth. Most important, they *chose to change.*

Today, five years later, Bob and Mary are transformed people. Their monthly spending is 30 percent of what is used to be. They're saving 50 percent of their after-tax income and giving 20 percent off the top to honor the Lord. Bob still practices medicine five to six days a week, but one of those days is donated to help meet the needs of those who can't pay. Mary spends 60 percent of her time in volunteer Christian service. The peace, contentment, and love radiating from their marriage and life is dramatic testimony to the transforming power of applying biblical truth to life.

Dee, David, and the Power of Commitment

One hot August afternoon, I received a call from our church pastor asking for help with a couple on the brink of divorce. Our pastor agreed to explain to Dee and David that my expertise was limited to the financial arena. Since they both recognized their money problems were aggravating their marital problems, we arranged a meeting.

At the first meeting, symptom number one surfaced in minutes: They both operated independently with their finances. Both of them wanted to preserve their marriage, but both wanted to maintain their financial independence. The problem (symptom) was obvious, but the cause was not.

Dee had been married previously and brought two children to the marriage, along with a lot of bills from her first husband, whom she identified as a con artist and a bum. David brought a premarital agreement to the marriage, several thousand dollars worth of inherited assets, and habits—not necessarily good ones—learned from his parents about handling finances.

Because David's parents had always maintained separate funds, David had created his spending plan to work the same way. The problem came because the plan was incomplete. Dee and David could agree on expenses for the child they'd had together, but they couldn't agree on who paid for what where Dee's children were concerned.

The real trouble had started when David wanted to buy a new van for the family, but Dee wouldn't commit any part of "her" money to the payments. As we worked through their opposition to each other, it became apparent that the root cause was their failure to commit themselves fully to each other. Neither was willing to combine their resources and operate as one, the way God intended them to.

David was afraid of being cheated out of his inheritance, so he protected himself with a premarital agreement. In David's home, his dad handled the finances like a benevolent dictator and gave David's mother an allowance. David's mother never knew what her husband earned, saved, or spent. She was even forbidden to open the mail, and if she needed anything, she had to sell David's father on the idea.

By contrast, in Dee's family, her mother controlled the finances. Every week, Dee's dad endorsed his check and gave it to his wife. Dee honestly believed the wife should handle the money. In her opinion, her first marriage had proved her correct.

What Dee and Dave had wasn't a complete marriage, it was a partial union with a financial arrangement rider attached. My suggested solution of total commitment, including combining income and assets, was not initially received well by either person.

"If I did that, I could lose my inheritance!" David said aggressively.

Dee countered, "You don't trust me! Besides, you don't have any common sense; you're a worse spender than the bum I was married to before!"

Here was symptom two: never had I seen a couple more different. Dee was a pack rat, and David saved nothing. David could really dream big, but Dee was a conservative, pessimistic realist. Dee was a night owl; David was a morning person. David was an outgoing person who loved people; Dee was introverted and task-oriented. Their ideas on everything were different—from raising children to earning and spending. I wondered how two people so different could ever have gotten married.

For Dee and David, the ultimate solution for the problems in their marriage and their finances was loving commitment to each other. The following Scripture passages were especially important in identifying what they needed to do:

> Do nothing out of selfish ambition or vain conceit, but in humility consider others better than yourselves. (Philippians 2:3)

> Be completely humble and gentle, be patient, bearing with one another in love. (Ephesians 4:3)

Dee and David needed to change how they viewed their personality differences—not as grounds for disagreements, but as complementary balances that God had most graciously provided for them. They began to learn that by approaching financial issues from different perspectives, they could emerge with a better, more balanced decision than either of them would have made alone.

David had wanted to raise their standard of living by getting the new van and a larger home. Dee had wanted to stay put until the bills from her first marriage were paid off, and then begin saving for their retirement. I'm pleased to report that, after much counsel and study of God's Word, they both saw the big picture realistically and began to soften their inflexibility and move toward a unified financial balance.

David ended up trading his existing car for a used van, and Dee agreed that paying off debt while building savings was wiser than funding their IRAs. Initially, both had wanted the other person to change, but neither was putting Christ first in his or her life. They had to come to a place of reckoning about the cost of discipleship, and the price they would have to pay to balance their finances, their marriage, and their spiritual lives. But as they grasped the power of commitment to Christ and each other, they began to experience the rewards.

There *is* a real price to pay for a financially balanced life. That price is learning to die to greed, selfishness, pride, and materialism. It takes effort and sacrifice to establish biblical habits in giving, saving, and living on a spending plan. The battle isn't a quick victory; it's a lifelong struggle to maintain the proper attitudes, habits, thoughts, and actions each day. It takes discipline to practice the repetition of truth over time.

But the good news is that, as believers and followers of Jesus Christ, we have the inside track because we know who wins the war! Our main responsibility is to stand firm and allow God to shape us, using money as a tool and a test for our testimony.

I am grateful for the opportunity to share with you the principles, ideas, and truths that God reveals to us in the Bible. I have tried to sow the seeds of truth. I hope that you will now provide a place for them to grow in your heart and mind. Together we can praise God, who conditions hearts to become good soil and causes the seed of His Word to grow and multiply. I look forward to hearing about the harvest you produce, both now and in the hereafter. May God bless you abundantly.

AUTHOR

Wilson (Jody) Humber is in private practice in Sun City West, Arizona. He is a Registered Investment Advisor, a General Securities Principal, and a member of the following organizations: International Organization of Financial Planners, Institute of Certified Financial Planners, and The Registry of Financial Planning Practitioners.

Jody Humber received a bachelor of arts degree in math and physics from Southern Methodist University and a master of arts in psychology from Arizona State University. He continued his education at the College of Financial Planning and became a Certified Financial Planner. Humber also holds degrees from Moody Bible Institute, Liberty Home Bible Institute, and Western Seminary in Phoenix, Arizona.